THE LOGICS OF BIOPOWER AND THE WAR ON TERROR

LIVING, DYING, SURVIVING

Edited by
Elizabeth Dauphinee
and
Cristina Masters

palgrave
macmillan

THE LOGICS OF BIOPOWER AND THE WAR ON TERROR

First published in 2007 by
PALGRAVE MACMILLAN™
175 Fifth Avenue, New York, N.Y. 10010 and
Houndmills, Basingstoke, Hampshire, England RG21 6XS
Companies and representatives throughout the world.

PALGRAVE MACMILLAN is the global academic imprint of the Palgrave Macmillan division of St. Martin's Press, LLC and of Palgrave Macmillan Ltd. Macmillan® is a registered trademark in the United States, United Kingdom and other countries. Palgrave is a registered trademark in the European Union and other countries.

ISBN-13: 978–1–4039–7465–5
ISBN-10: 1–4039–7465–9

Library of Congress Cataloging-in-Publication Data

International Studies Association, Meeting (46th : 2005 : Honolulu, Hawaii)
    The logics of biopower and the war on terror : living, dying, surviving / Elizabeth Dauphinee and Cristina Masters (eds.).
        p. cm.
    Papers from a roundtable delivered at the 46th Annual Convention of the International Studies Association in Mar. 2005 in Honolulu, Hawaii.
    Includes bibliographical references and index.
    ISBN 1–4039–7465–9
    1. War on Terrorism, 2001—Social aspects—United States—Congresses. 2. Violence—Political aspects—United States—Congresses. 3. Biopolitics—United States—Congresses. 4. Popular culture—Political aspects—United States—Congresses. 5. United States—Politics and government—2001—Congresses. 6. United States —Social conditions—1980—Congresses. I. Dauphinee, Elizabeth, 1974–. II. Masters, Cristina, 1974– III. Title.

HV6432.I57 2007
303.6'2502—dc22   2006048569

A catalogue record for this book is available from the British Library.

Design by Newgen Imaging Systems (P) Ltd., Chennai, India.

First edition: January 2007

10 9 8 7 6 5 4 3 2 1

Printed in the United States of America.

CONTENTS

Introduction: Living, Dying, Surviving I   vii
Elizabeth Dauphinee and Cristina Masters

Part I   Bodies, Lives, Deaths

1   Crossroads of Death   3
     Roxanne Lynn Doty

2   Missing Persons: Manhattan, September 2001   25
     Jenny Edkins

3   Body Counts: The Biopolitics of Death   43
     Cristina Masters

Part II   Cinematics, Culture, Aesthetics

4   Responsibility and Terror: Visual Culture
     and Violence in the Precarious Life   61
     Mark J. Lacy

5   Persistence of Memory? The (New) Surrealism
     of American Security Policy   83
     Kyle Grayson

6   Securitizing the Unconscious: The Bush
     Doctrine of Preemption and *Minority Report*   109
     Cynthia Weber

7   The Biopolitics of Security: Oil, Empire,
     and the Sports Utility Vehicle   129
     David Campbell

Part III Regulation, Securitization, Preemption

 8   Sovereign Contradictions: Maher Arar and
     the Indefinite Future   159
     David Mutimer

 9   Abject Spaces: Frontiers, Zones, Camps   181
     Engin F. Isin and Kim Rygiel

10   Biopolitics and the Tragic Subject of
     Human Rights   205
     Anne Orford

11   Living, Dying, Surviving II   229
     Elizabeth Dauphinee

Contributor Biographical Information   245

Index   249

INTRODUCTION: LIVING, DYING, SURVIVING I

Elizabeth Dauphinee and *Cristina Masters*

Collected in this volume are stories about the stories we tell. They are stories about the ways in which the political is inscribed on human bodies and human lives, and they explore the logics and contexts in which particular forms of violence are made possible and sustained. One of those contexts is the war on terror, though it is not the only one. The war on terror animates particular forms of political violence, while simultaneously obscuring the historical contexts in which these violences have emerged. Ascribing the violence of our current political situation to the events of September 11 and their aftermath erases the fact that many of these practices are not new. They have varying depths of historical salience that are rooted in the disciplinary representations associated with state and identity formation. In many ways, what September 11 introduces is a terrain of unquestionability and ineluctability, which in turn forms the "perfect alibi" for the evacuation of politics from memory. The violences that this volume foregrounds are, in the context of the war on terror, understood to be "necessary"—even "common sense." Particular individuals pose threats; terrorism requires response and containment; "rogue states" and "states of concern" must be acted against. In many ways, however, the war on terror is not what its architects claim it to be: it is both less and more and other than. The war on terror levels an obvious gaze at the places we expect to find it: in the narrow field of vision associated with "what counts" as "international relations"—in states and the administration of states and in the battlefields of war (physical, cyber, informational). But the war on terror also produces violences in the spaces where our gaze *is not*—where our disciplinary vision is murkier. To recognize this is to tell different stories and to tell stories differently.

Collected here are stories that ask questions not commonly associated with the war on terror—indeed, many of them ask questions that undermine and disturb the logics that are said to make the war on terror a necessary facet of contemporary global political practice. They are stories that ask personal questions. Very often they are painful questions. They are stories that inquire after the missing, the deported, the detained, the de-remembered, and the dead. By extension, they are also stories that ask us to ask ourselves who we think "we" are, and what the political imaginaries associated with that "we" demand of both ourselves and others. The authors of this volume find their stories in experiences of the everyday—and, indeed, the war on terror has become the everyday—even the mundane—leaking into the ordinary spaces of human lives in the form of airport security screening, the price of gasoline, and the entertainment we choose. But we might also say that the war on terror as produced in the experience of the everyday in turn produces spaces of the exceptional. Indeed, the violence that animates the practices associated with the war on terror increasingly produces an elision between the everyday and the exceptional. The exceptional bleeds into the everyday, and many of the lives chronicled in this volume are marked by a measure of exceptional violence that has, disturbingly, become the everyday. In this sense, we write, and perhaps *should* write, less as scholars and more as witnesses.

By extension, the stories in this volume can also be read as a mode of questioning. Each in its turn seeks to engage in an ethos of questioning with the aim of recovering the lives that are caught in the logics of sovereign biopower. In this way, it serves to unmask and refuse many of the questions that are associated with the war on terror—questions that inquire after citizenship status, place of birth and upbringing, religious and ethnic background, the language one speaks, and the friends one keeps. We know that questions always designate the form that answers can take. In the context of the war on terror, the dominant mode of questioning is one that seeks to constitute and mobilize particular subjects in ways that inevitably flatten the fragmented—and the political—textures of lived lives. Almost immediately following the attacks on the World Trade Center, a narrative emerged that sought to cohere and mobilize those whose lives were lost. The narrative became one of heroes, of sacrifice for the state, which in turn comprised the animating subject for the war(s) that followed, and perhaps for wars that are yet to come. These are narratives that thread the relationships between the bodies and lives of victims through the body and life of the state and through the public domain such that the victims were said to belong to all Americans. But, as Jenny Edkins demonstrates, the missing persons posters that plastered Manhattan following the collapse of the World Trade Center were images that evoked not the heroic sacrifice that was made but rather the complexity of the lives of the missing themselves and of their relationships to those who love them. Here, the public narrative is challenged by the intensely personal features of lives and deaths that are situated in families and in friendships and in communities—personal features that evoke and convey complexity while simultaneously rendering these almost impossible to express. The descriptions of the missing were both intensely unique and necessarily uniform; indeed, how could you ask after the person you love? How could you express who she or he is on a photocopied flier? These posters and the grief that animated their production created a rupture of the private into the public—a rupture that in some ways thwarts the attempts of the state to make sacrificial sense of the loss.

Exploring other narratives engenders the possibility of painting pictures that disrupt dominant conceptions of who "we" are, and of what that might mean in the politics of the war on terror. Understanding death as sacrifice situates bodies in a grid of social and political intelligibility that often conceals the complexity of the living, dying, and surviving that is at the heart—whatever that might mean—of human being and of human becoming. In many ways, it is the relationship between the living, dying, and surviving, and the ways in which each is in some sense made possible by the other(s), that weave the stories in this volume together. The war on terror is presumed to involve and privilege particular deaths and types of deaths—particular lives and types of lives. One does not include Mexican and other Latino migrants dying of heat and exhaustion in American deserts among the deaths accumulated and articulated within the war on terror. One does not include those who commit suicide in migration detention centers in the United Kingdom or France or Australia. Similarly, one does not include particular lives and kinds of lives in thinking about how the war on terror comes to be produced as such. One does not include the American moviegoer or the SUV (sport utility vehicle) driver or the Internet user in the context of lives that animate the need for the war on terror to be what it is—yet these are the lives whose particular contours and content are made possible by and in this war. And we know that the identification of lives that matter makes our identification of lives that don't possible.

We are mindful of the fact that the ability (which is different from the desire) to ask and answer questions at all rests on the primary assumption that it is the form of the question itself that produces particular economies of intelligibility. This enables us to think through the ways in which the questions posed in the context of the war on terror are posed such that only some answers are intelligible and "appropriate." The desire contained in these questions is to *make intelligible* within a political imaginary whose possibilities are increasingly narrow. One is, in many ways, required to situate oneself legibly in the dominant narratives of the war on terror. But those who become legible (the citizen, the sacrificial hero, the SUV driver) necessarily effect erasure with respect to what is illegible, unintelligible, and to what disrupts (the illegal migrant, the dead soldier, the missing). These erasures are, to be sure, founded in the realm of the conceptual, but they also necessarily have profound material effects on bodies and lives. For example, the conceptual boundary that marks the separation of the United States from Mexico makes possible our identification of some human bodies as "illegal migrants"—bodies that are already breaking down in the heat of the desert. The materiality of these bodies is constituted by the conceptual, but they also constitute and reconstitute the conceptual. As Roxanne Lynn Doty argues in chapter 1, the corpse of Ana Rosa Segura-Marcial, and countless others "whose dreams ended in the blinding glare of [the] sun," literally redraws the border as a space of exclusion and death.

The story of Ana Rosa is not intelligible in the context of the dominant narratives of the war on terror because the war on terror presumes to be only about specific spaces and individuals. In this way, the war on terror actively silences the livings, dyings, and survivings that make its larger claims possible. The war on terror hardens borders—responds to the territorial violation that occurred on September 11—and actively erases many of the lived consequences that follow from the desires of homeland security. Ana Rosa disrupts the dream of security without death.

The identity/security equivalent that the war on terror attempts to define appears to be based on economies of belonging and unbelonging. Yet the identity that the war on terror claims to secure is no security at all. It does not ensure one's life as politically qualified, as worthy of protection, even when one is apparently in possession of that which designates belonging. As David Mutimer argues in chapter 8, Maher Arar's Canadian passport did not afford him the rights and protections to which he was legally entitled. Interrogated and detained at New York's JFK airport as a suspected terrorist, Maher Arar was denied access to Canadian consular officials and was instead deported from the United States to Syria—his birthplace—where he was imprisoned and tortured for over a year. In the imperative to identify himself to the American state at the customs and immigration counter, Maher Arar's answer about who he was became meaningless. The question had already been answered for him by Homeland Security personnel and the Canadian federal police.

Although the contributors to this volume often work to refuse the questions asked within the context of the war on terror, in the lived realities of everyday existence the capacity to refuse becomes more and more difficult. One finds oneself already inscribed. The requirement to reveal oneself, and the contours of this revealing, are already formed and contained within the logic of the securitizing state. We are in possession of biometric passports; we have our fingerprints scanned at U.S. ports of entry; we produce our documentation on demand; and, when we cannot, we forfeit ourselves as politically intelligible—as eligible—subjects. We enter political space—the customs counter at JFK, for example—and are faced with certain kinds of questions, hoping that our answers will render us sufficiently intelligible that we may pass safely. Sovereign power attempts to capture us, and we are forced to make answer or to have answer made for us in the silence that would be our refusal. The imperative of sovereign power to *make known* is increasingly overwhelming—increasingly overpowering—but, also, as Anne Orford argues in chapter 10, fundamentally compromised in the awareness that omnipotent sovereign power is already always a failed project.

"Obscene Undersides"

This volume is also about the possibilities engendered by changing our scholarly imaginaries—by writing differently, by exposing ourselves and the worlds we conjure and encounter to challenge and scrutiny. For many of the contributors, this has resulted in the imperative to find a new voice, one that attempts to rethink and rewrite the subjects of scholarship—one that attempts to rethink the question of what our obligations might be and to whom we might be obligated. As Roxanne Lynn Doty has argued elsewhere:

> We may convey to readers illusions of truth with our authorial expertise, but often we are the hideous beings swallowed up by our scholarly clothes, the dancing fools under the fluorescent lights of our paradigms and theories that voraciously consume our thoughts, hammer the soul from our words, and drain our voices of any traces of humanity.[1]

Our invitation to the contributors was partially animated by a sense that International Relations scholarship has often obscured the human lives that are at stake in its conceptualization and its content. Framed through the identification of threat, preemption, security, and war, the dominant narrative of the war on terror as Attack on America produces phantasmic representations. These representations are variously populated by specific one-dimensional subjects who are mobilized in support of a political imaginary that makes certain kinds of narratives and responses possible. In this sense, the contributors reveal the violence in the microeconomics of particular human livings, dyings, and survivings, working to explore and expose the relationships between them. Here, we encounter what Slavoj Žižek, reading through Lacan, has called the "obscene underside"[2]—the recognition that the war on terror operates within the same frame of violence as that which it seeks to oppose. The exposure of the undersides in the context of the "making live" lies in the constitutive need to "let die." The obscene underside of the war on terror is the refugee who sutures his lips and eyelids to mark his abjection, the child in the Woomera detention center whose response to the trauma of her incarceration is to repeat, "Don't touch me I'm dead," the Mexican migrant whose death in the desert constitutes a strategy of "deterrence" that is necessary to prevent others from attempting the crossing, the SUV driver whose realization of "the American dream" is fueled by the persistence of war and its pervasive economy of death.

The contributors to the volume read through these obscene undersides, exposing their animating illogics. Theoretically focused on the relationship between Foucault's governmentality as articulated in *Society Must Be Defended* and Giorgio Agamben's notion of bare life, the chapters explore and extend the constitution of biopower as a set of regulatory practices that produce spaces of exception in which human beings are stripped of their political subjectivities such that any violence can be committed against them with impunity. This is a project that has to occupy every body—that has to situate all bodies relative to the ability and the imperative to, as Foucault puts it, make live and let die. This is the conceptual move that excises death from the repertoire of sovereign activities—which relegates death to a space of exception. Death is depoliticized. Killing takes place without responsibility, celebration, or remorse. As Foucault argues:

> In the right of sovereignty, death was the moment of the most obvious and most spectacular manifestation of the absolute power of the sovereign; death now becomes, in contrast, the moment when the individual escapes all power, falls back on himself and retreats, so to speak, into his own privacy. Power no longer recognizes death. Power literally ignores death.[3]

In the context of sovereign biopolitics, death needs to be made invisible because death, the underside of this politics, also undermines the sovereign claim that its primary activity is to "make live." In other words, death is expunged from the exercise of sovereign power—obscured as a primary effect of sovereign power—relegated to these undersides that are subsequently erased. Because sovereign power is understood as "making live," and not killing, it now operates across an apolitical terrain in which its moral credentials are apparently confirmed, thus preempting critique and challenge. Biopolitics hides its death-producing activities under the rhetoric of making live. Exposing death as the obscene underside of sovereign biopower exposes the politics that have been quietly emptied out of the biopolitical. It is death that exposes the biopolitical project of sovereign power. In his exploration of the contours of biopolitical power, Foucault asks:

> How can a power such as this kill, if it is true that its basic function is to improve life, to prolong its duration, to improve its chances, to avoid accidents, and to compensate for failings? How, under these conditions, is it possible for a political power to kill, to call for deaths, to demand deaths, to give the order to kill, and to expose not only its enemies but its own citizens to the risk of death?[4]

Part of the answer lies in the identification of a rupture in the field of the "human" that biopower controls: you cannot kill that which is not constituted as "living." It is this process of "desubjectification"—the construction of life as (potentially) bare life—that makes it necessary to read Foucault and Agamben simultaneously. Foucault provides us with a detailed historical account of the transformation of modern sovereign power from the right to "let live and make die" to the right to "make live and let die." Agamben deepens and stretches this transformation, locating the rise of biopower in the Nazi concentration camp and the violent formation of bare life—*homo sacer*—where the death of some sustains and makes possible the lives of others.

For both Foucault and Agamben, this fragmentation is inherently racialized. We can add that it is also gendered and classed. The fragmentations of race operate concomitantly with the identification of other fragmentations—technologies of disciplinary power are threaded into the exercise of biopower simultaneously—citizenship is an example, as marked through the technologies of citizenship—the passport is both disciplinary power and biopower—the constant reminder of the boundary, however precarious and chimerical, between belonging and unbelonging.

These narratives take us to the obscene sites of biopower—sites that must be actively de-remembered, depoliticized, and denied. They explore the war on terror not as it is dominantly described by the biopoliticians who underwrite its production, but rather through the sites that are not explored—the sites where human bodies succumb to technologies of death and are erased. There are multiple narratives associated with the war on terror that are partially articulated in architectures of sovereign power. These also play out in the spaces that have been politically excised—or rather depoliticized—as sites informed by the dominant conception of what the war on terror signifies. As Mark Lacy argues, this engenders a new imperative for scholarship:

> We need to look at how the logic of biopower in the war on terror—the state of emergency that prepares us for new forms of biopolitical control of populations and biocriminals—limits the chances of surviving the precarious life.[5]

Desire/Grief

The stories in this volume also revolve around the multifaceted experiences of grief and desire. Judith Butler argues that grief and desire are animated and marked by the same "undoing" of the subject. "Something takes hold of you: where does it come from? What sense does it make? What claims us at such moments, such that we are not the masters of ourselves?"[6] The grief and mourning associated with loss is made possible by the desire that was "always already" present.[7] For Butler, grief, mourning, and desire contain the possibility of the political—and the possibility of politics:

> Many people think that grief is privatizing, that it returns us to a solitary situation and is, in that sense, depoliticizing. But I think it furnishes a sense of political community of a complex order, and it does this first of all by bringing to the fore the relational ties that have implications for theorizing fundamental dependency and ethical responsibility.[8]

Throughout this volume, the contributors mark both grief and desire, which we understand as fundamentally related, both in the experiences that Butler describes and in the mutual constitution of grief and desire in the contexts of the war on terror: the desire to drive the SUV hinges on the grief of the violence and loss for others that makes the fulfillment of that desire possible. The grief of loss and death that emerges in the context of that violence is the condition that animates the desire for a livable life. Similarly, the immobility of the detention camp makes possible the mobility of the citizen; the loss or denial of subjectivity makes possible the politically qualified, eligible member of the contemporary nation-state (precarious as this qualification might be for Maher Arar and others). These are politics animated both by grief and desire. In its turn, grief lays bare all the unlivability in the war on terror, exposing the narratives that work to determine who/what counts and who/what does not.

Of course, the war on terror produces grief: lives are lost; people are incarcerated or simply disappear; cities and homes are destroyed. Yet this grief is manifest not only in the obvious spaces, but also in the form of what constitutes—and is felt to constitute—livable and valuable lives; and indeed, the question of grief often foregrounds its own absence in the questions we pose. For example, we operate in a sociopolitical realm that is obsessed with politically qualified "doing" as the only acceptable manifestation of human "being." Doing, claiming, and acting become the sole legitimate forms of qualified human existence. As Engin F. Isin and Kim Rygiel argue in chapter 9, those who are conceptually and physically relegated to spaces where they cannot make claim are reduced to what Agamben calls "bare life"—life that can be killed with impunity. The legitimate and legitimating "doing" is the mandate of the politically qualified subject. And yet, if we recognize grief as a politics, other possibilities for "doing" emerge. Exploring grief might provide opportunities to "do" differently.

It is not always clear within the contours of trauma and mourning exactly where one ought to begin. We recall one painful scene from Sri Lanka in which a man who had discovered that his wife and child had died in the December 26, 2004 Indian Ocean tsunami sat silently on a bridge spanning a swollen river. Bodies and debris floated by in the current. A Canadian Broadcasting Corporation journalist and camera crew approached him and asked him what he was going to do. The man who had lost everything looked up and answered that he did not know what to do. A subsequent interview with a Canadian medical team that had been dispatched to the region involved one of the physicians complaining that no one was doing anything. But what was there to "do" for a man who had lost his whole life—and those whom he loved? The man on the bridge had perceived that there was simply nothing to be done. If he "did" anything at all on that bridge, it was simply to grieve for those he loved. Was his grief not also a "doing"? We believe that it was. Grieving—mourning—is a doing that can disrupt dominant narratives that seek to co-opt and mobilize loss and mourning for violent political projects.

Here, we see a political imperative to cling to grief. In grief, the plans one lays and intentions one forms are destroyed. As Butler argues:

> There is losing, as we know, but there is also the transformative effect of loss, and this latter cannot be charted or planned. One can try to choose it, but it may be that this experience of transformation deconstitutes choice at some level. . . . I think one is hit by waves, and that one starts out the day with an

aim, a project, a plan, and finds oneself foiled. One finds oneself fallen. One is exhausted but does not know why. Something is larger than one's own deliberate plan, one's own project, one's own knowing and choosing.[9]

This awareness allows us to recognize that response is not automatic, nor is it animated by a singular possibility. In grief, we are exposed to one another in ways we could not have fully anticipated, and this exposure opens up a range of possibilities for the political.

In the context of a biopolitics that strives to deny the production of death, how might we begin to grieve lost lives? In some ways, this is a question that requires exploration of the interstices *between* life and death—the spaces of withdrawal and abandonment that constitute the contemporary states of exception in which more and more human beings find themselves. Livings and dyings are ruptured by survivings that are neither livings nor dyings, but which are otherwise: liminal spaces of abjection that are dangerously difficult to recognize. Where and what is the human body in this politics of exception? We tend to think of grief as tied to particular losses. In the case of death, it is the corpse that occasions the onset of grief and mourning. How do we grieve in a biopolitics whose primary activity is to remove that body from view? How do we grieve those whose bodies are simply devoured by the Sonoran Desert? How do we grieve dead soldiers when they are spirited back from "battlefields" under media whiteouts in body bags that have been rearticulated as "transfer tubes"? How do we grieve those who are neither living nor dead behind the razor wire of Guantánamo Bay, Yarl's Wood, Woomera? As Cristina Masters asks, "how do we grieve for those who have ostensibly been buried alive in prisons such as Guantánamo Bay and Abu Ghraib?" Here, we confront political death that is not properly "death," a state whose horror is as much contained in the unintelligibility of the category as it is in the physical and emotional trauma of abjectivity.

There is a concordant invisibility of these spaces and with those who are desubjected within them, such that they risk further erasure—the risk of complete historical omission. The war on terror has fundamentally relied on cultural technologies of coherent narrative production in spaces whose coherence is not immediately evident. Memory is fundamentally fragmented, both in time and space, and cannot provide a reliable "map." As Kyle Grayson demonstrates, one can even go as far as Leonard Shelby in the film *Memento*, tattooing images on his body in an effort to "remember" events whose meaning is already immediately lost, fragmented in contextual complexities that cannot be fully recovered in the scripting on/of the body. Cultural productions attempt to solidify a coherent "we" in the face of our inherent unruliness, and in the unreliability of our memories, interpretations, and desires. It is the pervasive fear of our unreliability and unruliness that animates national security imperatives, such as the Bush doctrine of preemption, which Cynthia Weber argues articulates an attempt to secure the unconscious mind in the immanence of its potential criminality. In many ways it is this unreliability and unruliness that marks even those within biopower's domain of making live as always already bare life.

A Note on Structure

The volume unfolds in three related parts: "Bodies, Lives, Deaths," "Cinematics, Culture, Aesthetics," and "Regulation, Securitization, Preemption" constitute a series of different attempts to explore lived lives in the shadow of the war on terror. These sections begin and end in the spaces that the biopolitical fundamentally obscures, and this is the logic through which they both open and close the volume. "Cinematics, Cultures, Aesthetics" (part 2) engages the dominant narratives of the war on terror, exploring the productive spaces through which its logics unfold. The authors in this section illustrate some of the cultural conditions that in turn make possible the content of the opening and closing sections. These are explorations of the sites of the everyday, cultural sites that, although seemingly obscure, are emphatically necessary for the articulation of the war on terror. As such, "Cinematics, Cultures, Aesthetics" interrogates the spaces where the articulation of hegemonic Americanness is both sustained and disrupted.

Cynthia Weber's reading of the film *Minority Report* identifies the dangers associated with preemption in the drive to securitize the unconscious. Recognizing the subversive content of the film's narrative on security, Cynthia also points to the ways in which the film—and the American political imaginary—makes use of the feminine as supportive and supplementary to the masculinized quest for security and tranquil domesticity. Kyle Grayson, in his analysis of the film *Memento*, points to what he calls the "delirium" of the American state in the war on terror. Kyle argues that, in its prosecution of the war on terror, the American state is always already unable to perform the "final act"—the failed revenge project insofar as the war on terror can never claim to have "eliminated" the enemy. Following on this point, David Mutimer argues in the closing section of the volume that the war on terror is articulated as an indefinite project in which the certainty of "winning" is permanently deferred.

Through this logic, the war on terror is also working to extend and sustain a particular way of life. For David Campbell, the cultural productions and desires connected to the attainment of the American dream implicate particular American (and other western) lived lives in the everyday politics of the war on terror. Indeed, as this section of the book demonstrates, it is not the spectacular violence associated with September 11 that mobilizes Americans as participants in the war on terror but rather the everyday consumptive desires associated with what it is said to mean to be "American." This underwrites the desire for geopolitical control through which a particular version of "Americanness" can be enacted and inscribed. The "national interest," as David demonstrates, is constituted in and by the everyday—in the choices we make about how to live our lives. Mark Lacy points to the textual and cinematic artifacts that work to provide the cultural purchase that emanates from the apparent necessity of the practices and people associated with the war on terror. Mark explores how the American cultural and political imaginary of the Bush administration produces scripts of moral absolution by narrating the administration as comprised of well-meaning, decent men and women caught in dangerous times.

All of the contributions tell us something about the places where the war on terror is playing out. They explore the cultural networks through which the war on terror is circulated and taken up in the experience of the everyday—in our encounters with others via E-mail, in the vehicles in our driveways, in the cinemas of our suburban neighborhoods, and in the articles of our "human interest" columns and magazines. Certain lives are premised and sustained through an entire economy, however fragmented, of literal and metaphorical deaths that in turn produce radically unlivable lives. It is these relationships that this volume seeks to explore.

Finally, while this collection is inescapably academic, it is our hope that the stories contained within it can find resonance both within our professions and across the terrain of the everyday. Though no doubt scholars in earlier and other times have voiced the same, it is our belief that we are currently caught in a particularly dangerous war. It is a war that is elusive and slippery, with concepts and logics that seem seductively simple. As such, it is a war that needs to be exposed and resisted. We hope that this volume will make some small contribution to these and other efforts.

Acknowledgments

This project originated as a roundtable entitled "Biopolitics: Boundaries, Borders, and the New Terrain of Global Politics," delivered at the 46th Annual Convention of the International Studies Association in March 2005 in Honolulu, Hawai'i. We would like to extend our warm gratitude to both Palgrave and the contributors to this volume for taking the chance on us, who proposed this project as graduate students with no established reputations. It is also our custom to thank those who provided us with nonacademic distraction in all the necessary moments. They will know who they are, and we are most grateful.

Notes

1. Roxanne Lynn Doty, "Maladies of Our Souls: Identity and Voice in the Writing of Academic International Relations," *Cambridge Review of International Affairs*, 17:2 (July 2004): 377–392, p. 378.
2. Slavoj Žižek, "What's Wrong with Fundamentalism? Part I," http://www.lacan.com/zizunder.htm.
3. Michel Foucault, *Society Must Be Defended*, trans. David Macey (London: Allen Lane/Penguin, 2003), p. 248.
4. Ibid., p. 254.
5. Mark Lacy, in this volume.
6. Judith Butler, *Precarious Life: The Powers of Mourning and Violence* (London: Verso, 2004), p. 21.
7. Ibid., p. 23.
8. Ibid., p. 22.
9. Ibid., p. 21.

PART I

BODIES, LIVES, DEATHS

CHAPTER 1

CROSSROADS OF DEATH

Roxanne Lynn Doty

Writing is writing what you cannot know before you have written.[1]

The crossroads in this story wind through the desolate landscapes of the Sonoran Desert where the Mexico/U.S. border becomes at once an intensely violent inscription and almost an afterthought. Sometimes this border seems meaningless, part of our deterritorialized global "reality." Sometimes the consequences are monumental, the difference between life and death. The official crossroads, represented by lines on the maps, have become impossible for some—for those whose names are destined for little white crosses, those who carry their dreams and lives on their backs, those who do not get cited in *our* academic journals. Those who are not *us*. *I* can still cross with relative ease. So can *you*. For an afternoon of shopping, cheap drink, trinkets, and souvenirs. Yes, it is different for *us*. For *others*, another story most of us will never read. *They* cannot cross where *we* can cross. But, there are many other ways, though infinitely more deadly. The deadliness of these other crossing points gives rise to this story and to the struggles I have in telling it in the way I think it should be told, with words worthy of the human beings who live it and those who die in it. Of course, I cannot claim that this story, which is ultimately my story, is the one *others* would tell were we to listen. I cannot pretend to know what *their* stories would be. For there are other unauthorized crossroads that snake through risky territory and these, too, must be considered. Crossroads between what we write and who we are. Between our words and our identities. I struggle because an *ethics of encounter* should include the ways in which we, as writers and human beings, confront what we write about and how we write, and there are no clear paths for doing this.[2] Michael Taussig asks, "how to write the nervous system that passes through us and makes us who we are?"[3] I struggle because who *we* are is so intrinsically connected to how we write our stories, our choice of words, their rhythm, the tone of our voices. There are crossroads between these things and our positions vis-à-vis those we write about. There are crossroads between those whose knowledge counts and those who become objects in our studies. Between the limitations of language and what lies beyond it. The nervous system that passes through our bodies and souls implicates us in all we write and it pulsates incessantly with uncertainty.

Death surrounds me (and you) as I search for a way to write this story, for a language that might restore a beating heart to words so often corralled into boxes, impossibly transformed into *indicators* and academic concepts meant to capture and control. I am searching for this language amidst blind promises, pretenses, and desires that bind scholarship into a soulless, self-validating enterprise that forces us to fall away from ourselves and the rest of humanity and utter words forever empty to everyone but *us*. I am looking for a way, a method if you will, to minimize the violence of my own writing, to soften "the very hard weapon with which one must inscribe."[4] Garcia Lorca spoke of *duende*, a clinging spirit associated with desire and demonic enthusiasm that rises through the body and courses through the veins; a spirit that cannot be rationalized away. Inspiration in the face of death.[5] Is it not such a clinging spirit disguised as rationality that courses through the veins of our disciplinary body as we write our fictions of international relations?

The words of Guatemalan poet, Otto Rene Castillo, echo as I ponder this writing: "What did you do—when tenderness and life were dangerously burning out?"[6] I do not have an adequate response to this question as I imagine a crossroad and a delicate implement that would burn through the cold, sanitized words in journals collecting dust on the shelves in my office, the ones very few will ever read because their pages are branded with the silent warning: these pages are for *us*. I am longing for a different sort of spirit to smoke through the reasons we write, a spirit that lingers at the edges of everything we must believe, in order for *us* and *our* discipline to exist. A spirit that haunts in the face of death as I struggle with the distance between words and *things* elusive/illusive. How can one traverse this distance so as to *know* not in the ways of an illusory social science but in a human way that would constitute an ethical encounter? How can I/we know the crossroads that must be traveled, the ones that have become sites where distinctions that frame our existence—international versus domestic, legal versus illegal, inside versus outside, presence versus absence, self versus other, fact versus fiction, rationality versus emotion, good versus evil—collapse in the face of desperate, dangerous journeys? Perhaps an answer lurks in the ghostly voices that resound throughout the landscapes in this story.

The Sonoran Desert is around 120,000 square miles and the hottest and driest of the four Arizona deserts.[7] On the crossroads cutting through it we discover the playing out of a logic born long before September 11, 2001 though intimately connected with, reinforced by, and now firmly entrenched in the post-September 11 imaginary. The sensibility at work in U.S. border enforcement policies testifies to the fact that the uniqueness of September 11 and the security-related policies it ushered in must always be qualified. What does it mean to be unique? Unique to whom? Unique in comparison to what? Of course, September 11 intensified the already powerfully present imaginary of danger and otherness. But, to those who must cross where *we* do not have to cross, this imaginary had already resulted in border enforcement policies informed by a kind of biopower at its most fundamental, physiological level zeroing in on the limits of human endurance in the face of an extremely hostile natural environment. Border crossers without the proper papers, *undocumentados*, had already been reduced to the barest of life through processes that seemed to obscure official responsibility for the human tragedy that has come to characterize the crossroads of death. But, official responsibility, statecraft, looms large if one chooses to see it. Even in the remotest of remote places statecraft hovers, hides, watches, and strikes. It lurks behind the face of every mountain, in the gullies and canyons, within every mirage of cool, crystal water. What does it want? It wants to suck the life out of the human beings at its mercy. It wants to watch them bake in the sun. No, it wants to save their sorry asses, to manage their rescue, to lock up the damned smugglers who abandoned them. No, it wants to turn its eyes the other way, pretend there is no desert, no crossroads, no "undocumented aliens (UDA), only Filibertos, endless citrus orchards, strawberry fields forever, and an eternity of cheap labor."[8] It wants all these things and nothing less. But, this is not all. There is no end to the desire of "the state." So, come with me to the crossroads in a relatively obscure place, but one that is an important microcosm of the workings of modern power and an instance of the tragedy that unfolds in many other locations. These crossroads are testimony to the fact that no location is so remote as to escape the consequences of statecraft.

Tierra, Viajes, Muerte

The land, he said, is a death trap.[9]

Landscape is an important, though often overlooked, element in the exercise of power.[10] Critical geographers have shown how spaces and places are both implicated in the use of power as well as themselves the products of coercion, struggle, and resistance. Landscape is simultaneously a thing and a social process, never fixed, natural, or unitary.[11] While appreciating the socially constructed nature of landscape, one can also give credence to an element of the raw physicality of nature in some areas, whose sheer being encompasses a degree of power, though the realization of that power is certainly not neutral or devoid of social/political practices and relationships. In the journeys that make up this story, the power of the land's terrain itself and the natural elements are key factors in the exercise of power. In its harsh extremeness the desert possesses a power that is nonetheless bound up with political and social relations that enable it to be realized. The "natural" power of desert terrains has also functioned, to a significant degree, to obscure official responsibility for the deaths of border crossers. In any case, the landscapes of the desert southwest have played a key role in the biopower of U.S. border enforcement policy. Let us visit this landscape, so we can see where *they* must travel, so we can begin to imagine their journeys.

I have chosen to describe a landscape(s) which has become particularly prominent in the story of deaths on the border. Or perhaps, it has chosen me. The desert has a way of working itself into your bones. This landscape has, in fact, been a key aspect of U.S. border enforcement policies over the past decade. I began to notice this several years ago when I developed something of a morbid obsession with stories of border-crossing deaths, which have become local, national, and international news. Springtime, with its increasing desert heat, marks the beginning of the dying season, the ultimate incorporation of human life into the dry land. Bodies of the dead and near-dead scatter across expanses of the earth that have become contemporary killing fields. The worst of it often lasts through October. A map on the wall above my desk reads "2003 Migrant Deaths and Humane Border Water Stations." Colored dots on the map indicate that migrant deaths cover a large portion of it. Red dots indicate death from heat, and there are far more of these than any other color (blue for vehicular deaths, green for deaths from trains, yellow for unknown causes, and brown for other causes). There are many ways to die in the vast desert between Mexico and the United States; an estimated 2,640 border-crossing deaths in the past ten years. Ten times more have lost their lives along this border than the Berlin Wall claimed during its entire 28 years in existence. The number of deaths is just a little short of the 2,749 lives lost in the attack on the World Trade Center.[12] The humanitarian group Humane Borders tracks these deaths and, with permission from the Border Patrol, puts water stations at locations where many are dying. There are a lot of these water stations but obviously not enough. Humane Borders was unable to complete their annual map project for 2004 because the Tucson sector of the Border Patrol has told them that they will only receive further information by employing the Freedom of Information Act.[13] A similar map could be produced for the other border states of California, New Mexico, and Texas. Maps could also be produced for the uncountable crossroads of migrant journeys all over the world. This story, though, unfolds in the Arizona desert around places whose names are unknown to many, invisible to the annals of academic International Relations.

We begin in El Sasabe, Mexico, which lies about 70 miles southwest of Tucson, Arizona. El Sasabe, a tiny border town of around 3,000 people has become a popular crossing point for human beings without documents. It's not a busy border town like Nogales, Tijuana, or Juarez with kids selling Chicklets chewing gun and brightly painted donkeys waiting for tourists to mount and be photographed. Tourists do not come to El Sasabe. There isn't much to it and it's not on the way to anywhere unless one is smuggling drugs or human beings, which is a big *unless*. To get there you take Highway 86, also known as Ajo Way, west from Tucson for about 22 miles to state Highway 286 that goes south for 46 miles to the U.S./Mexico border. Like many roads in this part of the world, Highway 286 traverses landscape so desolate the word *godforsaken* might come to mind. One might think of the word *badlands*, for it is true this is a land of drug smugglers, people smugglers, a place of promises and corpses, the long arm of the state, and those who seek to evade the law. *But*, it is beautiful and as we traverse this terrain I can understand why it and places like it have so often been constructed as "at once desirable and fearsome," intimidating, inviting, and luring.[14] I engage in my own romanticized construction of this landscape. I am in awe as I look out over the landscape and suspend all attempts to convey with words its sheer, surreal magnificence. But, of course, I am in a position to do this, as are you. This landscape is undoubtedly much different for those who cross it under conditions so different from mine. The vastness of the open desert is accentuated by mountain ranges in the distance: the Sierrita to the east, the Baboquivari to the west. Baboquivari Peak, sacred to the Tohono O'odham, rises 7,730 feet from the surrounding desert. Mario Alberto Diaz probably thought of this land in ways I cannot. He will die not too far from here in the steep foothills of the Sierrita. His body will be discovered in a deep creek bed after lying there for twenty days. Diaz is six feet tall, has a black belt in karate and is working on a master's degree in biology. But he is no match for this place and in a few months it will devour him.[15]

The day I travel this road, clouds drop to almost touch the peaks, creating the effect of one continuous sculpture connecting heaven and earth. Blurry, striated lines of gray indicate rain is falling over the mountains. A mystical air pervades. If one believed, one would almost expect to see God just over the summits. I do not, but still I think this is as close as I will ever come and I think of those who seek spiritual council before they cross, of the religious symbols often found on the pathways of their travels.[16] The other of language, the *thing* we can never reach with our words, seems to hang in the air over this vast space of magic and myth, as we make our way along the two-lane highway, a small caravan of three Borderlinks vans. The annual dying has not yet started on this cold, cloudy day in late February, though death is never very far away. *We* have come to see where *they* cross, the terrain they must navigate, where many must die.

As we pull up to the U.S. Customs station at the border between Sasabe, Arizona, and El Sasabe, Mexico the sky grows darker and a light rain begins to fall. A cold, damp wind rushes at us. There is a perverse irony in the desert where so many die from the heat. Diaz will not die until June when the temperatures begin to soar. But, sometimes the nights get so cold in the desert, crossers risk freezing to death. Agent Fred, a small bureaucrat in the big Homeland Security system, comes out to greet us with all the self-importance a minute spoke in the huge wheel of statecraft might be able to muster.[17] His first words are a warning that we should be ready if "something goes down." I pull out a camera that he notices immediately. He tells me not to take pictures of him or the other agents. He tells us this area used to be big in cattle ranching, but now it is mostly smuggling drugs and people. The whole town of El Sasabe, Mexico is smuggling, he says. When the students we are with begin asking him questions, he warms a bit and the thin bureaucratic veneer slips away. He's spent time on the U.S./Canadian border, but considers himself a desert rat. This is a point of connection for me. As he speaks I feel the deepness of the desert around us, its sheer unfathomableness, and the intensity of its openness. Distance stretches in all directions. We are just a few feet from the border, but it is nearly invisible, overpowered by terrain that knows only continuity.

We pass through a pale turquoise iron gate into Mexico, the guard waving us on, barely looking at us, the line separating the two countries not much more than flimsy chicken wire. A few feet ahead at the Mexican immigration checkpoint, a small beige and pink stucco building, the pavement ends. Again, we are waved on after a brief conversation with our driver. I note the sign stating that the border closes at 9 p.m. and momentarily reflect upon the meaning of this statement. The road turns rocky, gently curving with small inclines. We are on the main street. We pass a few restaurants scattered back off the road, modest homes, a yard with a child's swing set, and a couple of general stores until we reach what must be the center of town. The hub of activity seems to be a *tacqueria* on the corner of the main street and a small side alley. There is hardly anything here that would indicate how people make a living except the *tacqueria* and a small *supercito* down the street that could hardly support the population. We stop at the *tacqueria* for lunch. The light rain intensifies and the sky releases a heavy downpour as we all try to fit under the roof in the small outdoor eating area. The smell of desert rain mixes with lard, tortillas, and beef on the grill.

We are an obvious oddity on this late winter afternoon, three vanloads of *gringos* on a Borderlinks study trip, though an increasing number of reporters come here. For the remainder of the year 2004 I note a surge of articles in local papers about El Sasabe and its contemporary claim to fame. I notice a rather large number of late model pickup trucks and SUVs that race through town, speeding past the *tacqueria*—too many $25,000 and $30,000 vehicles for the economic base, which officially is cattle ranching, a brickyard, and fireworks. When the local policeman we visit later is asked about smuggling, he says that there is not much trouble here with coyotes (people smugglers) or drug smugglers. The thought occurs to me, without judgment, that he may be a smuggler himself. What else would one do here? Everyone knows that the shadow world of illegal border movements is the lifeblood in this remote little place in the middle of the desert and much of the surrounding area. The body of *el pollo* is now more valuable than drugs. Later in the day on a small dirt road in front of the office of Grupos Beta one of these expensive trucks screams around the corner preparing for that night's crossing.[18] But, the *undocumentados* will not cross in one of the shiny new vehicles. Their journey will begin on foot through the icy cold night. Their smuggler will likely promise to meet them somewhere close, after they have walked a short distance, at some prearranged site off Highway 86. They will probably walk much longer than expected, maybe for days. Perhaps the smuggler will meet them; perhaps not.

If you kept driving south from El Sasabe for about 50 miles, you would come to Altar, another small desert town where this road meets up with Highway 2, which parallels the Mexico/U.S. border for much of its length, dipping deeper into Mexico from Aqua Prieta to the east to Sonoita to the west. As many as 2,000 migrants a day arrive in Altar before journeying on to El Sasabe to cross over into El Norte. Most come from the south of Mexico, some from Central America. Many are not prepared for the parched desert terrain they will have to cross. Fidel Velasquez Perez, a 17-year-old boy from Guatemala, was not prepared. He arrived in Altar in late May 2003 and died on May 24 while crossing the desert.[19] The immi-grant rights group, Derechos Humanos, collected money to send his body back home to San Francisco. The landscape is overwhelming in its vastness and lack of reliable markers. "Everything looks the same," said Librado, a migrant from the tropical state of Veracruz. "I hope I will be able to tell whether I am walking forward and not backward."[20]

Directly east of El Sasabe, almost in a straight line, lay the border towns of Aqua Prieta, Mexico and Douglas, Arizona. For years, Douglas has been one of the busiest illegal crossing points along the U.S./Mexico border. It still is, but recently fortified enforcement technologies have led to the increasing popularity of El Sasabe, which still lacks adequate fencing, high-tech surveillance cameras, and the number of agents found in the Douglas area. Like El Sasabe, Douglas and Aqua Prieta are surrounded by desert and mountains. There are also many ranches, which on the U.S. side lead to a whole other story of vigilantism and "statecraft from below." It is another story for another time. On almost any day you can watch busloads of undocumented human beings exit big Border Patrol buses and shuffle toward the tall, steel turnstile that revolves continually as bodies pass through reentering Mexico, foiled in that day's attempt to reach El Norte. For me, this land recalls the words of Edward Abbey about the intangibil-ity of the desert, how it lures one on and then dooms one to an eternal search for its elusive heart. But it must be very different for *them*—an obstacle to be surmounted, an ever-threatening foreboding of death. Crossing *into* Mexico through the turnstile is easy. Crossing back is easy for you and me, even after September 11, 2001. But not for *them*.

Ana Rosa Segura-Marcial, a 15-year-old girl, crossed in this area a cou-ple of years ago. She traveled 1,200 miles from her home in San Fernando in central Mexico. She planned to meet her boyfriend in Guadalupe, a small village bordering Tempe, Arizona, which is home to Arizona State University. The group she traveled with arrived in Aqua Prieta, Mexico on August 9, 2002 and crossed the border in the desert near Douglas. She journeyed for an amazing distance. Her body was found three days later in an orange grove south of Gilbert, Arizona, an upscale town on the outskirts of Phoenix. In December the local paper will run a four-page special about Ana Rosa, and readers will undoubtedly feel bad about this tragedy.[21] A year and a half later, the anti-immigrant measure Proposition 200 will pass overwhelmingly.[22]

Two hundred miles west of Douglas, past El Sasabe, beyond the Baboquivari Mountains, lays the deadly Camino del Diablo (Devil's Highway), believed by some to be the heart of the Sonoran Desert. The average temperature increases as one moves into the western desert, and this is undoubtedly the deadliest area in which to cross. Camino del Diablo is a 4,100 square mile *despoblado* with temperatures reaching as high as 130 degrees Fahrenheit in the shade. It is full of death and unfulfilled dreams. Melchoir Diaz traveled this road in 1540 at the behest of Francisco Vasquez de Coronado in search of the mythical seven cities of Cibola whose streets were believed to be paved with gold. The Jesuit priest Padre Eusibio Kino explored the area in the seventeenth century. Seekers of gold traveled this road in search of riches in the mid-nineteenth century. Camino del Diablo is littered with the bleached bones of those whose dreams ended in the blinding glare of a sun screaming its power over this harsh landscape. One of the first "studies" of the effects of thirst on the human body occurred here in 1898 when ethnologist and explorer William McGee journeyed into this part of the Sonoran Desert to study the summer meteorology and biology of the area. On the second night, McGee discovered the near-dead prospector Pablo Valencia who had walked the desert, lost for eight days. Valencia was lying naked on the sand under an ironwood tree at the foot of Mesita de los Muertos. His lips were shriveled to thin black lines; his gums black and exposed. His eyes were open, and he was no longer able to blink. Amazingly, Pablo was still alive and over the course of the next several days, McGee was able to nurse him back to health. From this experience McGee wrote one of the first monographs on the effects of dehydration on the human system. The monograph was called "Desert Thirst as Disease" and was written before any clinical or detailed physiological studies of thirst had even taken place. This early attempt to describe the progression of dehydration's signs and symptoms was amazingly accurate and remains something of a classic historical document.[23]

More recently, the Camino del Diablo claimed the lives of 14 people out of a group of 20 who ventured into its deadly terrain in May 2001. They have become known as the Yuma 14. The group included small-plot farmers, coffee growers, a school boy, and his father. Most were from the tropical state of Veracruz in southeastern Mexico. Most had never seen a desert before. Luis Alberto Urrea tells the story of their tragic journey.[24] Experts say that the human body needs about two gallons (seven and one half liters) of water a day just to survive this environment, but writer John Annerino has recorded his own body's requirements for fluid when he made a 130 mile trek along Camino del Diablo for 6 days. The minimum he consumed was two gallons. On several days he drank as much as five gallons.[25] The walkers of May 2001 carried an average of eight liters for their journey that lasted five days.[26] It is physically impossible for most people to carry enough water.

The Bodies and the Theory(s)

A good theory has prescriptive richness. It yields useful policy recommendations.[27]

The bodies of 61 people have been found in Arizona's desert around Tucson since Oct. 1, reports from the Mexican government show. [28]

His remains lie in a white body bag in a 36-degree cooler. He was about 5 feet 5 inches tall and 29 years old. His body had been reduced to a skeleton before it was found in the desert.[29]

Despite the efforts of the Border Patrol and human rights groups, migrants continue to die in record numbers while crossing the Arizona border.[30]

Illegals dying at Record Rate in Arizona Desert.[31]

Migrant Deaths Hit Record High in Arizona.[32]

County Rents Truck to Use as Morgue.[33]

Corpse Overflow Stored in Trailer.[34]

The founding acts of violence, always visible though rarely seen by the eyes of humanity, are continually reenacted on these remote and unmarked crossroads in the scorching Arizona desert. Such acts enable *us* to be and our being is haunted by a logic that produces the borders running through the body of the earth, through our lives, our identities, our course catalogs, our publication outlets, our very souls. This logic defines and destroys us. We pull out our passports, pick up our pens, negotiate the boundaries, ignore the ghosts, and tell ourselves that boundaries must hold. Despite the violence. Despite the deaths. Despite the vicious arbitrariness of it all. All borders share the elements of violence, destruction, and arbitrariness. When we speak of one kind of border we implicitly invoke the trace of all the other borders that permeate our lives and our identities. The locus of U.S. border enforcement policy is the undocumented body as it moves across the surface of an intensely, obsessively documented earth, connecting and subjecting the human body, its physiological needs and desires with the body of the land and the rigors it imposes. And it is the undocumented body that suffers the founding acts of violence over and over again until this enormous desert is strewn with corpses, haunted by a brutality that begs the question of to whom and to what practices we should attach the words *terrorists* and *terrorism*.

A whole array of governmental bodies and programs exist to address various aspects of dying in the Sonoran Desert, to manage it, to facilitate it, to prevent it, to keep count of and tend to the corpses. These apparatuses operate far from what we generally think of as centers of power, though of course power is always a palpable presence hovering over arid landscapes like an ethereal presence. How to think about this? Conceptually? Theoretically? Morally? How to write about it? I struggle with the immense distance that separates theories from the human performances they seek to translate; the emotion, the passion, the desires that animate these performances. Like Babel, which Jacques Derrida suggests demands and simultaneously resists translation, this human drama cannot be dominated by any conceptualization or theorization we might offer. No theory will be able to translate this phenomenon of death in the desert, so incomprehensible to the part of our humanity still breathing beneath the bloodless stories that usually occupy us. No words are adequate.

Still, words, concepts are all we have to reach beyond language and I grasp at *biopolitics* as a concept that may offer insight into the logic and power behind all this dying. Michel Foucault used the term *biopower* to speak of a form of power exercised over *living* persons as members of a population, but in the desert there is often a fragile line between life and death, the living and the dead. Let me recall briefly the intimate connection between politics and the human body this concept suggests and how this connects up with interventions aimed at the social and political body. Let me recall how this concept can connect the local, everyday existence of human beings to the global. Drawing upon Giorgio Agamben's conceptualization of *homo sacer*, I suggest a kind of biopower that involves dead bodies rather than living ones, or rather a perverse combination of dead and living bodies. I would like to call attention to the fact that there is something happening on the desert crossroads that concepts such as surveillance and exclusion, which are certainly relevant to many aspects of the immigration issue, do not do justice to. The tale of U.S. immigration policies along its southern border has been told many times. The story I tell here interprets the border "operations," as they are officially called, through the lens of the camp as articulated by Agamben, that is, as the creation of biopolitical spaces "in which power confronts nothing but pure life without any mediation."[35] If the camp is the "hidden matrix and nomos of the political space in which we are still living," then surely the many desolate and dangerous crossing areas are an important modern manifestation of it.[36]

Agamben suggests the camp as a biopolitical paradigm of the modern, cautioning us that every time we encounter the materialization of the state of exception and the creation of a space in which bare life and juridical rule enter a threshold of indistinction, we find ourselves in the presence of a camp whatever its denomination and specific topography.[37] Agamben's paradigm of the camp begins with the concept of *homo sacer*, who may be killed but cannot be sacrificed. For Agamben, *homo sacer*, an obscure figure of archaic Roman law whose life was included in the juridical order solely in the form of its exclusion (i.e., its capacity to be killed) continues to serve a function in modern politics and can thus tell us something about contemporary workings of sovereign power. Sacred man and sacred life do not refer to lives warranting honor and respect, to be treasured and protected at all costs. Rather, they imply just the opposite. "In the case of *homo sacer* a person is simply set outside human jurisdiction without being brought into the realm of divine law."[38] The killing of *homo sacer* is classified neither as a homicide nor a sacrifice. For Agamben, this violence opens up a sphere of human action, the sovereign sphere, in which killing can occur without the commission of a homicide and without celebration of a sacrifice. Sacred life is the life that has been captured in this sphere.

The concept of bare life is synonymous with sacred life and is, according to Agamben, the originary activity of sovereignty. "The sacredness of life, which is invoked today as an absolutely fundamental right in opposition to sovereign power, in fact originally expresses precisely both life's subjection to a power over death and life's irreparable exposure in the relation of abandonment."[39] Bare life fully entered the structure of the state, becoming the foundation of the state's legitimacy and sovereignty with the French Declaration of the Rights of Man and Citizen in 1789. At the same time, though, this bare life vanished into the figure of the citizen in whom rights are preserved. Rights are attributed to man "solely to the extent that man is the immediately vanishing ground (who must never come to light as such) of the citizen."[40]

The desert crossroads approximate the camp, but not exactly as Agamben suggests. The state of exception here is not so much the "ordering of space" or "taking of the outside" so as to define and create the space in which the juridico-political order has validity, though what is going on is not unrelated to this endeavor. The state of exception as it pertains to dangerous border crossings is rather the creation of a space or spaces that, while technically within the juridico-political order are de facto "beyond the pale"—a no man's land where sheer physical survival is a feat and often a miracle, a place where rule of law is momentarily suspended, where the fate of those who wander is left to the natural elements and the harsh terrain. Border enforcement operations involve the creation of *nonmoral* spaces where whatever ethics and morality are present within the social/political order are suspended, where encounters are anything but ethical. This kind of place exists in many parts of the world, geographically remote, sparsely inhabited if at all, but increasingly necessary for the validity of the juridico-political orders that constitute the world today.[41] The existence of these camps is also increasingly undermining of much of the world's juridico-political orders because these juridico-political orders are never what they pretend to be, never what is so widely and repetitively disseminated throughout our institutions of government and of higher learning, that is, the stable, fixed, eternally legitimate entities embodying exemplary principles of democracy, liberty, and justice.

In contrast to the concept of governmentality as articulated by Foucault, wherein he suggests the idea of governmental concern/preoccupation with the management of population in all its numerous aspects from health, wealth, and poverty to birthrates, death rates, needs, desires, and aspirations resulting in a "governmentalization of the state" by which it increasingly exercises a form of micropower over its population, the lens of the camp enables a more complex understanding of the functioning of U.S. border policies.[42] The biopower associated with the concept of governmentality can illuminate many aspects of the immigration issue, for example, the use of high-tech surveillance mechanisms such as biometric fingerprinting, identification cards, and other policing practices. But in the case of illegal immigration as it has been dealt with through border enforcement policies in the southwestern United States, the concept of governmentality fails to fully capture the ways in which statecraft yields its power, sometimes briefly relinquishes it in order to maintain legitimacy, and effaces its complicity in the inhumane consequences. The ordering of space that is relevant to U.S. border enforcement strategies is not a "taking of the outside," not an incorporation of the everyday life of border crossers into the domain of the state, but a banishment to spaces that are simultaneously both and neither outside and/or inside, which marks a decision about life that does not deserve to live. Here the desert functions as a kind of endless hinterland into which illegal bodies can disappear and the contradictions they embody be deferred, at least temporarily. According to Agamben, "He who has been banned is not, in fact, simply set outside the law and made indifferent to it, but rather *abandoned* by it, that is, exposed and threatened on the threshold in which life and law, outside and inside, become indistinguishable. It is literally not possible to say whether the one who has been banned is outside or inside the juridical order."[43] This calls our attention to a way in which modern power works that *does not* require a fixity of place, but rather works on human bodies in the moments of their mobility.

One can only wonder about the calculations that went into the border "operations" that are the enactment and realization of this power that forced crossers into the extreme terrains where they would likely meet their deaths. Calculations about how many would attempt such a journey, how many would survive, how many would perish, how many would be deterred. One can only wonder because these calculations were not spoken of openly. At least not very often. But, one can piece together the story, the way it unfolded, the assumptions that underlay it, the silences that were necessary

for a coarsening of the moral fiber required to put these "operations" into
practice, and to suspend reflection on their ethical consequences.[44]

Far from the halls of official power, in Washington, D.C., a man with
some local power in the border town of El Paso, Texas, had a theory about
the living human beings whose hearts still beat, whose blood was still warm
as it coursed through the arteries of their dreams. He had a theory about
these crossers, and how to manage them, control them, deter their desire to
move freely. The force of the theory depended on some deaths. Not that
the man necessarily gave any conscious thought to this. By all accounts he
is a decent and respected man and in fairness, perhaps dead bodies were far
from his conscious mind. They were essential, though. In fact the theory
would have been meaningless without them. No deaths, theory rejected.
The theory was not articulated in the sense that academics generally think
of theories. It was more like just your average, nonacademic Joe saying
"I have a theory about this or that." But of course this man was not your
average Joe, even though at the time he was fairly low on the official chain
of powerful people. His theory was powerful and infinitely more conse-
quential than average Joe theories and even most academic theories. It was
called *deterrence*, a killer word that deadens our moral sensibilities. Behind
deterrence lay a technology of the human body: its need for water and
what happens when it has none. The man with the power did not say too
much about this. But it was at the heart of his theory. It had to be. The
horror of a human body without enough water was absolutely essential to
the theory. True, other hazards such as dangerous terrain, the extreme cold
of desert nights, drowning in water rushing through canals could also act as
a deterrent, but it is inconceivable that given the geography and climate of
the border areas, the issue of water (and the lack of it) would not be
relevant, would not be absolutely essential to the success of the theory. It is
equally inconceivable that those who promoted deterrence and the policies
that followed from it could have been unaware of this at some level, some
human level beneath the bureaucratic, problem-solving veneer. The
theory said that death would be so likely and the deaths would be so
horrible as to deter others from attempting to cross. The advocates of this
theory likely never heard of Pablo Valencia or what happened to his body
in the heat of Camino del Diablo, but this vulnerability of the human body
was at the heart of the logic of deterrence.

Deterrence also entailed some presumptions about the human spirit and
what could defeat it, though again this was not clearly articulated.
Deterrence absolutely depended on defeating the human spirit, that part of
the human spirit that desires more: a job, food, a better life. It depended on

the presumption that the spirit of would-be illegal border crossers could be defeated with the implicit threat of death by dehydration, that such a horror would overpower the desire for what was believed to lay on *el otro lado*. Deterrence depended on killing both the body and the spirit in some cases, just the spirit in others. If enough potential crossers witnessed or heard about the horrors of thirst, dehydration, and ultimate death, *they* would be deterred. *They* would be absolutely scared shitless to cross the barren badlands. Nothing would be worth the risk of such an experience. *They* would lose their spirit, their determination to get to El Norte, to the strawberry fields, the citrus groves, the meatpacking plants, the kitchens of our restaurants, the laundry rooms of the very hotels in which *we* hold our academic conferences. The man was wrong about this part of the theory, though, as attested to by the countless stories of the many that cross despite the warnings, despite the deaths. Perhaps the human spirit is more difficult to theorize.[45]

Silvestre Reyes, the Border Patrol chief in El Paso, Texas, was the man with the theory. Its official name was Operation Hold the Line, so named after its original Operation Blockade proved offensive to the Mexican government in the El Paso border region.[46] The practices ushered in by this and the subsequent border operations from Gatekeeper in San Diego to Safeguard in Tucson and Nogales to the many enforcement operations of the "prevention through deterrence" doctrine, constitute a micropolitics of the body based on its need for water, among other things.[47] This is biopolitics at its most fundamental physiological stratum, entailing an intervention at the level of individual human beings and their bodily requirements and aimed at management of the social body, that is, the social body that includes would-be illegal border crossers as well as the social body of sovereign citizens in whose names "border integrity" was/is being upheld. The technology of the body behind deterrence was never clearly articulated. It did not need to be. It is undoubtedly true, as others have suggested, that border enforcement operations are, at least in part, elaborate public performances aided by the mass media to enhance the impression of control.[48] Policy makers may or may not actually believe that *deterrence* will truly once and for all stop the movement of people, but the important point here is that the "success" of such a public performance depends on the *visibility* of the enforcement operations and the *invisibility* of border crossers. The presumption behind the new border enforcement operations was/is that the likelihood of crossers surviving in the areas where they would be forced to cross would drastically decrease, thus leading to a decrease in crossings. The result would be a diminished threat to the integrity of the border itself and the officials of the state who uphold that integrity. Some, of course, would make it through, but many would not and those who did would do so by a route much less visible than before. The presence of illegal border crossers could be deferred to the desert spaces, beyond the pale, to modern camps of contemporary *homo sacer*. Border enforcement operations may be, in part, symbolic public performances, but this does not detract from their deadly serious nature or the inhumane consequences that have resulted. Nor does it obviate the need to understand the logic at work in these policies.

The illegal immigrant, the UDA, the *undocumentado*, the *sans papiers*, as a figure of modern politics is similar in many respects to the refugee and we should not make too much of the distinction between the categories. We can agree with Michael Dillon that refugees are a scandal for politics because their very existence constitutes a reproach to the political orders and subjectivity that gives rise to them.[49] The same can be asserted regarding illegal immigrants. However, the latter are arguably closer to Agamben's *homo sacer* in that they are afforded no legal status of being and are devoid of any political existence. Illegality erases not only legal personhood but arguably in the moments of crossing, the time of the journey, any notion of personhood at all is obliterated. Only bare life remains. The illegal immigrant elicits significantly less empathy or sympathy than the refugees whose tragedy is generally recognized, even if actions to ameliorate their plight are woefully insufficient. Illegal immigrants' very existence as human beings in a certain time and place is subject to legal sanction by the very political order(s) in which they seek "refuge." The illegality of their being opens the possibility of a violence sanctioned by the law, relegating them to the status of human litter on the world's crossroads of death.

The story of border-crossing deaths suggests that illegal immigrants are today's "sacred men," banished to spaces that remain outside the normal juridico-political order, excluded from all political life, their existence stripped of every right, reduced to perpetual flight. Yet, they are in a continuous relationship with the power that banishes them in that at every instant they are exposed to an unconditional threat of death, caught in the sovereign ban, reckoning with it at every moment, searching for the best way to elude or deceive it.[50] Border enforcement policies of pushing crossers into areas where the landscape is harsh, the weather extreme, and chances of survival infinitely smaller than more visible and safer crossing points constitute a decision on life that can be killed without commission of a homicide, eliminated without punishment. These strategies feed upon sovereign authority whose very nature is inextricably connected with its power to dispense with human life.

Words

"The State as the model for the book and for thought has a long history."[51]

A density of statistics spreads across a white surface illuminated by fluorescent ceiling lights in a windowless conference room. The numbers are neatly aligned in rows and columns like soldiers in formation awaiting our inspection. We are deeply immersed in these numbers as if something profound might be found in the probabilities and significance levels attached to them. Rumors of truth silently circulate with the chilled air. I sense a deep desire pumping through our nervous systems. It is the glue that holds us together here. Words run lengthwise along the left margin, ostensibly orienting the numbers toward a world beyond their own self-validating authority. But, they have been eviscerated, stripped of any connection to flesh and blood. "Immigrant contact," "humanitarianism," and "border enforcement" have become *variables*, and we are doomed to celebrate "empirical findings," forever silencing any insight and wisdom not reducible to the statistics. The names, the faces, the bodies have been indefinitely deferred from our consciousness.

My colleagues' questions form a dim background buzz as they assess the tightness of the argument presented, the certitude with which it has been made, the prestige of the words uttered. My thoughts are momentarily suspended in the enormous space between the reductions in this room and the humanity that so often seems to evade social science scholarship. There is death in the words uttered in this room, just as surely as there is death on the desert crossroads. Statecraft echoes in every question posed, masquerading as disinterested rationality. Agamben tells us that today there is no longer any clear figure of sacred man because, perhaps, we are all virtually *homines sacri*.[52] I believe he has a point. All of us in this room are "new living dead men," though there are no readymade social scientific indicators through which we could come to know the "truth" of this.

For a brief moment, after the May 2001 deaths on the Devil's Highway, in the *other* tragedy of that fateful year, there was a glimmer of hope for a more humane border policy in the United States. It briefly seemed as if George W. Bush and Vicente Fox were on the verge of personally eradicating the Mexico/U.S. border. But of course, just the opposite occurred. The dying continues, and the word *terror* echoes over every hallowed boundary marker that characterizes our post-September 11, 2001 world, mapping numerous bodies as sites of danger. Despite the recent discussions about a guest worker program and amnesty for illegal immigrants, "deterrence" remains a cornerstone of U.S. border enforcement policy. But it did not begin with September 11. This day and all it has come to represent merely functions to more firmly entrench an already existing sensibility that for many years has defined border policies.

Bare life. Like all concepts there is an inherent instability to this one. Human beings cannot indefinitely and without objection be stripped of their humanity, pigeonholed into an arbitrary category of identity that by its very nature permits killing without punishment. The natural characteristics of the harsh landscapes of the U.S. Southwest have enabled a deferral of official responsibility for the deaths and functioned to obscure the power that has created a modern day *homo sacer*. The desert, however, does not offer endless deferral. The invisibility of border crossers is not permanent. Dead bodies eventually are found, at least many of them. In Pima County, Arizona, the bodies found in the desert pile up awaiting autopsies and identification. As they come in, the chief medical examiner analyzes dental records and any personal items found near them in an attempt to give a name, an identity to the heat-ravaged corpses. Lori Baker, a forensic anthropologist at Baylor University in Texas, has started a project of identifying the remains of migrants who die in the sunbaked deserts of Arizona, the scrublands of Texas, and the waters of the Rio Grande. Her goal is to reunite the bodies with their relatives.[53]

These bodies exercise something of a counterpolitics sparking projects like Baker's as well as resistance to the policies that are responsible for the dying as indicated in the numerous immigrants' rights and humanitarian groups such as Humane Borders, National Council of La Raza, Borderlinks, National Immigration Forum, Citizens for Border Solutions, and many others. There is a form of everyday resistance, even a poetics in the deaths of border crossers as well as in their journeys that disrupt notions of territoriality, citizen/human distinctions, and modes of representation and writing that are supported by these dominant and dominating conceptualizations. A troubling connection weaves through the many border-enforcing practices being carried out in numerous locales today. The territorial politics in the display of statistics and the discussion surrounding them is not so different from that practiced in the desolate southwestern desert. They censor unauthorized crossings and reinforce *our* identities against some *other*. They stifle the possibility of connecting to those not cited in our academic journals but whose ghostly presence haunts all we write about. Such stifling, though, rattles the nervous system, and it is only by the thinnest of threads, the most sustained studied effort, that a blindness to all that is excluded by such practices can be sustained. How should we write? How should we tell our stories? How much can we stifle before the life burns out of us?

Notes

1. Helene Cixous, *Three Steps on the Ladder of Writing* (New York: Columbia University Press, 1993), p. 38.
2. I borrow the phrase, "ethics of encounter," from Michael J. Shapiro in "The Ethics of Encounter: Unreading, Unmapping the Imperium," in *Moral Spaces: Rethinking Ethics and World Politics*, ed. David Campbell and Michael J. Shapiro (Minneapolis: University of Minnesota Press, 1999).
3. Michael Taussig, *The Nervous System* (New York: Routledge, 1992), p. 10.
4. Jacques Derrida, "Circumfession," in *Jacques Derrida*, trans. Geoffrey Bennington (Chicago: University of Chicago Press, 1993).
5. Edward Hirsch, *The Demon and the Angel-Searching for the Source of Artistic Inspiration* (New York: Harcourt, Inc., 2002).
6. Otto Rene Castillo, "Apolitical Intellectuals," in *Tomorrow Triumphant: Selected Poems of Otto Rene Castillo*, trans. Roque Dalton Cultural Brigade and ed. Magaly Fernandez and David Volpendesta (San Francisco: Night Horn Books, 1984).
7. The other three deserts are the Great Basin, the Mojave, and the Chihuahuan. Unlike the Sonoran, these are all classic rain-shadow deserts, having developed in the rain shadows of mountain chains. See Alex Shoumatoff, *Legends of the American Desert: Sojourns in the Greater Southwest* (New York: Harper Perennial, 1997), pp. 55–57.
8. UDA (undocumented alien) is the official acronym for illegal immigrants.
9. Ginger Thompson, "The Desperate Risk Death in the Desert," *The New York Times*, October 31, 2000, section A, page 12, col. 1.
10. Patricia L. Price, *Dry Places: Landscapes of Belonging and Exclusion* (Minneapolis: University of Minnesota Press, 2005), p. 56.
11. See Don Mitchell, *The Lie of the Land: Migrant Workers and the California Landscape* (Minneapolis: University of Minnesota Press, 1996), pp. 30–35.
12. See Wayne Cornelius, "Evaluating Enhanced U.S. Border Enforcement," *Migration Information Source*, May 1, 2004 and Eric Lipton, "New York Settles on a Number that Defines Tragedy: 2,749 Dead in Trade Center Attack," *The New York Times*, January 23, 2004, section B, p. 7, col. 1.
13. Robin Hoover, *Desert Fountain*, Humane Borders' fiscal year end report, October 2004, www.humaneborders.org.
14. See Price (2005), pp. 33–60 on ways in which the desert southwest has been subject to such constructions as well as gendered, racialized, and generally made available for exploitation and conquest.
15. Richard Bourdeaux, "Deadly Journey of Hope," *Los Angeles Times*, October 13, 2004.
16. Migrants often leave religious symbols on the paths they have crossed. Volunteers who maintain water stations in the desert have discovered antlers atop their water stations, a symbolic Yaqui blessing. In Tijuana, migrants pray at a shrine dedicated to Juan Soldado, a folk hero said to perform miracles for migrants. See Annabelle Garay, "Migrants' Journey

a Spiritual One, Too," *The Arizona Republic*, December 26, 2004, p. B11. On the legend of Juan Soldado, see Price (2005), chapter 6.

17. The agent's real name isn't Fred, but I never asked his permission so I cannot use his real name.

18. Grupos Beta is a federal agency in Mexico. Members carry no weapons and have no police authority and cannot detain drug or people smugglers. They are trained in first aid and offer help to all migrants. Migrants, who are distrustful of other authorities, tend to trust the members of Grupos Beta. The agent we spoke with was a young man who had been working with the agency for nine years. He began with his father and said he liked the idea of helping those who cannot afford to pay for services.

19. Michael Marizco, "Wanted: One Last Trip Home," *Arizona Daily Star*, June 11, 2003, http://www.azstarnet.com/border/30611BODYRETURN. html.

20. Thompson (2000).

21. Ray Stern, "The Tragic Journey of Ana Rosa Segura-Marcial," special report for *The East Valley Tribune*, December 15, 2002, pp. 1–4.

22. Proposition 200 was a controversial citizens' initiative in Arizona, modeled after California's Proposition 187.

23. William McGee, "Desert Thirst as Disease," *Atlantic Monthly*, April 1898, pp. 483–488.

24. Luis Alberto Urrea, *The Devil's Highway: A True Story* (New York and Boston: Little, Brown and Company, 2004).

25. John Annerino, *Dead in their Tracks: Crossing America's Desert Borderlands* (New York and London: Four Walls Eight Windows, 1999), appendix B.

26. Urrea (2004), p. 101.

27. Stephen Van Evera, *Guide to Methodology for Students of Political Science* (Cambridge, MA: Defense and Arms Control Studies Program, Massachusetts Institute of Technology, n.d.).

28. Michael Marizco, "Arrests, Deaths Surge Along Border," *Arizona Daily Star*, May 3, 2004, http://www.azstarnet.com/dailystar/printDS/ 20502.php.

29. Luke Turf, "Border Crossers' Bodies Await ID," *Arizona Daily Star*, April 18, 2004, http://www.azstarnet.com/php-bin/clicktrack/print.php?

30. Joseph A. Reaves, "Tillman, Migration Among '04 Top Stories," *Arizona Republic*, December 26, 2004, pp. B1–B2.

31. Dennis Wagner, "Illegals Dying at Record Rate in Arizona Desert," *USA Today*, August 19, 2005, http://usatoday.com/news/2005-08-19-border-deaths_x.htm.

32. Arthur H. Rotstein, "Migrant Deaths Hit Record High in Arizona Desert," *East Valley Tribune*, September 3, 2005, p. A05.

33. Associated Press, "County Rents Truck to Use as Morgue," *The Arizona Republic*, September 2, 2005, p. B10.

34. Eric Swedlund, "Corpse Overflow Stored in Trailer," *Arizona Daily Star*, September 1, 2005, http://www.azstarnet.com/dailystar/printDS/ 91340.php.

35. Giorgio Agamben, *Homo Sacer: Sovereign Power and Bare Life* (Stanford: Stanford University Press, 1998), p. 171.
36. Ibid., p. 171.
37. Ibid., p. 174.
38. Ibid., pp. 82–83.
39. Ibid., p. 83.
40. Ibid., p. 128.
41. The Mexico/U.S. border is not the only location of deadly crossroads that human beings much journey along. Similar journeys take place through the Sahel Desert, over the Straits of Gibraltar, on the Caribbean Sea and the highways of Iowa as countries increasingly fortify their sovereign borders. See Ali Bensaad, "Sahel: Caravan of Despair," *Le Monde Diplomatique*, September 2001, http://mondediplo.com/2001/09/04sahel; Frank Bruni, "Perilous Immigrant Crossings Frustrate Italy," *The New York Times*, December 3, 2002, section A, page 12, col. 4; Kirsten Scharnberg, "Pipeline of Peril for Migrants," *Chicago Tribune*, January 6, 2003, p.1; and Dana Canedy, "As TV Cameras Roll, Haitians Dash From Stranded Boat to Florida Shore," *The New York Times*, October 29, 2002, section A, page 20, col. 1.
42. See Foucault's "Governmentality" and the other often-cited articles in "*The Foucault Effect: Studies in Governmentality*," ed. Graham Burchell, Colin Gordon, and Peter Miller (Chicago: University of Chicago Press, 1991).
43. See Agamben (1998), p. 28.
44. For an excellent account of the origins of Operation Gatekeeper, which has become symbolic for all the other border operations that have attempted to make it more difficult to illegally cross into the United States from Mexico, see Joseph Nevins, *Operation Gatekeeper: The Rise of the "Illegal Alien" and the Making of the U.S.-Mexico Boundary*" (New York and London: Routledge, 2002).
45. Am I making an unquestioned presumption here about the existence of *the human spirit*? Yes, I suppose I am. We can never fully escape presumptions, nor do I think we would want to escape this one entirely. Given the enormous number of human beings who undertake unbelievably dangerous and impossible journeys across territorial borders today, I think it is reasonable to imagine *something* like a human spirit that drives them on.
46. Nevins (2002), pp. 90–91.
47. See "INS' Southwest Border Strategy: Resource and Impact Issues Remain After Seven Years," GAO-01-842, August 2001 and "Chaos on the U.S.-Mexico Border: A Report on Migrant Crossing Deaths, Immigrant Families and Subsistence Level Laborers," Report 5, Catholic Legal Immigration Network, Inc., 2004, http://www.ilw.com/lawyers/articles/2004,1006-Clinic.pdf.
48. See Peter Andreas, *Border Games: Policing the U.S.-Mexico Divide* (Ithaca and London: Cornell University Press, 2000); J. M. C. Heyman, "Putting

Power in the Anthropology of Bureaucracy: The Immigration and Naturalization Service at the Mexico-United States Border," *Current Anthropology*, 36:2 (1995), pp. 261–287.

49. See Michael J. Dillon, "The Scandal of the Refugee: Some Reflections on the 'Inter' of International Relations and Continental Thought," in *Moral Spaces: Rethinking Ethics and World Politics*, ed. David Campbell and Michael J. Shapiro (Minneapolis: University of Minnesota Press, 1999), pp. 92–124.

50. See Agamben (1998), pp. 183–184.

51. Gilles Deleuze and Felix Guattari, *A Thousand Plateaus* (Minneapolis: University of Minnesota Press, 1987), p. 24.

52. See Agamben (1998), p. 115.

53. Lee Hockstader, "Remains of Migrants Haunt DNA Expert," *Washington Post*, April 21, 2003, p. A03.

CHAPTER 2

MISSING PERSONS: MANHATTAN, SEPTEMBER 2001

Jenny Edkins

Disaster

To look again at the photographs of the missing that were pasted on the walls of Manhattan in 2001 is for me to feel once more the urgency and the disturbance of the first few hours and days after the destruction of the World Trade Center. A jumble of incomprehensible events came one after another in rapid, staccato succession. An explosion and fire at the top of tower one—a bomb perhaps, or a plane hitting the skyscraper by accident? Some saw the plane collide; most assumed it was a horrific accident. People phoned their friends: "Switch your television on!" Huge flames and black smoke could be seen from near the top of the 110-story North Tower. Then, this time observed by those on the streets of Manhattan and the viewers worldwide watching the live coverage, a second plane flew straight into the South Tower. This had to be deliberate: or at least the aircraft made a definite turn to head for the tower at speed. Gigantic fireballs appeared and debris began to fall. People watching on the streets were tormented by the fate of those in the buildings. There would be escape routes, surely? Staircases would be there if the lifts were out of action. People would get out. Yet those watching could see to their disbelief and horror people falling from the buildings to their deaths. Not just one or two "jumpers," but a steady stream of figures spewed out alongside the rubble and debris as it fell.[1] Television viewers were not shown these shots, but they could see in close-up figures waving from the upper stories. Chaos and confusion prevailed: rumors of planes hijacked, of other targets, of

explosions on Capitol Hill, in the Pentagon. And the incredible collapse of
the buildings. Shock—those still evacuating the buildings, those desperately signaling their plight from the windows, the rescue teams helping:
they were surely trapped within this horrible thundering descent of
concrete and steel collapsing into itself. This could not be happening. But
shock was followed quickly by panic and action as the clouds of dust and
debris sped through the streets, engulfing those too slow to run. Finally,
an eerie silence fell as people on foot streamed outwards, across Brooklyn
Bridge, or up the avenues of central Manhattan, toward their homes or in
search of temporary lodging.

In this immediate context some of the questions that have been raised
since seem to me less pressing or, rather, too abstract. Many have asked to
what extent the reaction to this event in the United States and elsewhere
was an overreaction. In terms of the numbers killed, the significance of
what happened as a turning point in world politics, and the conflicts and
deaths in other places, and of other people, which arose from the response
to what happened in New York, Washington, and Pennsylvania, the
devastation of September 11 is maybe not so striking. Civilian casualties
elsewhere, in Afghanistan and Iraq in particular, have by now far exceeded
the deaths brought about on that day.[2] And these other deaths have
arguably been as deliberate: despite the claimed care that has been taken to
minimize them, military action has taken place in the knowledge that
civilian deaths would be an inevitable if regrettable consequence. In sheer
quantity, the dead and missing in the Indian Ocean tsunami in December
2004, numbering in the hundreds of thousands, exceed by several orders of
magnitude the thousands killed on September 11.[3] And the roster will continue. But since when has it been adequate to measure death in numbers?
Or to categorize sudden death by its cause? Is there not a demand to address
each death as in some sense unique in terms of both personal and political
consequences?

There is no doubt that the deaths in New York have been drawn on and
their significance amplified in a certain way to justify a number of foreign
and domestic policy moves in a series of states: not only the wars in
Afghanistan and Iraq but also the Patriot Act and the Department of
Homeland Security in the United States and similar powers of arbitrary
detention and surveillance in the United Kingdom, and, to a lesser extent,
in other European countries. Remembering the dead of September 11 risks
playing into the hands of those who support such policies.[4] Remembering
is always a risky strategy, but so too is forgetting. And the one is in any case
haunted by the other. What is perhaps also important here is that there is
always more than one way of remembering. Remembering does not have

to play into the hands of those who wish to "use" the dead to support their militaristic responses; it can in fact be a particularly strong way of opposing those policies.[5]

We can see this when we look at practices of memory and remembrance in relation to World War I in Europe or the Vietnam War. Both the Vietnam Wall in Washington and the Cenotaph in London were highly contested memorials and the site of opposition to state practices of military action: to war, in other words. Often, memorials are considered to be the very place where the "nation" is reaffirmed. Certainly that is what state authorities attempt. After a war, a story of heroism and sacrifice is necessary to legitimate the horrors of war and the deaths of conscripts. The nation-state relies on a claim that it and it alone can guarantee the safety and security of its citizens, and that the deaths in war that it demands are a necessary part of that security.[6] It depends on a story of its own inevitable origins in the heroic acts that brought the state into being and that have sustained it in a smooth linear narrative time ever since. This story, this heroic account, is vital for the state's claim to authority, as is the concealment of the violence that accompanies the emergence of states. Remember that Max Weber's definition of the state is "that human community which (successfully) lays claim to the *monopoly of legitimate physical violence* within a certain territory."[7] When we read this we tend to focus on the violence, and forget the fact that for Weber the important thing is the *successful claim* to *legitimate* violence. This legitimacy is established through a narrative, and for the narrative of the state to work it has to establish a particular linear, homogeneous, empty time against which its claim to origin and legitimacy can be successful. Unsurprisingly, this form of time suits, and arose alongside, industrial production and capitalism.[8] The state relies on a view of time as a continuous movement from one second to the next in a regular or regularized fashion. It has a point of origin and a sense of purpose, progress, and continuity: the state will survive, and in particular will survive *us*.

When it comes to violence, and particularly the violence of state-led wars, the state encounters a problem. Those who have fought have been put in a position where they want to question stories of heroic actions and patriotic struggle. Veterans have experienced the brutality of killing and the disorganization and error that characterizes military action. They have seen their friends killed, and they have killed people themselves. Often there is a sense of betrayal: those in charge have not proved omniscient but on the contrary fallible and indecisive. For many, the encounter with brutality and death in war is traumatic. I don't intend to imply here that veterans will suffer what we now call posttraumatic stress. Rather, I want to suggest that their experience has been of a particular type, one that we call "traumatic."

By this we mean, on the whole, that it is something that they are not prepared for; it is an unexpected and shocking encounter with brutal realities
outside language. There are many things that are unspoken or that cannot
be spoken. It can be argued that our everyday existence is only possible—it
is only possible to carry on, in other words—by forgetting these things or
by even forgetting that there are such things. And indeed this is what we
do, most of us, most of the time. We become who we "are"—rational,
separate individuals—through a forgetting of who we might be—
inevitably so bound up with each other that the death of another creature
is shocking. But such forgetting is not possible in war when we are faced
with the traumatic immediacy of death and survival.

If we cannot forget, we cannot go along with the stories that the state
wants to tell us in the aftermath of war. On the contrary, we feel betrayed
by these stories. The smooth time of the state makes no sense when it is set
alongside the disjunctive, fragmented time of trauma, the time that I have
called "trauma time."[9] A traumatic event is not experienced when it
occurs: it does not fit in "ordinary time." It is only experienced later when
it is recalled, not as a memory, but as a reliving. A traumatic event produces
a fissure in smooth time; it reveals its artificial, constructed, narrative
nature. This is of course dangerous for the state, which, as I have argued,
relies on smooth linear narrative time for its very existence. Trauma time
and the time of the state are in conflict. The state has to move as quickly as
possible after a war to a reinstatement of linear time, and a forgetting of
trauma time. It has to remember *in a particular way*—through stories of
origins and heroic sacrifice. Remembering in the name of the state is
always a difficult project, fraught with the risk that the memory of the
trauma will resurface, unbidden. This is why traumatic memories are such
an important site of resistance and contestation. The state is vulnerable at
this point. It works through violence, yet it risks always that the violence
in which it engages will reveal the fracture in smooth time that so threatens its own legitimating narrative. So there are two dangers: first, the
danger that the state will use the memory of the dead to justify its acts of
"revenge," and second, the danger that threatens the state itself—the
danger that people will not forget the trauma and, not forgetting, will not
be able to remember in the way the state demands.

Despite, or perhaps because of, these opposing dangers, coming face to
face with the photographs of those who disappeared in the rubble and dust
of the World Trade Center towers is a disturbing experience, even for
people not intimately involved with the events, and I write from that
perspective. I was in London at the time of the events, on a day trip visiting
exhibitions. My own immediate instinct was to head home. The first time

I visited New York after that was around the time of the six-month anniversary; this proved to be the start of a series of visits over the following months from which much of the material in this chapter is drawn. Looking again at the photographs I took during those visits of the missing posters that were still on the walls of lower Manhattan reminds me of my own first encounter with what was at the time, for me at least, stunningly unexpected, unbelievable even: the use of passenger planes, full of people, as weapons to be flown deliberately at skyscrapers. I still find it difficult to comprehend how anyone could find it possible to do such a thing; I'm not sure I would call it courage, as Susan Sontag famously implied, but certainly it entailed a way of thinking that for me is beyond the imagination.[10] In recalling the chaos and confusion that followed, amplified of course by the totally unexpected collapse of the towers, we are taken back to how at the time the hospitals were put on alert to receive thousands of casualties, people flocked to donate blood, and rescue squads rushed to recover the survivors assumed to be buried under the rubble. It was a while before it became clear that of the majority of the thousands killed only the smallest traces would remain, if anything remained at all. The missing would disappear. The cloud of dust that hung over Manhattan for some days afterward was all that lingered of many of the dead.[11]

The line between presence and absence cannot be drawn clearly for those whose relatives or friends cannot be found after a disaster, and maybe not at all, for any of us. An exploration of the photograph is apt in this context. While a photograph appears to record a moment that has inevitably passed, in itself, as a photograph, it is equally clearly present. The eyes in the photograph still gaze determinedly directly at us, undaunted by the impossibility of this look.[12] The photograph *is* the person. As Roland Barthes points out:

> Show your photographs to someone—he will immediately show you his: "Look, this is my brother; this is me as a child," etc.; the Photograph is never anything but an antiphon of "Look," "See," "Here it is"; it points the finger at a certain *vis-à-vis*, and cannot escape this pure deitic language.[13]

We find this same language used in the New York photographs: "Have you seen this man?" "If you see this person . . ." "If you see or have seen this person, please contact the following people . . ." It is much more unusual to have the inscription "Attached is a picture of . . ." The photographs of the missing are a precious remnant, a proof that this person exists. This is a person, a missing person, they proclaim. Here is my sister, my husband, my son, my friend. Here they are: *I did not just imagine them.* They have not come home, but they must be somewhere. "Please help!" say the inscriptions, "Please call if you have any information"; "Have you seen my daddy?"

Searching

It was in the chaos and confusion of the first few hours after the World Trade Center towers collapsed that the missing posters came to be produced. People who were deeply worried about relatives and friends they had not heard from and who had failed to return home gave up watching television, with its repetitions and its lame attempts at making sense of what had happened in terms of "attacks" and "terrorists," and they took to the streets. One of those searching, Tommy Mackell, was quoted as saying, "We're not interested in watching any more TV. We have no time limit. We'll just keep walking."[14] This was part of a general move for people to gather in public spaces, notably Union Square. This park was the closest people could get to the site where the World Trade Center had been—the whole tip of Manhattan Island below that point, in other words below 14th Street, had been closed off. Union Square became a focal point for groups to gather and talk and to begin to absorb what had happened. For those searching for the missing, there was no official coordination at first, no central place they could go. It was not until late on the Wednesday, more than 24 hours after the collapse, that the New York Armory was opened to allow those seeking information on friends and relatives to complete forms with details of those missing.[15] In the meantime, people took to the streets in search of others who might have information, who might have been in the towers and escaped, or who might have seen the people they were looking for. They took photographs of their relatives with them to show to those they came across. An obvious next step, given the availability of photocopiers and computers, was to make their own fliers to hand out to people they met and to post on the walls by the hospitals where they came to check lists of those admitted. In a situation where everyone wanted to do what they could to help, copy shops were providing as many free copies as the relatives wanted.

In addition to handing out posters, relatives talked to the press and to others searching. It is the conversations with the press that I remember. I wasn't in New York until quite some time later, as I have already said, so I didn't see the posters appear on the streets, on bus shelters, on cars, on pizza restaurants. But I did see the broadcast interviews with the relatives. The press had nothing much else to show. There were no injured being ferried to hospitals, no people being dramatically recovered from the rubble, no dead bodies being pulled out that we could avert our eyes from though we did have our eyes averted for us from the body parts that lay on the streets and the roofs of surrounding buildings. There was only this chaos of people needing to walk the streets with their fliers, searching—hopelessly, endlessly searching. I remember one interview with someone who actually found the person she was looking for. I cannot remember the details for certain, but I think that the reunion was actually filmed. One minute we were talking to a woman with her son looking for the missing father, and the next he had miraculously appeared. I don't know if this was staged or what. I remember thinking at the time it seemed highly improbable. Maybe I dreamed it. Mostly what we saw were people anxiously but determinedly giving details of the person they were looking for, holding the picture close to their chest to make sure it was in view of the camera, refusing to surrender what hope remained, refusing to cry out.

The Fliers

On the whole the fliers people produced were basic and all very similar to one another: each carries a photograph accompanied by text. A full name is always given and alternative or nicknames too; sometimes the correct pronunciation is even spelled out. Then there are details of where the missing person worked, personal information such as age, height, weight, and distinguishing marks, and finally a contact telephone number or numbers. Some fliers were handwritten, most produced on a word processor. The photographs were generally in color, only occasionally were they black and white. The posters were overwhelmingly the same size, printed on standard, white, letter-size paper.

The language on the posters is direct and unambiguous: "AON Insurance. 101 floor. Missing. Please call. . . . Last seen 78th floor waiting for elevator. Anyone from AON who knows Edward please call"; "5ft 10in, 175lbs, brown hair, brown eyes; WTC 104th floor— Junk Bonds. Contact . . ." Personal details are given without flinching: "6+ ft tall; Heavy set; Blond; Pale skinned; Wedding band"; "Extremely overweight approximately 6 feet tall, wearing a navy blue polo shirt, black pants, and black Rockport lace shoes"; "Tattoos: panther—left forearm (looks more like a dogs head), 'Jim'—upper right arm (both poorly done); Gold wedding band; Watch with gold band; Dressed business casual"; "Female, Indian (Brown complexion) . . . prominent mole on upper right cheek below eye, a mole on right thigh"; "Small gap between upper two front teeth."

A confusion of tenses betrays the uncertainty the relatives are trying to hold on to. While what the missing were wearing or where they worked is described most usually in the past tense, "Hugo was an employee on the 84th Floor of the Second Tower. He was last seen wearing a Black Shirt and Blue Jeans," their distinguishing marks are detailed in the present: "He has a tattoo on his right shoulder." The type of information given on the posters changed as speculation about likely outcomes altered. At first they were hopeful, giving just name, picture, and workplace; later, less optimistic people listed information about scars, dental implants, and tattoos.[16] To us now, of course, it is obvious that certain locations were an almost automatic death sentence. People didn't know that then.

Occasionally as well as the information to help identification, we are given other details: "Expecting first child this week"; "Wife is pregnant with twins and due next week. He also has a two year old son at home who has just said his first sentence: 'I want my daddy' "; "Her family is in Bermuda and unable to come to the USA due to restrictions. PLEASE HELP." We are often told where people were last seen—"Possibly seen outside the WTC after the crash"; "Last heard evacuating the 86th floor of tower 2"—and sometimes we are given the whole story as far as it is known: "The last call we had from her was that she was trapped in the elevator on the 12th floor #2 WTC and she couldn't get out since about 8.50am. Then we lost contact with her. If anyone was with her at that time and was able to escape from the elevator, please contact us and tell us what happened." There is a desire to know not just whether a friend or relative is alive, but what happened to them. How did they die? How come they didn't get out? *What was it like for them?*

It is difficult to read these details, but it can be easier to read the inscriptions than to look at the photographs themselves.

Most of those who died were people who either worked in a particular office block, or were visiting it for one reason or another that day, or those who had come to rescue them. The photographs on the missing fliers do not show these people. They show a woman with her child, in a garden, another woman in a strappy dress with a bouquet of flowers, a man in a tuxedo and bow tie. A man sitting back on a leather sofa, relaxed, arms spread wide, with a broad smile on his face. A couple in dark glasses, arms around one another, smiling. Another couple in a garden, older but also happy and smiling. A graduation photo. Another in a bow tie. A couple and their baby. Another couple with two children gathered around the table to blow out the candles on a birthday cake: a third birthday, it looks like, though the child seems too small. A family on a beach, the daughter riding high on her father's shoulders. A wedding day. Another celebration: champagne. An evening out in a restaurant. A couple at home at Christmas, she sitting on his lap. A father holding his newborn child. More parties. A backpacking holiday. A boat trip. And one that really haunts me: someone that has a look just like someone I know.

Occasionally there is a posed, official photograph, but for the most part these are intimate, personal photographs, snapshots intended for the privacy of the album, not the walls of New York City. Taken by family or friends, they recall holidays, celebrations, births, marriages. The people are smiling, happy, relaxed, if occasionally a little awkward at being photographed but sublimely unaware of what the future is to bring. These are the people that worked in the World Trade Center, the people New Yorkers saw around them every day, on the subway, the buses, the sidewalks, in the parks. But these are their private faces. They are not the public, city-walking, streetwise New York faces that people show to the world. Yet here they are, torn from the private world and pasted on walls, bus shelters, lampposts. They are faces that do not suit the context in which they now appear, exposed to public gaze alongside the sometimes embarrassing details of their distinguishing marks.

In the Asian tsunami a similar form of missing poster was found. The United States Holocaust Memorial Museum in Washington contains what is called the "Tower of Victims."[17] The tower contains hundreds of photographs taken from the Yaffa Eliach Shtetl Collection, covering Jewish life in a small town in Lithuania.[18] The three-story tower is "covered with a pastiche of photographs depicting ordinary people in ordinary situations: weddings, new babies, school and religious rites of passage, working, or playing—simply people living."[19] Visitors are told that all but 29 of the Jewish residents of the town were killed in 1941 and that no Jews live there today. Like the New York missing posters, these photographs show people before the disaster, unaware of what was about to happen, and disconnected from context in which their images would be shown. This is felt to be one of the most powerful exhibits in the museum.[20] The photographs are from a period where the snapshot photograph was rarer. They are posed photographs taken by a professional photographer. They depict family groups and individuals from the Jewish community, and like the missing posters in New York, the sitters smile out at us or sit composed and reflective, ignorant of what the future is to bring. The photographs contrast starkly with those elsewhere in the museum, taken when prisoners were admitted to the camps, or when victims were shot.

In New York, the workers in the World Trade Center were normally concealed behind the corporate façade of the buildings. Much of the shock on September 11 could be traced to our most basic fantasies about buildings.[21] They are seen as a form of protection from danger that has to be solid because their occupants are fragile. In practice, however, a corporate office

building like the WTC works to hide those that work there both from the
outside world and from each other. To the corporation, the occupants are
irrelevant: "the corporation veils the actual bodies of those whom it networks together and controls from afar and even those who carry out that
control."[22] These normally concealed faces suddenly appeared on the
streets of New York after the disaster:

> When the façades came down the faces of the invisible occupants who were
> lost came up, filling the vertical surfaces of the city in pasted photo-
> copies. . . . They formed a new kind of façade, a dispersed image of diversity
> in place of the singular monolithic screen—each face, each personality, each
> story suddenly in focus. . . . It was precisely those who were missing, those
> who the building did not protect, who had their horrifying disappearance
> marked by a sudden visibility.[23]

In other words, those who had been presented as faceless and invisible by
the system within which they worked were suddenly given individuality.
Those of us wandering the streets could see clearly the mix and variety of
people who had been in the buildings that day. We could see them as private people, with their families, their children, their dogs, their special
occasions. All things that the corporation lives on and makes its profits from
yet chooses to ignore. We may not have felt that they were people we had
much in common with, or would have been particularly likely to have as
friends, but that was unimportant. We now knew who they were and that
they had been disappeared, rubbed out, vanished.

What was most shocking was the way this disappearance revealed to us
their inevitable invisibility—they were in any case the disappeared, the bare
life of the city-state:

> What might be really horrifying in the end is precisely what was already there.
> The collective sense that everything had changed that morning may have more
> to do with no longer being able to repress certain aspects of contemporary life.[24]

This is always the way with trauma—trauma is a betrayal. This particular
event reveals "the economy of violence" that we live within.[25]

Afterlife

By the time I photographed the missing fliers posted outside St. Vincent's
Hospital on 11th Street it was more than one year after the tragedy. The
original fliers had been joined by others saying things like "Loved and
missed by all . . . 12.22.69—9.11.01" rather than "Missing." People had

added newspaper cuttings—"Reality-TV champ missing in rubble"—or memorial cards—"In loving memory of . . ." Others posted what they hoped were helpful poems—"gone but not forgotten"—messages from children, or religious or patriotic symbols: "Proud to be an American." For the most part though, the initial posters were still there and still the same: still asking for information, still telling us dates of birth, eye color, distinguishing marks. New York was indeed "a city that lived alongside its missing and dead."[26]

Why did New Yorkers do this? Why were the missing posters left up for so long and even annotated or replaced? The explanation generally given is that by the time people realized that for "missing" they should read "presumed dead," the posters had become shrines where people could remember those killed. There was a range of different types and forms of impromptu memorial that appeared around the city, as has been chronicled by City Lore and the New York Historical Museum in their exhibition "Missing."[27] But I think they were more than memorials. The missing posters in New York trace the way in which personhood—its absence or its presence and the boundary between absence and presence, or death and life—figures in contemporary politics. "Missing" as a category opposed to "dead" or "alive" is interesting here. How does that category work in relation to contemporary forms of sovereign politics and political life?[28] In New York there was a swift move to resolve the missing into the dead. Death certificates were offered rapidly in the aftermath. This was not the case in the Asian tsunami of 2004: Why was there this contrast? And why then did the missing posters remain on the streets of New York for well over a year after the event?

But why did it seem appropriate to continue to display such private things in a public place? Remember that the posters included not only pictures of private events and personal moments, but also details of old surgical procedures, intimate tattoos, pregnancies, personal peculiarities. This is not the sort of information that is usually placed in a memorial context.

Perhaps the persistence of the posters was like a collective scream, an open wound, a refusal to close over the trauma of loss, a refusal of the incorporation of the bodies of the missing as heroes of the state. Those people who had turned off the television to take to the streets had a view of what had happened that was starkly different from the account that was by then being broadcast by government and media:

> [W]hen the only president we have talked to us [in George W. Bush's tele-
> vised broadcast that evening] about "terrible sadness" New Yorkers weren't

impressed. When he gave us clichés about the day's events many of us were furious. "We know what happened, we weren't in a bunker," one shouted at the set. As for the government functioning and the economy continuing . . . "Who's he kidding? Wall Street is under dust." . . . In lower Manhattan at least, it's clear that this president has no idea what happened today. "That's the scariest part of all," some people said. There was no leadership coming from politicians tonight. Nor pundits, try as they might.[29]

On the morning of September 12, Secretary of State Colin Powell said on ABC's *Good Morning America* that "[t]he American people have a clear understanding that this is a war. That's the way they see it." Laura Flanders wrote, "I beg to differ. In Manhattan, we aren't in a state of war, we're in a state of mourning. And for the whole country to join us right now would be a really good idea."[30] In the aftermath of what was being called "the attacks" the federal authorities had moved swiftly to reestablish narratives of state control. The traumatic events were followed very rapidly by an attempt to reinstate narratives of nation, sacrifice, and heroism. In fact, these attempts began even as the events were still unfolding.[31] As I argued earlier, the state can only survive with its legitimacy intact if the trauma of violence is concealed. The persistence of the missing posters on the streets of New York was testimony to the trauma, to the ineffectiveness of the state in safeguarding those it claimed to protect, and to the lies of heroism and sacrifice. These were ordinary people who went to work and were overtaken by disaster, not heroes who sacrificed their lives for America. Just take a look at the pictures.

Bare life was exposed in the missing fliers—in the portrait photograph and in the details—scars, eye color, race.[32] Through the display of fliers, bare life, the life of the home, has insistently become politically qualified life, life that demands its place in the public sphere. In an interesting reflection of the place of "home" in all of this, Judith Greenberg suggests that "the intimacy produced by the 'Portraits of Grief' section in the *New York Times* and the 'family album' quality of the missing person fliers publicly attempted to bring the grief of the broken private home to the broken public home."[33] The "Portraits of Grief," the short obituaries published for each of the missing focused, as did the photographs, on family life. In the majority of cases, the men and women were remembered for their connections to family members, and rather than just mentioning those who survived the deceased, as happens at the end of a traditional obituary, family relationships are vividly portrayed. But their function was in a sense the opposite of the traditional obituary. While the latter "typically highlight what the deceased did to distinguish themselves, to set themselves apart, the portraits celebrated *ordinary* qualities."[34]

The collective scream, with its insistent display of the life of the home in public, was a form of contestation of state or sovereign power and its exclusion of bare life. Agamben argues that since the beginning of western patriarchal politics, there has been a distinction drawn between two forms of life: bare life, or the life of the home, and politically qualified life, the life of the polis or public sphere.[35] Sovereign power has relied since the start on this separation. The life excluded from politics is a life in some senses unworthy of consideration—a life that can be killed without that killing constituting murder—though it was necessary for politics, in that something had to be excluded for the political community to be constituted as bounded and sovereign. Agamben traces an alteration in contemporary sovereign politics, which increasingly operates under the "state of exception"—a state in which the life excluded from political life no longer remains on the margins, in what Agamben called zones of indistinction, but extends its sway to occupy all the spaces of politics as politics becomes biopolitics. When politics becomes biopolitics, all life becomes bare life—life with no political voice. This is what, according to Agamben, has happened increasingly everywhere since the Nazi camps.

The posters remind us that it is this very bare life that in the end is what is important to us. All our politics, all our systems of government or economics, all these are of little value when set alongside our personal lives. These posters do not ask us to look out for the person who was in charge of the office, the one who had the biggest paycheck, the one from the most prestigious family or with the most qualifications. Each and every person represented in the fliers has their own value—as a life that is interwoven with other lives, none of which will any longer be the same.

The fliers are also a symbolic reminder of the fact that these people are indeed *missing*—there are no remains, they are not "dead"—the dead have corpses. It is expected that up to 1,000 people will remain missing: that not even the smallest remains of these people will be identified, despite the best efforts of forensic scientists. Many bodies were fragmented on impact and burned or crushed and mixed with other debris on the huge site. Increasingly, fragments located and identified by DNA are linked to people who have already been identified, with as many as 200 body parts matched to one person.[36] The missing are not dead; they are not alive either. They are neither dead nor alive. *There are no bodies to insist that these people once lived, only the pictures.* These pictures insist, alongside the Madres de Plaza de Mayo that "they took them away alive—we want them back alive!"[37]

There was a move to issue official death certificates very early on in the process, ostensibly to help relatives. It took some while for a final count of the dead to be decided. Two weeks after the attack, 6,886 people were reported missing. This reduced rapidly and then remained at 2,792 from December 2002 until October 2003, when 40 unsolved cases were removed from the list. The number settled on in January 2004, when three more names were removed, was 2,749, the same as the number of death certificates that had been issued.[38] This is no doubt a tidy solution, but it does not reflect the uncertainties that are bound to remain. A number of people have been prosecuted for falsely claiming relatives missing in order to benefit from compensation payments; there are very likely to be also people killed on September 11 who have not been listed as missing by anyone.

The missing posters protested this tidiness and insisted on the raw, traumatic brutality of loss. The photograph exaggerates the non-sense that death makes. How can someone be there one minute and have vanished the next? The photograph demands action, refuses easy ways out—the missing must be found, but in some sense all the dead are missing. There is no place for them in our politics: the dead and the unborn are excluded. Our attitude is that since they can no longer feel pain or know what's going on, what happens doesn't matter to them, and their views don't count. Though the dead, like the unborn, have certain rights in law, the respect they are accorded is limited: they do not fully count. The bereaved do not behave like this: often they carry on as if responding to someone who is no longer there. More seriously, once anonymous, the dead can be co-opted into political projects: they can be the heroes who sacrificed their lives in a noble cause or the victims whom we invoke as triggers of retributive action.

Not only did the posters remain on the streets long after everyone had realized that none of the people depicted were going to return, but people were also taking photographs of these photographs: "I took pictures of pictures, of people looking at pictures, of people taking pictures."[39] This seemed incomprehensible, but it was widespread. It was perhaps in part a record of the politicization of bare life and in part the need to record what the journalists were not recording. What was missing was not the images of the disaster but the images of those bearing witness to the disaster—bearing witness to the missing. It was not a question of remembering the dead but of bearing witness to their deaths and the manner of their deaths. It could not be done the usual way: these were not usual deaths.

Photographs also appear on government websites.[40] An exhibition of missing posters was put together and two versions of it toured the country, attracting some controversy.[41] Photographs of the missing posters appear in books and exhibitions. Credit is given to the person who photographed the photograph but not the person who took the photograph itself. Nor is permission sought from the relatives of those whose photograph is shown, just as I have not sought their permission to talk about their photographs here.

Conclusion

In the events in Manhattan in September 2001 life was instrumentalized, both by those who organized and carried out the so-called attacks on the World Trade Center towers and by those who claimed the lives lost as lives sacrificed for the U.S. state. This instrumentalization of life, its production as bare life rather than as politically qualified life is not, of course, unique to such events, but in general it remains invisible. What happened that day made it plainly visible. The missing posters that appeared around Manhattan in the aftermath could be seen, I have argued, as constituting an assertion of the instrumentalization of life both before and after 9/11. They functioned too as a reminder of the traumatic impact of the events in the face of the state-sponsored practices of memorialization that narrated an account of a heroic response to a dastardly attack. These posters, and in particular the photographic portraits they carried, seemed to be particularly effective this way.

When I traveled through New York in March 2005, the posters I had photographed two and a half years earlier on the wall outside St. Vincent's hospital on West 11th Street were, to my surprise, still there. They were much faded then, with some colors fading more rapidly than others to give a blue tinge. But they remained, a haunting presence on the streets. Nobody had yet felt it appropriate to take them down.

Born out of necessity and public silence, the posters became a call to a different form of politics, one that starts in the street, in the home. They contest the neat boundaries that the authorities wanted to impose in the form of death certificates. They remind us of our responsibility to the dead, a responsibility that can only be fulfilled to each as an individual and that means resisting their invocation en masse in support of causes or nationalism. The folk memories embodied in the missing posters are not to be dismissed as sentiment. They remain dangerous: they invoke the betrayal of the World Trade Center workers by their buildings, and their incorporation by state remembrance, as well as their victimization by those piloting the planes. They were obliterated in the name of what? The answer is twofold: They were obliterated by those who killed them and by those who write their deaths as sacrifice. They did not sacrifice their lives: what would that mean anyway? They went about their ordinary business. They were always already missing—excluded from our politics. The state has no time for persons, only for bare life that it can regulate and control.

Notes

Versions of this essay were presented at the 46th Annual Convention of the International Studies Association, Honolulu, Hawaii, March 1–5, 2005, to the University of Warwick Poststructural Politics Group on October 20, 2005, and at the British International Studies Conference, December 19–21, 2005. Thanks are due to participants at these meetings for their engagement and their comments, and to Maja Zehfuss for her comments on an earlier draft of the chapter.

1. Certainly scores, and according to one estimate as many as 200 people. Kevin Flynn and Jim Dwyer (of *The New York Times*), "Mystery Surrounds those who Jumped," *International Herald Tribune*, Saturday, September 11, 2004, available in *The IHT Online*, http://www.iht.com/articles/538337.html. See also Dennis Cauchon and Martha Moore, *USA Today*, September 2, 2002. A version of the latter article is available online at http://forum.ogrish.com/forum/archive/index.php/t-8318.html; some of the sites that show such material are now semipornographic.

2. Marc Herold, "A Dossier on Civilian Victims of United States' Aerial Bombing of Afghanistan: A Comprehensive Accounting," http://pubpages. unh.edu/~mwherold; The Iraq Body Count Project, http://www. iraqbodycount.net/links.htm. See also Marc Herold, "The Bombing of Afghanistan as Reflection of 9/11 and Different Valuations of Life," September 11, 2002, http://www.cursor.org/stories/heroldon911. htm.

3. There was some discussion at one point as to whether more *Americans* had died in the tsunami than on September 11. See Keith Olbermann, "MSNBC's Countdown," January 4, 2005, Bureau of Consular Affairs, U.S. Department of State, http://travel.state.gov/travel/cis_pa_tw/tsunami/tsunami_2048.html.

4. Maja Zehfuss, "Forget September 11," *Third World Quarterly*, 24:3 (2003): 513–528.

5. I develop this argument in more detail in Jenny Edkins, *Trauma and the Memory of Politics* (Cambridge: Cambridge University Press, 2003).

6. Here I am using the shorthand of referring to "the state" as if it were an unproblematic entity, though I would prefer in general to disaggregate "the state" and examine instead the actions of those people whose practices constitute what we call "the state."

7. Max Weber, *Weber: Political Writings*, trans. Ronald Spiers, ed. Peter Lassman and Ronald Spiers (Cambridge: Cambridge University Press, 1994), pp. 310–311 (original emphasis).

8. And alongside the Calvinist view of predestination. Max Weber, *The Protestant Ethic and the Spirit of Capitalism*, trans. Talcott Parsons (London: Unwin, 1930).

9. Edkins (2003), p. xiv.

10. "In the Matter of Courage (a Morally Neutral Virtue): Whatever May Be Said of the Perpetrators of Tuesday's Slaughter, They Were Not Cowards," Susan Sontag in "Talk of the Town," *The New Yorker*,

September 24, 2001, http://www.newyorker.com/talk/content/? 010924ta_talk_wtc. See also Susan Sontag, "Of Courage and Resistance," *The Nation*, May 5, 2003, http://www.thenation.com/doc.mhtml?i= 20030505&c=1&s=sontag.

11. Laura Kurgan, *New York, September 11, 2001. Four Days Later* . . . Installation using high resolution Ikonos satellite imagery of New York on September 15, 2001. Control_Space, ZKM, Karlsruhe, Germany, Opening October 2001, catalogue, http://www.princeton.edu/~kurgan/sep15/text.html.

12. At the same time this impossibility is made apparent. See Jean-Luc Nancy, *Le Regard Du Portrait* (Paris: Galilee, 2000). The subject is exposed as nonpresent to itself. I discuss this more fully in Jenny Edkins, "Exposed Singularity," *Journal for Cultural Research*, 9:4 (2005): 359–386.

13. Roland Barthes, *Camera Lucida*, trans. Richard Howard (London: Vintage, 1993), p. 5.

14. Jane Gross and Jenny Scott, "The Missing: Hospital Treks, Fliers, and the Cry: Have You Seen . . . ?" *The New York Times*, September 13, 2001, http://www.nytimes.com/20001/09/13/nyregion/13MISS.html.

15. David Usborne, "It Has Taken Me My Whole Life to Find Him," *The Independent* (London), September 14, 2001, p. 5 and "Normal Life Resumes," *The Independent* (London), September 15, 2001, p. 3.

16. Jonathan Wallace, "The Missing," *Year Zero*, September 29, 2001, The Ethical Spectacle, http://www.spectacle.org/yearzero/missing.html.

17. Jeshajahu Weinberg and Rina Elieli, *The Holocaust Museum in Washington* (New York: Rizzoli in collaboration with the United States Holocaust Memorial Museum, 1995).

18. [Photograph #N03043], http://www.ushmm.org/uia-cgi/uia_doc/query/10?uf=uia_RdpfZw.

19. Billie Jones, "Employing Identification in Online Museums," papers from *Museums and the Web 2000*, Archives & Museum Informatics, http://www.archimuse.com/mw2000/papers/jones/jones.html.

20. Richard Crownshaw, "Performing Memory in Holocaust Museums," *Performance Research*, 5:3 (2000): 18–27.

21. Mark Wigley, "Insecurity by Design," in *After the World Trade Centre: Rethinking New York City*, ed. Michael Sorkin and Sharon Zukin (New York: Routledge, 2002), pp. 69–85.

22. Ibid., p. 75.

23. Ibid., pp. 82–83.

24. Ibid., pp. 83–84.

25. Ibid., p. 84.

26. Jeanne Henry, "What Madness Prompts, Reason Writes: New York City September 11–October 2, 2001," *Anthropology and Education Quarterly*, 33:3 (2002): 283–296, p. 285.

27. City Lore, "Missing: Streetscape of a City in Mourning," http://www.citylore.org/911_exhibit/911_home.html.

28. This is interesting in relation to "Wanted" posters, where someone is described as "Wanted: Dead or Alive."

29. Laura Flanders, Live reports from Manhattan, filed 10.35 p.m. EST Tuesday, September 11, 2001. Working Assets, WorkingforChange, http://www.workingforchange.com/printitem.cfm?itemid=11899.

30. Laura Flanders, Live reports from Manhattan, filed 1.05 p.m. EST Wednesday, September 12, 2001, Working Assets,WorkingforChange, http://www.workingforchange.com/printitem.cfm?itemid=11899.

31. Jenny Edkins, "The Rush to Memory and the Rhetoric of War," *Journal of Political and Military Sociology*, 31:2 (2003): 231–251.

32. "Bare life" is Giorgio Agamben's term, also sometimes translated as "naked life." He uses it to refer to the life that since the ancient Greeks has been excluded from the *polis*; as a form of life "bare life" has in the past included slaves and women. See Giorgio Agamben, *Homo Sacer: Sovereign Power and Bare Life*, trans. Daniel Heller-Roazen (Stanford, CA: Stanford University Press, 1998).

33. Judith Greenberg, "Wounded New York," in *Trauma at Home: After 9/11*, ed. Judith Greenberg (Lincoln and London: University of Nebraska Press, 2003), p. 23.

34. Janice Hume, " 'Portraits of Grief,' Reflectors of Values: The New York Times Remembers Victims of September 11," *Journalism and Mass Communication Quarterly*, 80:1 (2003): 170.

35. Agamben (1998).

36. "Many WTC Remains Are Unidentified," *CBS News*, August 14, 2003, http://www.cbsnews.com/stories/2003/08/14/attack/main568168.shtml.

37. http://www.madres.org/.

38. "Final WTC Death Toll Said Down to 2,749," *The Associated Press*, January 23, 2004, http://www.voicesofsept11.org/medical_examiner/012304.html. See also Eric Lipton, "New York Settles on a Number that Defines Tragedy: 2,749 Dead in Trade Center Attack," *The New York Times*, January 23, 2004.

39. Marianne Hirsch, "I Took Pictures: September 2001 and Beyond," in Greenberg (2003), p. 69.

40. U.S. Department of State International Information Programs, *New York City: Three Months After: Pictorial Essays Developed during Three Days in December 2001 Capture the City's—and the Nation's—Indomitable Spirit*, http://usinfo.state.gov/topical/pol/terror/album/newyork/.

41. *Missing: Last Seen at the World Trade Center September11, 2001*, a touring exhibition of missing person fliers, initiated by Louis Nevaer, funded by the Mesoamerica Foundation, http://www.bronston.com/missing/.

CHAPTER 3

BODY COUNTS: THE BIOPOLITICS OF DEATH

Cristina Masters

Where was the dead body found?
Who found the dead body?
Was the dead body dead when found?
How was the dead body found?

Who was the dead body?

Who was the father or daughter or brother
Or uncle or sister or mother or son
Of the dead and abandoned body?

Was the body dead when abandoned?
Was the body abandoned?
By whom had it been abandoned?

Was the dead body naked or dressed for a journey?

What made you declare the dead body dead?
Did you declare the dead body dead?
How well did you know the dead body?
How did you know the dead body was dead?

Did you wash the dead body
Did you close both its eyes
Did you bury the body
Did you leave it abandoned
Did you kiss the dead body

—Harold Pinter, "Death"[1]

Metrics of Violence

The body count of dead American soldiers in Iraq now exceeds 2,000.[2] To date, there is no official body count of Iraqis killed—civilian or combatant[3]—in this most recent war on terror. U.S.-led coalition forces have not kept count, and in the words of General Tommy Franks; "We don't do body counts." Iraq Body Count, a nongovernmental organization unofficially sponsored by the United States and United Kingdom, estimates the civilian deaths resulting directly from coalition military action between 28,000–32,000 casualties.[4] A number of independent studies, however, such as the much-denounced study led by Dr. Les Roberts and published by the *Lancet*, have estimated the number of Iraqi civilian casualties at more than 100,000, an estimate that Dr. Roberts claims is based on rather conservative assumptions.[5] In responding to this study a Pentagon spokesperson stated: "[T]his conflict has been prosecuted in the most precise fashion of any conflict in the history of modern warfare."[6] While the loss of any "innocent lives" is tragic, he went on to say, and something coalition forces have worked hard to avoid, there is no way to confirm the accuracy of the report and, more importantly, that any report on civilian casualties must consider how "former regime elements and insurgents have made it a practice of using civilians as human shields, operating and conducting attacks against coalition forces from within areas inhabited by civilians."[7] In other words, while U.S. precision-guided bombs and bullets may be what kill Iraqi civilians, it is "former regime elements" and "insurgents" who are ultimately responsible for the deaths of civilians.

This displacement of responsibility has become a primary modus operandi of the U.S.-led coalition attack on Iraq. A news report on a "battle" between U.S. forces and Iraqi "insurgents" in May 2005 reads: "Through Sunday night and into Monday morning, the foreign fighters battled on, their screaming voices gradually fading to just one. In the end, it took five Marine assaults, grenades, a tank firing bunker-busting artillery rounds, 500-pound bombs unleashed by an F/A-18 attack plane and a point-blank attack by a rocket launcher to quell them."[8] In the words of Gunnery Sergeant Chuck Hurley, commander of the team that battled the insurgents in a one-story house in Ubaydi: "*They came here to die. They were willing to stay in place and die with no hope. All they wanted was to take us with them.*"[9] The choice of words tells its own story, wherein the moral grammar of the statement suggests a suicide mission: "they came here to die," "willing to die with no hope," "all they wanted was to take us with them," with the effect being to dislocate agency and responsibility onto the "insurgents." They alone become responsible for their deaths. At the same time

signaling that any Iraqi resistance to the U.S.-led war as illegitimate by
constituting any who resist as "insurgents," "foreign fighters," "former
regime elements," and "irregular soldiers."

It is estimated that 75 "foreign fighters" died in this particular attack,
demonstrating that while the United States does not tally the total number
of enemy combatants killed in battle, it will release numbers on estimated
deaths in tightly managed instances. Not surprisingly, perhaps, is the
willingness to circulate the number of Iraqis killed in suicide attacks and car
bombings. Headlines read as follows: 27 killed in a car bombing outside of
a hotel in Baghdad, 54 killed in a car bombing while applying for jobs at a
police station, 109 killed in a suicide bombing, 30 killed in an attack on a
café. These body counts, much like the color-coded security alert system,
serve as a constant reminder of the "necessity" of the war on terror, while
also subtly reinvoking the memory of September 11. These body counts
also work to reproduce fear, reminding Americans, and people in the West
more generally, that they need to be afraid.

This discrete management of body counts, no doubt, has its roots in the
Vietnam War. With approximately 60,000 soldiers sent back to the United
States in body bags, not including the tens of thousands injured and
maimed, and horrific instances of Vietnamese civilians killed by the U.S.
military, such as the more than 300 civilians brutally killed at My Lai
including the rape of at least one girl, the U.S. administration has worked
hard to ensure that body counts do not find their way into American living
rooms. Or if they do find their way into the American imaginary they
ensure that they tell a story of victory, rather than stories of defeat and
horror. Such was the case with the Gulf War of 1991. The U.S. administration was more than willing to take ownership of the body count—
only 147 U.S. soldiers died in combat, effectively erasing the trauma of
the Vietnam War from the American body politic through a highly stylized, techno-war displayed nightly on our television screens. In both the
Vietnam War and Gulf War, however, the hundreds of thousands
Vietnamese and Iraqis killed largely remain absent from the dominant
narratives of war.

While we recognize that death permeates the experience of war, the
"givenness" of death actually renders it outside of politics. How does the
death of some go unnoticed? Dead bodies do much discursive work for
sovereign power, however, who is working on their behalf? In other
words, who is doing the discursive work for the dead? One of the questions
that lingers, then, is how to make present the absences marked by death,
both for who and how bodies are counted. This chapter, therefore, critically seeks to interrogate death as a site productive of political meaning.

It explores the paradox raised by Foucault's theorization of biopolitics that while the injunction to make live appears as the central task of biopower, indeed, killing in the name of making live has become the key signifier of sovereign power. As Agamben argues, the "sovereign sphere is the sphere in which it is permitted to kill without committing homicide and without celebrating sacrifice."[10] Not surprisingly, then, killing has been profoundly depoliticized in the war on terror. In *Society Must Be Defended*, Foucault argues that power over life—biopower—"no longer recognizes death. Power literally ignores death."[11] That death is ignored suggests that it needs to be a central site of inquiry, not least of which because biopolitical practices underwrite and secure claims to sovereign power through their depoliticization (or celebration) of death. The imperative to depoliticize hinges on the capacity to read death in very particular ways—or through the denial of death altogether. Yet, the imperative to "read" death in ways supportive of sovereign power must also presuppose that there are ways to read death that are more politically dangerous in the threats that they pose to the claims of sovereign power.

> Violence immediately suggests the end of dialogue, enacting not just the destruction of the body, but of its capacity to speak, to articulate agency and history. Even as the oppressed are allowed to speak, they have already and irretrievably been silenced. . . . But even as the embodied self is silenced and destroyed, it re-emerges in its deathly aura, as the sight of memory and ultimately a political agency that seeks to remind the audience of its perpetual presence.[12]

Considering that violence has become a central modality through which American economies of representation have been constructed, to resist these particular representations is necessarily to take up the responsibility of other representations. Knowing that the abject others created in these performances cannot always speak for themselves, but they can always be read differently and, and more importantly, subversively.

Increasingly, there is a need to understand death as the exposed body that faces, subverts, and otherwise thwarts attempts at assimilating the body-in-death into the imperatives associated with security and survival. Indeed, the body-in-death has the potential to be profoundly destabilizing to hegemonic claims because it is the site not only upon which biopower is inscribed but also where it can be subverted in the refusal of the narrative assigned to it or in the articulation of other narratives. This awareness first reveals that death is not simply a singular experience undergone by the "I" who faces death—rather, death is experienced in the plural; the body-in-death must be buried or cremated, explanations must be given and made meaningful to those who survive (individuals, communities, nations) and who also narrate. Thus, there are always multiple ways to "read" the significance of death and its relationship with both the social political imaginary and the expression of sovereign power.

This chapter, however, is not an economy of violence. It does not assume that getting the count right or that counting altogether is the way in which we can unravel the complexity of this most recent "terrorizing war." It does not assume that numbers speak for themselves and that the numbers alone will tell us "The Story," as though there is a singular, definitive story to be read through numbers. While at the same time, there is no doubt that body counts do tell a story. Dead U.S. soldiers, for instance, get counted. They tell a story about which bodies count as politically qualified life—in other words, those worthy of being counted. The body counts of dead U.S. soldiers are intended to tell us a story of how well the "precision of conflict," made possible by the so-called revolution in military affairs, is working. The body counts of dead U.S. soldiers can also be read as a narrative of sacrifice and protection on behalf of the American people. We would do well, however, to be suspicious of the body counts the U.S. administration circulates for us. They don't include, for instance, the deaths of private military contractors. As David Levi Strauss argues, the Bush administration "uses these contractors to mask the real costs of occupation."[13]

But these aren't the only stories worth telling about the body counts of U.S. soldiers. Biopoliticians of the U.S. administration and their refusal to participate in the funerals of American soldiers killed in Iraq, and the shift in discourse in and around soldiers killed in battle, potentially provide us with the opportunity to read these body counts differently. In the past, these moments have been an opportunity to (re)articulate the patriotic, heroic, honorable self killed in his duty to nation. These dead soldiers killed in their duty to nation, however, have ironically been marked as other—as potentially contaminating of the body politic. This sense of contamination is invoked in the official discursive designation of "body bags" as "transfer tubes" where these "bodies-of-violence" now have become "bodies-in-violence."

> In order to continue to sell an increasingly unpopular Iraqi invasion to the American people, President George W. Bush's administration sweeps the messy parts of war—the grieving families, the flag-draped coffins, the soldiers who have lost limbs—into a far corner of the nation's attic. No television cameras are allowed at Dover. Bush does not attend the funerals of soldiers who gave their lives in his war on terrorism.[14]

This sanitization of dead soldiers in body bags can be read in several ways. We can maintain the dominant narrative that these dead soldiers represent the hegemonic self. We can also place these bodies outside of resistance because they can no longer speak for themselves. Or we can do the more difficult thing and read these bodies back at the self by "rendering delirious" their contamination, allowing them to infect the body politic with the trace of the other. Especially with the rank and file of the U.S. military increasingly composed of racial, ethnic, class, and gendered minorities, the willingness to expose some to death in the name of life—pitting bare life against bare life—needs to be critically engaged.

Lori Ann Piestewa, a Hopi Indian and the first American woman to be killed in combat and the first Native American to be killed in the war, was raised in the Navajo reservation in Arizona. Paradoxically, "if Lori had been born a century earlier, the United States government would have considered her an enemy."[15] Lori grew up in and around Tuba City where the unemployment rate hovers around 20 percent. She played sports in high school and made commander in the Junior Reserve Officer Training Program. By the age of 17 she was pregnant with her first child, Brandon. She married the father of her son, but shortly after her daughter Carla was born her marriage fell apart. Joining the U.S. Army and leaving her kids behind was her way of pursuing what would have been difficult otherwise—a college education and a steady job. Like many others in the same position, the reality of being sent on a tour of duty in Iraq was most likely a distant possibility. But Lori didn't go to Iraq against her will, indeed she was still recovering from surgery when her company was called to deploy. She could have stayed behind.

Lori also wasn't the first in her family to go to war. Her father, Terry, was drafted and fought in the Vietnam War. He went because he did not want to go to jail, as his two brothers-in-law had when they refused the draft during the Korean War. In different ways, but in both instances, there is an ambivalence in Lori and Terry's participation in war; one that seems noteworthy in resisting particular representations. There is a messiness to war that fails to be captured in the neat borders that body counts ascribe. Lori Ann Piestewa—Private First Class of the 507th Army Maintenance Company—is at the same time both more and less than this representation. Lori has become "known" in the war on terror as a dead U.S. soldier, but she also exceeds this representation that has quite literally taken hostage her dead body. She can be made present differently by reading the absences that mark the borders of this singular identity.

Casey Sheehan, a Humvee mechanic in the U.S. Army's 1st Cavalry, was killed by a roadside bomb on April 4, 2004. He was 24 years old. His death marked the day that the U.S. administration announced an end to major military operations in the war on terror in Iraq. His mother Cindy

Sheehan has has taken up the difficult endeavor of challenging sovereign power, setting up camp outside of President Bush's ranch in Texas, leading protest marches in Washington against the war, and, as some have argued, single-handedly "reenergizing" the U.S. peace movement. In her words it is "patriotic dissent."[16] And as Jean Franco argues, "constellations of meaning accrue around powerful cadavers"[17]—cadavers that are made powerful precisely in the possibility of critical (re)readings of death. Cindy Sheehan has done this with her son's death, recasting her son's body with a political agency that now haunts the U.S. administration.

The significant point is that even as Lori Ann Piestewa and Casey Sheehan are made present by their inclusion in official U.S. body counts, there is much that body counts can't tell us, and therefore, much that remains absent. These absences are invitations that need to be taken up, calling on us to tell different stories. What body counts can't tell us, for instance, can be captured by the poem introduced at the beginning of the chapter by Harold Pinter entitled "Death." These are some of the questions that body counts don't ask, questions that are excluded from our critical inquiry. Body counts, for instance, don't ask questions about Lori Ann Piestewa's life, her children, her decisions, and her pain in the last moments of her life. Did someone hold her hand? Did someone kiss Lori's dead body? Did someone kiss Casey's dead body? Who declared his dead body dead? Who buried his body? These are questions that can be only asked if we advance the claim that bodies indeed do count. When they don't count, and aren't counted, are they grievable lives, in other words, lives worth mourning? As the primary site through which power and violence operates and materializes, the body needs to be central to our critical inquiries.

While this chapter explores death across a variety of registers, there is one register in particular that stands out. This particular register of death captures the imperative to read death in more politically subversive ways. This register, however, falls outside of the frame of body counts, not least of which because no, or only a few, dead bodies are produced to count—"they are those who were missed by the bombs."[18] In doing so, I would like for us to consider at least the double entendre in the title of the chapter: what bodies do count? This particular register of death can be found in the prisons we have seemingly become intimately and horrifyingly aware of because some U.S. soldiers thought they were moments worthy of being photographed, in other words, "Kodak moments." These are the photographs of U.S. soldiers torturing Iraqi prisoners at Abu Ghraib. These are the individuals who have been cast as life not worth living by the biopoliticians of the U.S. administration, making it unnecessary to name "them."

While the chapter has so far asked after those bodies made intelligible in particularly violent ways, the reminder of the chapter asks after those denied intelligibility—the bodies that fail to materialize as living, loving, longing life.

Ritual Burials

I would like to read the prisoners of places such as Abu Ghraib and Guantánamo Bay, and the technologies of the prison, through historical practices of live burial. These practices of live burial, while rare, offer us interpretive possibilities for reading the contemporary context of the war on terror. In particular, I want to read the indefinite detention of prisoners and the space of the prison they occupy through the live burials of vestal virgins in the ancient Roman Republic, where live burial was the punishment enacted on vestal virgins accused of impurity or sexual immorality. While these burials were rare, they almost always coincided with times of crisis, wherein the "immorality" of the vestal virgin was understood as jeopardizing the safety of Rome. It needs to be pointed out that the actual guilt of a vestal virgin was of little importance. As jeopardy to the state, the vestal virgin would be buried alive in an underground chamber. The chamber contained a bed, a lamp, and small portions of the bare necessities of existence—some bread, water, milk, and oil.

The provision of the barest necessities stands out, not least of which, because it firmly placed the "when" of dying in the hands of the vestal virgin. She, and she alone, would be left to decide how much to eat and drink, either extending her life and delaying death or bringing about the quickest death possible under the circumstances. What is significant for interpreting the indefinite detainees of the U.S. administration is that

> [g]iven the problematic status of the condemned, the punishment was carefully crafted to displace responsibility and blame. At the moment of its enactment, live entombment placed the condemned woman neither among the living nor among the dead. Ensconced in a space beyond the living and yet undead, the sacrificed vestal is contained in a way that it meant to inhibit her return. Within the earth, she is removed from the sensory perception of the living. She can make no claims on them. But not yet dead, she is not due the rituals of mourning, the remembrance of her life and contributions. She is erased.[19]

The 70,000 prisoners held by the United States, mostly in undisclosed locations around the world, have equally been removed from the sensory perception of the living. They have been erased. And as alive but not alive, dead but not dead, they have also been denied the rituals of mourning, grieving, and remembering.

The state of emergency invoked in the ritual burials of vestal virgins in the Roman Republic reflects the state of emergency underwriting the suspension of international law by U.S. sovereign power. The same way that the so-called immorality of the virgin jeopardized the safety of the state, the constitution of the detainees as "high value terrorist targets" has equally been framed as jeopardizing the state. And much like the live entombment of vestal virgins, the imprisonment of the individuals has little to do with the actual or real guilt of the prisoners. "The hooded prisoner being forced to masturbate in front of Lynndie England is named Hayder Sabbar Abd, and he was picked up for 'getting out of a cab in a suspicious manner.' "[20] The vast majority of the prisoners in these ostensibly nonplaces have been picked up in random raids where their only crime is seemingly being Arab and male.

This sovereign power, as Foucault argues, has been fundamentally articulated in the last century through the category of race. We were first witness to this power in the Nazi concentration camp, now witnessed in the prison. This visuality of difference through which sovereign power is operating figures significantly within American representational politics as evidenced in the institutionalization of categories of identity and difference, wherein one emerges within the representational frame *as* a gendered, raced, and sexualized *body*. The body, as the key signifier of identity and difference, perhaps now more than ever, has taken on the disproportionate weight of representation within American identity politics. This is evident in American security practices wherein what one looks "like" has become essential to identifying threat. As Giorgio Agamben points out, all life has the potential of being rendered as bare life. This trope of visibility, thus, is two-pronged. While it appears first and foremost about rendering visible particular subjects, it is also necessarily about rendering subjects invisible— a politics of active *de*representation.

The denial of habeas corpus perhaps most graphically captures the derepresentation marked by the figural death and ritual burial of prisoners indefinitely detained in the war on terror. Literally translated as "you shall have the body," the question of habeas corpus has been a central site through which the ritual burial of the prisoners held in Guantánamo Bay has been enacted. "Living entombment in this instance, it would seem, constitutes a death sentence without an executioner, a means of delivering the polity from a political evil without an assumption of responsibility for producing a corpse."[21] In the same way that live burial in the Roman Republic denied vestal virgins from making a claim on the living, the denial of habeas corpus by the U.S. Republic has had a similar effect. The prisoners of Abu Ghraib and Guantánamo Bay have been fundamentally denied the possibility of making claims on the living, whose very existence they underwrite. Importantly, this denial has the profound effect of expunging U.S. biopoliticians of any responsibility. With no body placed in front of the law, and no body produced in a court of law, there is *no body* to be responsible to. "[T]he legal architecture of the war on terror is visible only in an illusive language that makes border zones like Abu Ghraib not simply susceptible to human rights violations, but renders dramatic dislocation of cultural responsibility acceptable."[22]

Much like "[t]he trials and executions of the Vestals are never referred to as—what they so palpably are—human sacrifice,"[23] the torture and death of the prisoners held by the United States are also never referred to as human sacrifice. This would actually require that the prisoners be recognized as politically qualified life, life cast within the realm of the human. Instead as bare life, they can be killed or tortured with impunity—it is neither murder nor sacrifice, marking the prison as camp. "Even while different sovereign authorities might fight over an inmate's future, whether 'dead or alive,' what is clear is that the sovereign produces bare life whereby taking it is neither a crime nor is it the sacrifice of a fully 'human life.' "[24] At the same time that the U.S. Supreme Court in *Rasul v. Bush* has extended habeas corpus to the detainees held at Guantánamo Bay, it has left unanswered the legal status of the territorial space itself, maintaining "the prisoners in a limbo between military rule and civil rights."[25] These limbo spaces abound for the prisoners detained by the United States.

Some differences stand out, namely the refusal to allow prisoners to take their lives into their own hands. In the words of Joshua Colangelo-Bryan, the American lawyer assigned to one of the prisoners at Guantánamo Bay: "Detainees see it as the only means they have of exercising control over their lives. . . . Their only means of effective protest are to harm themselves, either by hunger strike or doing something like this."[26] There have also been dozens of hunger strikes, and more than two dozen detainees are currently being fed by force. In response to the more than 30 suicide attempts at the prison, the spokesman for the Joint Task Force Guantánamo stated: "We treat prisoners humanely, we don't let them commit suicide. . . . No detainee has died at the military prison."[27] Paradoxically, the humane thing in this instance could very well be the extension of the only agency and resistance left them—literal death at their own hands.

Amnesty International has been instrumental in tracking the numerous violations of the U.S. administration, both domestically and internationally. In doing so they have advanced the argument that

> [t]he US cannot have it both ways. It cannot speak the language of human
> rights while at the same time violating human rights and disregarding interna-
> tional law. Either it is for human rights in deed as well as in word, or it will
> continue to be denounced as a human rights violator and, especially given its
> power, reach and influence in the world, a global threat to the rule of law and
> security.[28]

But the United States can have it both ways precisely because of the
operation of sovereign power that is at the same time *the law* and *above the
law*. As Agamben tells us, this is the essence of sovereign privilege.
"Precisely because it is a power established and sanctioned by the law that
cannot be subject to legal rules, clemency marks the boundary of law
itself."[29] Living up to the law is no longer sufficient, or possible, as sovereign power "comprises a central contradiction. Its first necessity is to
uphold the law. Its second necessity is to be outside the law so that it is able
to impart the law, since anything already bound by law cannot initiate
law."[30] It is this contradiction that needs to be challenged.

Unintentionally, the photographs of U.S. soldiers torturing Iraqi
detainees have enabled, in some way, the return of the "not yet dead" who
populate these prisons. They have been made figurally present, if only
partially and grotesquely, in these Kodak moments. We see *them* as we have
never seen them before. At the same, and with the same gaze, however, we
do not see *them* at all. The subject of the text slips from Hayder Sabbar Abd
to Lynddie England, from *them* to *us*. An "us" that is both recognizable and
unrecognizable. These representations have effected a double erasure of the
prisoners in Abu Ghraib—erasure in the first instance through the violence
enacted upon them, and erasure in the second instance because our feelings
of horror are not for them but rather for us, because it is "us" who are
reflected back.

> In them, we are represented with a seemingly unsustainable contradiction: an
> image of liberators engaged in torture, of a democracy acting sadistically in a
> totalitarian setting. We are confronted with America decentered publicly and
> unavoidably, its "imagined community" disrupted by way of a hyper-
> aggressive patriotism. Simultaneously, we are not surprised at all.[31]

Not surprised, because there is a familiarity gestured to in the photographs.
At the same time legible and illegible. So familiar that one must look twice,
they require a double take, not least of which because these Kodak
moments paradoxically capture iconic American culture—walking a dog

on a leash, pyramids of cheerleaders, fraternity-hazing rituals, and its obscene undersides, pornography, capital punishment, and lynchings. Some images more familiar to some than others. The image of an Iraqi prisoner, hooded, standing on a box, hands stretched out, without a doubt resonates with black Americans' historical memories, seeing themselves in the very borders of the photograph. American cheerleaders recognizing the mainstay of their supporting acts at all-American football games. College boys intimately familiar with the rituals of initiation into fraternities across the country. Perhaps this is the subversion—seeing ourselves, in all of our horror, reflected back through violent enactments on *other* bodies.

Conclusion

The case of Terri Schiavo raises complex issues. Yet in instances like this one, where there are serious questions and substantial doubts, our society, our laws, and our courts should have a presumption in favor of life. Those who live at the mercy of others deserve our special care and concern. It should be our goal as a nation to build a culture of life, where all Americans are valued, welcomed, and protected—and that culture of life must extend to individuals with disabilities.

—President George W. Bush[32]

In the context of the prisoners occupying zones of indistinction in Abu Ghraib and Guantánamo Bay, this statement by President Bush raises so many critical questions and stark contradictions, not least of which, because the ambiguity extended to Terri Schiavo, has been denied to the indefinite detainees held by the U.S. administration in the war on terror. Instead, their lives have been captured by a representational singularity and totality that has placed them outside of relationality, outside of the realm of the human. Our care and concern has not been extended to these individuals who live at our mercy. Rather, they have been ritually buried for us—to save us, if only from ourselves. Terri Schiavo's life ended in death, and her life was mourned, grieved, and memorialized. The living dead in these prisons have not been extended the same gifts—gifts that mark livable, memorable life. A culture of life fundamentally premised and sustained, however, on the death of others is no culture of life at all.

It's rather ironic that nonstructuralists are invariably accused of losing sight of the body through the rhetorical critique that if everything is discursive, how do we even know if we really exist? The question I would ask back to the critics, in particular those who have actively participated in legitimizing this latest war on terror through just war traditions, is this: where is the body in U.S. sovereign power? I would argue that there is no *body* to be found—the technologies of the prison, like the technologies of violence employed by the U.S. military such as precision-guided munitions, produce no living, loving, grievable bodies. The men and women who populate these spaces are actively dehumanized, desubjectified, derepresented, in other words they are D.E.A.D.

> The terms by which we are recognized as human are socially articulated and changeable. And sometimes the very terms that confer "humanness" on some individuals are those that deprive certain other individuals of the possibility of achieving that status, producing a differential between the human and the less-than-human. These norms have far reaching consequences for how we understand the model of the human entitled to rights or included in the participatory sphere of political deliberation. . . . Certain humans are recognized as less than human, and that form of qualified recognition does not lead to a viable life. Certain humans are not recognized as human at all, and that leads to yet another order of unlivable life.[33]

Cast outside of the social—the social being a necessary modality of subjectivity—the prisoners of Abu Ghraib and Guantánamo Bay have been fundamentally denied the relationality necessary for subjective existence. They are the living dead, or in Žižek's words: "[T]hey are between two deaths," in the zone of indistinction.[34]

There's a profound arrogance in claims to security as they have been articulated in the U.S. war on terror, not least of which because these claims to security come at the expense of radical insecurity for most of the people and places upon which these practices play out, both inside and outside the state. As Agamben succinctly points out, a state that has security as its central task and as the source of its legitimacy runs the risk of turning itself "terroristic."[35] It seems that the United States has already crossed the threshold. To advance an alternative politics, one that isn't premised on security and terror,

> [t]he task seems to be about distinguishing among on the one hand the norms and conventions that permit people to breathe, to desire, to love, and to live and on the other hand those norms and conventions that restrict or eviscerate the conditions of life itself. What is most important is to cease legislating for all lives what is liveable only for some, and similarly, to refrain from proscribing for all lives what is unliveable for some. The difference in position and desire set the limits to universality as an ethical reflex. The critique of norms that legislate difference must be situated within the context of lives as they are lived and must be guided by the question of what maximizes the possibilities for liveable life, and what minimizes the possibility of unbearable life or, indeed, social or literal death.[36]

One possibility is espousing an ethics of making strange oneself rather than perpetuating strategies of making others strange to us and for us. The desire is to participate in political practices that make life livable rather than participating in an international politics premised on profoundly uninhabitable and unlivable lives. Bodies do matter as registers of multiple livabilities.

Notes

1. In Harold Pinter, "Art, Truth & Politics," *Nobel Lecture* (The Nobel Foundation, 2005), p. 12.
2. See Iraq Coalition Casualties at http://icasualties.org/oif/default.aspx.
3. The discursive move by U.S. biopoliticians of labeling enemy combatants "irregular soldiers," "insurgents," and so forth has laid the groundwork for circumventing Geneva Conventions rules that stipulate for body counts of both civilians and enemy combatants. This "third" category, created by the U.S. administration has enabled the superceding of international norms of war.
4. http://www.iraqbodycount.net/ (accessed March 3, 2006).
5. Dr. Les Roberts et al., "Mortality Before and After the 2003 Invasion of Iraq: Cluster Sample Survey," *The Lancet*, 364:9448 (November 20, 2004): 1857–1864.
6. Quoted in "Iraqi Death Toll 'Soared Post-War,'" *BBC News*, October 29, 2004, http://news.bbc.co.uk/2/hi/middle_east/3962969.stm (accessed April 4, 2005).
7. Ibid.
8. Ellen Knickmeyer, "They Came Here to Die," *Washington Post*, May 11, 2005, http://www.washingtonpost.com/wp-dyn/content/article/2005/05/10/AR2005051000221_pf.html (accessed October 11, 2005).
9. Quoted in ibid., emphasis added.
10. Giorgio Agamben, *Homo Sacer: Sovereign Power and Bare Life*, trans. Daniel Heller-Roazen (Stanford: Stanford University Press, 1998), p. 83.
11. Michel Foucault, *Society Must Be Defended*, trans. David Macey (London: Allen Lane/Penguin, 2003), p. 248.
12. Vivienne Jabri, "Pinter, Radical Critique, and Politics," *borderlands: ejournal*, 12:2, http:www.borderlandsejournal.ade . . . u.au/vol12no2_2003/jabri_pinter.htm (2003) (accessed December 2, 2003).
13. David Levi Strauss, "Breakdown in the Grayroom: Recent Turns in the Image War," in *Abu Ghraib: The Politics of Torture* (Berkeley: North Atlantic Books, 2004), p. 92.
14. Tim Harper, "Pentagon Keeps Dead Out of Sight," *Toronto Star*, November 3, 2003.
15. Osha Gray Davidson, "A Wrong Turn in the Desert," *Rolling Stone*, May 27, 2004, http://www.oshadavidson.com/Piestewa.htm (accessed October 18, 2005).

16. See Cindy Sheehan's website "Truth Out: One Mother's Stand," http://www.truthout.org/cindy.shtml (accessed December 12, 2005).

17. Jean Franco quoted in Mary Hawkesworth, "The Semiotics of Premature Burial: Feminism in a Postfeminist Age," *Signs*, 29:4 (2004): 983.

18. Quoted in Slavoj Žižek, "Between Two Deaths: The Culture of Torture," *London Review of Books*, 26:11, June 3, 2004, http://www.lrb.co.uk/v26/n11/zize01_.html (accessed November 7, 2005).

19. Hawkesworth (2004), p. 977.

20. Strauss (2004), p. 101.

21. Hawkesworth (2004), p. 977.

22. Michelle Brown, " 'Setting the Conditions' for Abu Ghraib: The Prison Nation Abroad," *American Quarterly*, 57:3 (2005): 977.

23. Holt N. Parker, "Why were the Vestals Virgins? Or the Chastity of Women and the Safety of the Roman State," *American Journal of Philology*, 125 (2004): 585.

24. Jenny Edkins and Véronique Pin-Fat, eds., "Introduction: Life, Power, Resistance," in *Sovereign Lives: Power in Global Politics* (New York: Routledge, 2004), p. 10.

25. Amy Kaplan, "Where is Guantánamo?" *American Quarterly*, 57:3 (2005): 847.

26. Josh White, "Guantánamo Desperation Seen in Suicide Attempts," *Washington Post*, November 1, 2005, A01.

27. Ibid.

28. Amnesty International, "Guantánamo and Beyond: The Continuing Pursuit of Unchecked Executive Power," May 13, 2005, p. 11 (accessed March 3, 2006).

29. Austin Sarat, "At the Boundaries of Law: Executive Clemency, Sovereign Prerogative, and the Dilemma of American Legality," *American Quarterly*, 57:3 (2005): 617.

30. Michael Dillon, "Correlating Sovereign and Biopower," in *Sovereign Lives: Power in Global Politics*, eds. Jenny Edkins et al. (New York: Routledge, 2004), p. 48.

31. Brown (2005), p. 973.

32. President's Statement on Terri Schiavo, March 17, 2005, http://www.whitehouse.Seegov/news/releases/2005/03/20050317-7.html (accessed October 25, 2005).

33. Judith Butler, *Undoing Gender* (New York: Routledge, 2004), p. 2.

34. Žižek (2004).

35. Giorgio Agamben, "Security and Terror," *Theory & Event*, 5:4 (2002), http://muse.jhu.edu/journals/theory_and_event/v005/5.4agamben.html (accessed February 26, 2006).

36. Butler (2004), p. 8.

PART II

CINEMATICS, CULTURE, AESTHETICS

CHAPTER 4

RESPONSIBILITY AND TERROR: VISUAL CULTURE AND VIOLENCE IN THE PRECARIOUS LIFE

Mark J. Lacy

In *Precarious Life: The Powers of Mourning and Violence*, Judith Butler argues that 9/11 produced a "dislocation" of "First World privilege" for citizens of the United States. Watching the events of 9/11, the "secure" in the first world were exposed to a feeling of vulnerability that is usually experienced in "failed states" and "disaster zones." For Butler, this dislocation of first world privilege does not have to result in acts of violent protection or retaliation:

> That we can be injured, that others can be injured, that we are subject to death at the whim of another, are all reasons for both fear and grief. What is less certain, however, is whether the experiences of vulnerability and loss have to lead straightaway to military violence and retribution. There are other passages. If we are interested in arresting cycles of violence to produce less violent outcomes, it is no doubt important to ask, what, politically, might be made of grief besides a cry for war.[1]

Butler goes on to comment that

> [I]f national sovereignty is challenged, that does not mean it must be shored up at all costs, if that results in suspending civil liberties and suppressing political dissent. Rather, the dislocation from First World privilege, however

temporary, offers a chance to start to imagine a world in which that violence might be minimized, in which an inevitable interdependency becomes acknowledged as the basis for a global political community.[2]

These "other passages"[3] are limited by a "hegemonic field of vision" that translates vulnerability into the desire for the violent protection of borders, "the sublimity of destruction." This chapter looks at the role that popular visual culture plays in the (re)production of what Butler refers to as an "imagined wholeness" that requires the creation of a "desensitizing dream machine" of a "resuscitated US military power."[4]

One of the key lines of inquiry that is developed through *Precarious Life* concerns the determination of a hegemonic consensus in the United States on the global war on terror. The determination of hegemony takes place through the production of consensus in the public sphere on what certain terms will mean, how they can be used, and who the legitimate political actors are that can respond to our vulnerability and insecurity. The point Butler wishes to underscore is that "a frame for understanding violence emerges in tandem with the experience, and that the frame works both to preclude certain kinds of questions, certain kinds of historical inquiries, and to function as a moral justification for retaliation."[5] As Jacques Derrida observed, the dominant power "is the one that manages to impose, and thus, to legitimate, indeed to legalize (for it is always a question of law) on a national and world stage, the terminology and thus the interpretation that best suits it in a given situation."[6]

This determination of hegemony is not simply an issue of legitimating certain acts as terrorist/evil for juridico-political purposes; the dominant power must produce a hegemonic consensus that the violence it perpetrates is legitimate violence, violence that serves a just purpose, violence perpetrated with an ethos of responsibility and care (unlike what is viewed as terrorist violence: irresponsible violence that has no respect for life). This legitimation is not only an important strategy in terms of building consensus internationally, but is also significant in terms of the identity of citizens in liberal democracies, many of whom will tolerate violence and suffering in the form of a *virtuous* war.[7] Citizens in liberal democracies, desiring to be responsible and *good*, need to maintain a moral distance from the violence that is perpetrated in their name. Butler observes:

> When a bleeding child or a dead body on Afghan soil emerges in the press coverage, it is not relayed as part of the horror of war, but only in the service of a criticism of the military's capacity to aim its bombs right. We castigate ourselves for not aiming better, as if the end goal is to aim right. We do not,

however, take the sign of a destroyed life and decimated peoples as something for which we are responsible, or indeed understand how that decimation works to confirm the United States as performing atrocities. Our own acts are not considered terrorist.[8]

Acts of preemptive "policing" against terrorism become legitimate policies through the way that presidential speech acts promising protection and security resonate with the derealization of violence and the policing of debate in the public sphere; responsibility for *our* violence—in all its forms—becomes easier to silence, to actively forget.

Precarious Life is a meditation on the strategies that translate our vulnerability into the violent protection of society and the control and destruction of human beings that exist outside our hegemonic moral geographies. Butler shows how, on the one hand, the public sphere, shaped by a media structured by implicit and explicit censorship, maintains a separation between grievable and ungrievable lives, maintaining a distance from the intentional—and unintentional—deaths that emerge from the *global war on terror*.

There is less a dehumanizing discourse at work here than a refusal of discourse that produces dehumanization as a result. Violence against those who are already not quite living, that is, living in a state of suspension between life and death, leaves a mark that is no mark.[9]

On the other hand, a hegemonic grammar comes into play that limits what can be said in the public sphere about this condition, with "raw public mockery of the peace movement" in a manner that "profoundly marginalizes antiwar sentiment and analysis, putting into question in a very strong way the very value of dissent as part of contemporary US democratic culture."[10]

Butler outlines the narrative dimension of the explanatory framework that emerges with the hegemonic grammar of 9/11. She points to the way that in the United States "we begin the story by invoking a first-person narrative point of view, and telling what happened on September 11." The story can begin earlier but there are only a few narrative options, primarily the type of stories that focus on the personalities of bin Laden and his followers. For Butler, this type of narrative suggests to the citizenry that there is a "personal pathology at work."[11] This narrative dimension "resituates agency in terms of a subject, something we can understand, something that accords with our idea of personal responsibility, or with the theory of charismatic leadership that was popularized with Mussolini and Hitler in World War II."[12]

Butler goes on to comment that "those who commit acts of violence are surely responsible for them; they are not dupes or mechanisms of an impersonal social force, but agents with responsibility."[13] But these "individuals are formed, and we would be making a mistake if we reduced their actions to purely self-generated acts of will or symptoms of individual pathology or 'evil.' "[14] For Butler, both the discourse of moralism and individualism assume the "first link in a causal chain that forms the meaning of accountability."[15] The ethico–political challenge is to go beyond this hegemonic grammar of moralism and individualism in order to be able to ask: "What social conditions help to form the very ways that choice and deliberation proceed?"[16]

This narrative of individualism and moralism comes to legitimate a condition where the U.S. acts unilaterally to secure its populations from terror:

> Nations are not the same as individual psyches, but both can be described as "subjects," albeit of different orders. When the United States acts, it establishes a conception of what it means to act as an American, establishes a norm by which subjects might be known. In recent months, a subject has been instated at the national level, a sovereign and extra-legal subject, a violent and self-centered subject; its actions constitute the building of a subject that seeks to restore and maintain its mastery through the systematic destruction of its multilateral relations, its ties to the international community. It shores itself up, seeks to constitute its imagined wholeness, but only at the price of denying its own vulnerability, its dependency, its exposure, where it exploits those very features in others, thereby making those features "other to" itself.[17]

This point about "imagined wholeness" requires elaboration. As Jürgen Habermas remarks, the attacks on 9/11 destroyed

> an icon in the household imagery of the American nation. Only in the surge of patriotism that followed did one begin to recognize the central importance the towers held in the popular imagination, with their irreplaceable imprint on the Manhattan skyline and their powerful embodiment of economic strength and projection toward the future.[18]

Similarly, Jean Baudrillard observes that the towers are both a "physical, architectural object and a symbolic object (symbolic of financial power and global economic liberalism)": "Imagine they had not collapsed, or only one had collapsed: the effect would not have been the same at all. The fragility of global power would not have been so strikingly proven."[19] The towers were part of the "imagined wholeness" that Butler refers to, the promise of overcoming the precarious life, the promise of future security.

What if the UN building in New York—symbolic of a security and democracy to come—had become a ground zero rather than the World Trade Center? The symbolic force of the act would have been different: the World Trade Center towers are the promise of a better future orchestrated by a nurturing U.S. global economic liberalism; the towers are a symbol of *permanence* but are intimately connected to the promise of the overcoming of vulnerability through techno-scientific transformations, transformations that promise to secure a permanent identity at the same time as they create changes in our mode of existence, transformations that create uncertainty over forms of life that were supposedly once secure, that form a desire for a solid, "authentic" identity. Global economic liberalism does not offer security and justice for everyone in the present, but it is the *promise* of a better future for everyone in the future, and the promise of continued development in war against "biocriminal" threats to populations: that the twin towers are imbued with such meaning is testament to the power of the hegemonic consensus that has depoliticized the inequality, insecurity, and uncertainty of the world that global economic liberalism creates. September 11 (9/11) was an attack on U.S. strategies of protection and its projection toward the future, hence the symbolic force of the attack activated forces that more easily lend themselves to the reassertion of a violent and self-centered subject.

A hegemonic consensus is produced on how to understand 9/11 and develop the global war on terror; Butler's *Precarious Life* is useful in the way that it shows how a hegemonic consensus is produced in the public sphere, but the focus is primarily on "official" discourse and news media/popular intellectual commentary. To be sure, Butler is aware of the way that the hegemonic consensus operates through other forms, such as the way the twin towers work to create the image of "imagined wholeness," but the determination of the hegemonic consensus needs to be taken further: this chapter looks at how the determination of hegemony emerges with other forms of representation (such as comics, magazines, Hollywood films, and documentaries used for political marketing).

Jacques Derrida, commenting on the repetition of the images of the attacks on 9/11, argues that "repetition always protects by neutralizing, deadening, distancing a traumatism."[20] Yet repetition operates in other ways, (re)creating the imagined whole of the nation. In a discussion of media and "integrated world capitalism," Felix Guattari comments that

> IWC forms massive subjective aggregates from the most personal—one could say infra-personal—existential givens, which it hooks up to ideas of race, nation, the professional workforce, competitive sports, a dominating

masculinity [*virilité*], mass-media celebrity. . . . Capitalistic subjectivity seeks to gain power by controlling and neutralizing the maximum number of existential refrains. It is intoxicated with and anaesthetized by a collective feeling of pseudo-eternity.[21]

The U.S. war machine needs to be presented in a way that distinguishes its destructive capabilities from *terrorist* violence, maintaining the hierarchy of responsible violence and irresponsible violence, grievable and ungrievable life; we need to be intoxicated with and anesthetized by the war machine. What Butler refers to as "this violent and self-centered subject" is presented not only in the terms of the hegemonic grammar as a *responsible* and "expert" authority—but also the only authority capable of (re)securing a population through the mastery of cyber and geopolitical space, and as Cynthia Weber's chapter illustrates (chapter 6), through the desire to securitize the unconscious, with the military-scientific technologies that emerge from the "projection toward the future." Pentagon futurist, Andrew Marshall, comments on the future of war: "There are ways of psychologically influencing the leadership of another state. I don't mean information warfare, but some demonstration of awesome effects, like being able to set off impressive explosions in the sky. Like, *let us show you what we could do to you*. Just visually impressing the person."[22] Post-9/11, a demonstration of awesome effects— what Butler refers to as the "sublimity of destruction"—is required to visually impress the population at home. And in a reversal of the way that the enemy is individualized and moralized, so those orchestrating the response to terror are also individualized and moralized (as good, civilized, careful) as agents of responsible violence, but a violence that is awesome, delivering the population from the terror of uncertainty.

I have selected four different cultural products to explore the repetition— and restoration—of these representations of responsibility, authority, and terror, exploring how desire for the "imagined whole" forms "massive subjective aggregates" from the most personal existential givens, "controlling and neutralizing the maximum number of existential refrains":[23] an article on the Bush administration published by *Vanity Fair* in February 2002; a documentary on the Bush administration entitled *Faith in the White House* released during the U.S. presidential campaign in 2004; an issue of *Spiderman* published shortly after 9/11; and a film about a U.S. citizen seeking "justice" for a murdered child in Mexico and *Man on Fire*, released in 2004, a film about a U.S. citizen.

Vanity Fair

In February 2002, *Vanity Fair* published an article entitled "War and Destiny: Historic Portraits of the White House in Wartime," which contained a collection of photographs by Annie Leibovitz that set out to capture "the spirit of Washington's mission control."[24] The text that accompanies the photographs is concerned with restoring confidence in the Bush administration's ability to manage the nation in a time of uncertainty and terror. The editorial of the issue makes this strategy explicit: Graydon Carter, after telling us of the memorable images that *Vanity Fair* has produced since World War I, informs us that it is not just "strength but images of strength that matter in this 21st-century war." *Vanity Fair*, Carter likes to believe, has taken on a "status equivalent to the High Sierra of the Public Images."[25]

The pictures that dominate the article could have been produced by someone who had studied Roland Barthes' essay "Photography and Electoral Appeal," where Barthes sets out the signs that are used to produce "a veritable blackmail by means of moral values: country, army, family, honor, reckless heroism."[26] Although, in this case, the narrative that develops is concerned with displaying responsible and careful heroism.

In the text that accompanies the portraits the narrative is of a politician commonly viewed as inexperienced, and perhaps even unsuited to the role of president, transforming into a great leader. The article admits that Bush got off to a "rough start" by flying *away* from Washington on 9/11. And he "evinced a Bushian aptitude for the jarring phrase: we would find 'those folks' who attacked us." His transformation into a war president has an easy explanation because "Bushes are cool in crisis. It's the breeding, stupid—blue Wasp *sang* at its most froid."

The war on terror is the destiny of George W. Bush, and a destiny for which "breeding" has prepared him. But the article does not reduce the war on terror to the destiny of Bush, although the first main image is a close-up of his face. As Barthes observed, a full-face photograph underlines the "realistic outlook" of the candidate: "Everything there expresses penetration, gravity, frankness: the future deputy is looking squarely at the enemy, the obstacle, the 'problem.' "[27] Bush is not seeking reelection yet but he is seeking the restoration of his authority after the dislocation of his first world privilege.

The article contains portraits of the team Bush has around him, aiding him to fight terror. The article tells us—reassures us—that Bush is surrounded by an experienced and diverse team; a talented team that will deliver us from terror. The article individualizes and moralizes the complex war machine that is fighting the global war on terror. And the text that accompanies the "War and Destiny" article tells us about the "family" that is looking after us, an embodiment of the state apparatus through clearly defined characters, with the pictures titled with captions that allude to popular culture like "The Rock" (for Dick Cheney), "The Confidante" (for Condoleeza Rice), "The Conscience" (for Colin Powell), "The Protector" (for Tom Ridge), "The Lieutenants" (for Richard Armitage, Paul Wolfowitz, and Stephen Hadley), "The Consiglieri" (for Karl Rove and Karen Hughes), and "The Heat" (for John Ashcroft). Some members of the team are celebrated for their strength: "You thought this was going to be pretty? Well, tough times demand a tough man. . . . In the aftermath of 9/11, Ashcroft has overseen the roundup of more than 1,000 terror-probe detainees and has nimbly arranged things so that investigators can sidestep some of those pesky constitutional issues." But we also get to see the humanity (and femininity) of the multicultural team: "Beloved by both Bush generations—it was Bush *père* who introduced 'Condi' to his son—Rice is living proof that, in times of crisis, friendship counts most." Alongside the photograph of the first lady, we are told that the person who is probably closest to Bush is not afraid to rein in her husband when "he starts sounding like Jack Palance."

The text for each "player" reduces their character to a simple role; producing an image of the administration that reads like a real-life performance of the television series *The West Wing* (it even includes pictures and descriptions of the real-life "Spin Team"). The image produced is one where the sheer diversity of personalities of the administration—the balance of care and toughness—will create a *balanced* and authoritative form of governance, overcoming individual frailty with a body that represents and embodies the values that make up the state: there is a team of "experts" that represent the diversity of the nation working to protect us. And it is the possibility of such diversity shown on these glossy pages, next to images of a stylish and luxurious existence, that makes us *good*.

The descriptions and pictures are full of representations that have roots in the historical imagination of the United States. Dick Cheney sits in front of what appears to be an antique map: the map is titled "A Map Showing the Route taken by Samuel Fletcher Cheney Captain 21st Regiment." These people have experience of war in their "blood" and "breeding": we can feel safe while they are in control. The description of Tom Ridge, director of Homeland Security, concludes with an observation from a White House official that this imposing six-foot-three man is designed to become a "brand": "When people see him, we want them to think, 'My babies are safe.' "

The article is followed by "The Big Guns," an article that informs the reader about the military experts that are securing us: here we learn that Tommy Franks, commander in chief of U.S. Central Command, was raised in "Bush country" and they refer to him as "Pooh," a move that humanizes him (and the war machine he directs) as a family man who will look after us. A few articles later, we are reminded of our vulnerability: we arrive at "Inside Saddam's Terror Regime," an interview with the most senior officer ever to defect from Iraq, giving us an exclusive on his "strong belief that Iraq was involved in the September 11 attacks."

Faith in the White House

Faith in the White House is a documentary film, "produced independently and without help from the White House," that was released during the run-up to the presidential election in 2004. The success of Michael Moore's attempt in *Fahrenheit 9/11* to use documentary filmmaking to contribute to the public sphere has led to a conservative response in the form of *Celsius 41.11* and *Faith in the White House* (which includes a DVD extra on "Responses to *Fahrenheit 9/11* for further Enjoyment and Study"), films that do not have a theatrical release but aim to influence people in the same way that conservative writers and radio presenters do. At the same time, John Kerry's experiences in the Vietnam War were explored in *Going Upriver: The Long War of John Kerry*, a documentary that presents itself as a serious account of Kerry's political journey: "Some Men Are Changed By History . . . Others Make It."[28] Both *Faith in the White House* and *Going Upriver* are about the suitability of the candidates to manage a war on terror. Using a combination of interviews and dramatic recreations of significant moments in Bush's life, *Faith in the White House*

> is a unique insider's look at how one man's dedication to prayer and the daily application of God's word transformed his life and leadership. His dependence upon God gave him the clarity of vision and quiet confidence needed to lead us through the 9/11 terrorist attacks and the ensuing wars in Afghanistan and Iraq. Witness President Bush's remarkable journey of faith, and decide for yourself whether it has been good for America. But whatever you decide, it will change and inspire you!

In the *Vanity Fair* article an attempt is made to provide the images of strength/responsibility, the reassuring spectacle that the team around the Bush administration are the experts that will deliver the nation from the terror of uncertainty; at the same time, the article is designed to show that—unlike the enemy—the war machine is in the hands of responsible human beings. *Faith in the White House* shows the extent to which the administration understands that the line of separation between responsible violence and irresponsible violence is not secure and is in need of constant (re)production to appear natural and legitimate. The narrator informs us that "[m]isguided critics have gone so far as to suggest that since the terrorists are driven by religious zeal, Bush's claim to religious beliefs makes him no different than the enemy. This reasoning suggests that somehow the spectre of a Muslim terrorist strapping a bomb to his 24-year-old son is the moral equivalent of President Bush gathering a 14-year-old girl into his arms and hugging her to his chest—a girl whose mother was killed in the World Trade Center bombings."

Sensitive to the "culture war" that they see raging in the United States, the makers of the film are aware of the way that the hierarchy of responsible and irresponsible violence is problematized by intellectuals such as Susan Sontag in the public sphere. As Butler comments, positions that are considered " 'relativistic' or 'post-' of any kind are considered either complicitous with terrorism or as constituting a weak link in the fight against it."[29] The limits of debate in the public sphere that emerged (i.e., the claim that "either you're with us or you're with the terrorists") produced a situation where to develop "more responsible distinctions" was pushed aside in the "claims of vengeance."[30] Charles Krauthammer, for example, made these comments about remarks by Susan Sontag on understanding 9/11: "This is no time for obfuscation. Or for agonized relativism. Or, obscenely, for blaming America first. (The habit dies hard.) This is a time for clarity. At a time like this, those who search for shades of evil, for root causes, for extenuations are, to borrow from Lance Morrow, 'too philosophical for decent company.' "[31] Ann Coulter comments that Al Gore wanted to put the war on terrorism in a "lockbox": "Instead of obsessing over why angry primitives hate America, a more fruitful area for Democrats to examine might be why the Americans are beginning to hate them."[32]

Faith in the White House is the story of a man who struggled to find meaning in his life until he discovered God (and the moral certainty so cherished by both Krauthammer and Coulter). The film depicts a flawed man—drinking and cussing—who discovers God on his fortieth birthday and realizes his destiny on 9/11. Much of the film is told through flashbacks where Bush is played by an actor: one scene depicts Bush working on his father's campaign for the White House where a young woman attempts to seduce him by the photocopier. Bush's solid moral foundation enables him to reject the seduction and political corruption in Washington. Indeed, a theme that runs through the film is that Bush, while being deeply respectful of the White House, is able to reject the temptations of an institution that can easily corrupt: in response to the claim made in *Fahrenheit 9/11* that Bush was an absentee president, inattentive to serious issues of policy, the film is suggesting that the distance Bush has from Washington (e.g., on his ranch) allows him to maintain faith in the White House and responsible governance. And through creating faith in the White House, Bush is able to maintain his humanity in an institution corrupted by "liberals" such as Bill Clinton.

"But whatever you decide, it will change and inspire you!" The filmmakers are aware of the difficulty of convincing the viewer of the truth of Bush's religious beliefs. Those concerned with creating the image of George W. Bush in the public sphere must be all too aware of his image as cowboy in Washington, acknowledging in the *Vanity Fair* article that Laura Bush has to rein in her husband when "he starts sounding like Jack Palance." Yet image makers can use this image, an image that is extremely easy to satirize, to their advantage, enabling them to focus on his humanity; his mistakes are part of a normality and decency that critics such as Moore exploit in a vindictive manner.

Faith in the White House is punctuated by moving, emotional moments that show the caring and responsible side of Bush. These scenes have an emotional power and these moments in *Faith in the White House* may be more significant for the viewer than the historico-political narrative. A number of scenes show how, in moments of sadness for U.S. citizens, Bush is willing to step outside his role as president to offer care and spiritual consolation: irrespective of his religious beliefs, Bush is capable of stepping outside of his role in guiding a complex bureaucracy and war machine and act like a human being. An African-American man whose son died in a car accident while working for the Bush administration tells us how Bush made it clear, while flying on Air Force One, that he was available to the family if they needed him. Told by a tearful father over music that feels to be building to some dramatic event (the destiny of George W. Bush), the scene is moving and, although it is far briefer and much less harrowing, produces an affective power similar to the Lila Liscombe scene in *Fahrenheit 9/11*.[33] Similarly, a father of a young boy with a terminal illness tell us how Bush gave up his time in the week before the war began in Iraq to meet his family; Bush went against policy to carry a gift (a Bible) from the boy onto the plane. Bush promises a young soldier who had lost a leg in Afghanistan that he would run with him once the man could run a mile again. So, while we might not believe in his religious turn, and he might seem ill suited to the job, he is a *good* man.

Both *Fahrenheit 9/11* and *Faith in the White House* show the deterritorialization of emotion, the way emotion can be "cut and pasted" for different political ends.[34] This is what Guattari describes in terms of power that operates through "controlling and neutralizing the maximum number of existential refrains."[35]

Spiderman

Paul Virilio suggests that the state's "only original existence is as a visual hallucination akin to dreaming."[36] Comic books are part of this "visual hallucination" and superheroes represent the desire for a better security. In an age of cynicism about politicians and corporations lying to citizens, the superhero represents an individual who cannot be easily corrupted. Superheroes embody the problems of living with responsibility and terror, presenting an ideal view of the United States in comforting comic book colors where life is *brighter*. Peter Parker is the "geeky" (intellectual), thoughtful, and caring young man; Spiderman is blessed with awesome superhuman powers—the result of research initiated by an obsessed businessman—that enable him to protect those around him, to protect the "good."[37]

An issue of *Spiderman* published shortly after 9/11 follows a shocked Spiderman as he arrives at Ground Zero.[38] A man and woman escaping from the smoke ask Spiderman: "Where were you? How could you let it happen?" Spiderman offers a sermon—a presidential speech from an icon in the imagined whole—from the pulpit of Marvel Comics. We see an older superhero, Captain America—"He's the only one who could know. Because he's seen it before"—standing in Ground Zero with Spiderman observing, "I wish I had not lived to see this once. I can't imagine what it is to see it twice."

The comic produces a hierarchy of good and evil, responsible violence and evil violence. We see the heroism of everyday people: Spiderman makes a plea for tolerance ("Do not do as they do, or the war is lost before it is even begun"); in response to the question of what to tell the children, Spiderman asks: "Do we tell them evil is a foreign face?" The final image is of a multicultural United States urged to "Stand Tall."

The story focuses on the sense of horror and regret felt by the superheroes. The Spiderman story reinscribes the view that for all the insecurity that the event has caused, it is possible to return to the security of community; even the enemies of Spiderman put aside grievances and mourn with him. Spiderman makes this observation about a tearful Dr. Doom: "Because even the worst of us, however scared, are still human. Still feel. Still mourn the death of random innocents." Even Dr. Doom—Spiderman's enemy most of the time—is still human, reinforcing the view that those who committed the acts are inhuman, in a dead zone beyond our moral community and our understanding.

In a condition of insecurity we can overcome difference and rivalry inside the state for the greater good ("We have become one in our grief"), recreating the projection toward the future. On this level, the comic is a response to the terror of uncertainty through the promise of a political and moral community that is renewed through fear ("You wanted to send a message, and in so doing you awakened us from our sense of self-involvement"). At the same time, Spiderman recognizes the fundamentalism of "Holy Warriors" in the United States, and he includes the speech of a Christian fundamentalist who declares: "All of them who have tried to secularize America . . . [t]he pagans and the abortionists and the feminists and the gays and the lesbians and the ACLU . . . I point the finger in their face and I say 'You helped this happen.' "

But these fundamentalists are not the ones protecting us. The comic is concerned with a justice waged with responsible violence, telling us, over the image of an aircraft carrier, we should listen to the voice that says "do not do as they do, or the war is lost before it is even begun": "We live in each blow you strike for infinite justice. But always in the hope of infinite wisdom." It is clear that justice will be sought using military means: "Look for your reply in the thunder." This will be a responsible violence, unlike the violence orchestrated by "madmen": "Only madmen could contain the thought, execute the act, fly the planes. The sane world will always be vulnerable to madmen, because we cannot go where they go to conceive such things."

Man on Fire

Tony Scott's film *Man on Fire* (2004) tells the story of a U.S. citizen, a former counterterrorism agent, seeking revenge for the murder of a child that he failed to protect. The film begins by informing us that "[t]here is one kidnapping every 60 minutes in Latin America. Seventy percent of the victims do not survive."[39] We then meet Creasy (Denzel Washington) as he visits a friend in Mexico City. Creasy has been "movin' around . . . Colombia, a couple of places I can't name." As he relaxes with his friend, Ray (Christopher Walken), over some drinks it becomes clear that Creasy is tormented by his past, which we learn involves 16 years of military experience, including extensive counterterrorism activities: "You think God'll forgive us for what we've done?" "No," replies his friend. "Me, neither," Creasy agrees. Ray runs a private security business and finds Creasy a job looking after Pita, the child of a U.S. citizen and Mexican businessman. Creasy's drinking problem has weakened him but the job seems unlikely to become difficult and, anyway, the businessman only wants to employ Creasy for a short time for insurance purposes. The businessman's wife trusts Creasy because he is an American. The precocious blond Pita tries to befriend the world-weary Creasy, but he attempts to keep his distance, spending his evenings drinking liquor.

Creasy warms to the child, gives up drinking, and coaches her to improve her swimming technique. But, in a shootout where Creasy sustains major injuries, Pita is kidnapped. The police get involved and help the father and his lawyer organize the ransom. The handing over of the money goes wrong, resulting in the nephew of the kidnapper being killed. The kidnapper informs the family that Pita will be killed. As Creasy regains his strength he is informed of Pita's death. Pita's mother asks him what he is going to do about her murder: "What I do best. I'm gonna kill 'em. Anyone that was involved, who profited from it, anybody who opens their eyes at me." The mother responds: "You kill them all."

With the help of a local journalist, Creasy begins to track down and kill people in the complex network of organized crime protected by La Hermandad, a brotherhood that protects corrupt police and organized crime. This leads him to discover that Pita's father was involved in arranging the kidnapping. The father did not realize that his daughter would be killed, and he commits suicide after his wife tells Creasy to kill him. But Creasy discovers that Pita is still alive and so arranges for her to be released. The condition: he must hand himself over to the kidnappers.

Man on Fire is similar to many films where an antiheroic father figure must avenge a murdered child (*Mad Max*) or protect a child from violence (*Ransom*). The film constantly makes the viewer aware of Creasy's spiritual crisis. One night, while he lives in the flat in the complex owned by Pita's parents, he attempts suicide but the bullet does not fire. He phones Ray who tells him: "[A] bullet doesn't lie." Later in the film he gives the bullet to Pita's father and it kills him, an act of divine intervention. As he prepares his rocket launcher in the flat of an elderly Mexican couple, an old man informs Creasy that Christianity is about forgiveness. He replies that he just arranged the meeting with God. He is spiritually renewed through his love for Pita—a love that gives him the strength to "expertly" avenge those who supposedly killed her and to give up his own life for her. It is a narrative similar to that developed in *Faith in the White House*: a lost sheep (re)discovers God and is spiritually renewed to be able to act as God's messenger on earth and administer divine violence: "He'll deliver more justice in a weekend than ten years of your courts and tribunals. Just stay out of his way."

In *Beyond Good and Evil*, Friedrich Nietzsche wrote, "He who fights with monsters should look to it that he himself does not become a monster."[40] Nietzsche is acknowledging that human beings commit "monstrous" acts, and we sometimes have to take action to protect ourselves. The dangers in declaring an enemy *evil*—a monster—is that it installs a mode of securing where *everything is permitted*, reproducing cycles of violence and the desire to create a sanitized public sphere. This sanitization of the public sphere then intensifies the impact of further acts of violence, closing down spaces of reflection and moral anxiety on our actions, and increasingly calling for violent retaliation for those who hurt us. Spiderman warns us: "do not do as they do, or the war is lost before it is even begun"; *Man on Fire* warns us that the battle is lost as soon as the enemy is understood as a monster occupying a dead zone beyond the human.

In the war on evil in *Man on Fire* everything is permitted. It has been common in Hollywood movies for acts of torture to be carried by evil characters; post-9/11 our heroes can creatively and expertly torture the enemy in the search for justice. In the first act of torture in *Man on Fire* Creasy cuts off the fingers of a man in a car parked on waste ground—and then stops the bleeding by cauterizing them with a cigar lighter. This scene is explicit but strangely unaffecting, and we see the violence very clearly. Brian De Palma's *Scarface* depicts a drug deal gone wrong and a gangster saws off the limbs of Tony Montana's friend with a chainsaw in a hotel room, a locational normality that makes the violence even more disturbing. We never see the act or any severed limbs; De Palma lets the camera drift to Montana's friends, listening to the radio and talking to a woman, in the street outside (a move that builds the tension as they are meant to be on the lookout for trouble) and then drifts back to focus on Montana's blood-splattered face. The horror of the scene, a horror that makes the scene uncomfortable to watch, is played out through Montana's face as he tries to look away. The soundtrack is made up of television noise (the sound of sirens as the scene begins that alerts us to the violence to come, unsettling the viewer) and some ominous low-key synths as the deal starts to go wrong. The dominant sound then becomes the violent and repetitive buzz of the chainsaw.

The scene in *Man on Fire* is far more visually explicit but a comfortable viewing experience. Scott utilizes a variety of cinematic techniques and textures, layering image over image, cutting in images of Pita (as if to remind us of the legitimacy of the violent act, like the repetition of images of the twin towers), which make the scene frenetic and visually *interesting*. Our senses are overloaded with images and sound: the soundtrack moves from hard rock to a remix of Santana's "Oye Como Va" through to a 1980s pop song, concluding with "Nessum Dorma" (for the final act of divine violence); the scene plays out like an MTV music video. The scene neutralizes our senses with its overloading of sound and vision and, perhaps, also through the fact that a Mexican is being tortured by an

African-American, a move that plays down the potential for racial anxieties over acts of colonial violence by a U.S. citizen. The cinematic power of *Man on Fire* is controlling (the drama of the film is the sport of hunting down the criminal network) and neutralizing (torture carried out by our hero is entertainment).

Far from being a potential warning about the desire for revenge and security, the film displays the extent to which we can be intoxicated with and anesthetized by cinematic techniques, techniques that proliferate through our visual culture. Guattari would argue that such images become part of a "degenerate" social ecology; as Jean Luc Goddard comments after being asked about Quentin Tarantino's admiration for Goddard's work: "What is never said about Tarantino is that those prisons we are shown pictures of, where the torture is taking place, are called 'reservoir dogs.' "[41]

In the next act of revenge, our hero inserts an explosive into the rectum of the leader of La Hermandad, who is stripped down to his boxer shorts and tied over a car. As Ray says, Creasy's art is death and he is "about to paint his masterpiece."

Concluding Remarks

Butler concludes *Precarious Life* after thinking, along with the writings of Emmanuel Lévinas, about the difficulties of developing a public sphere that can respond to the vulnerability of existence, asking: "But what media will let us know and feel that frailty, know and feel at the limits of representation as it is currently cultivated and maintained? . . . We would have to interrogate the emergence and vanishing of the human at the limits of what we can know, what we can hear, what we can see, what we can sense."[42] This chapter has explored popular cultural products that code the restoration of the imagined whole as the only response to the precarious life. Butler goes on to comment that the "media becomes entranced by the sublimity of destruction, and voices of dissent and opposition must find a way to intervene upon this desensitizing dream machine in which the massive destruction of lives and homes, sources of water, electricity, and heat, are produced as a delirious sign of a resuscitated US military power."[43] This chapter has sought to show how popular cultural products code the sublimity of destruction as responsible violence.

The possibilities for a future public sphere in the United States that can challenge this "desensitizing dream machine" seem bleak. The next time a state of exception is created and preemptive "policing" action is pursued—and after the difficulties of postwar reconstruction in Iraq this may be some time—it appears likely a configuration of forces in the public sphere will suggest that technological advancement will make *this* war more responsible than the last: the technology will be both more deadly and precise; we will have learned from our mistakes. Just as global economic liberalism rests on the promise of a better tomorrow for everyone, so the waging of war is presented in terms of the promise that the next one will be different and necessary for our survival—what Paul Virilio refers to as *military-scientific messianism*.[44]

The ethico-political problem, however, is not simply how to challenge this desensitizing dream machine and its military-scientific messianism; we need to look at how the logic of biopower in the war on terror—the state of emergency that prepares us for new forms of biopolitical control of populations and biocriminals—limits the chances of surviving the precarious life. Biopolitics is concerned with the strategies that make possible "healthy" societies shaped by flows and mobilities—wealth, labor, diseases, pollution, images, information, and technologies—able to respond to the aleatory phenomena that emerge from human/nonhuman habitats and networks (as well as emerging from the interaction of human/nonhuman habitats and networks), reducing the uncertainty of existence: "security mechanisms have to be installed around the random element inherent in a population of living beings, so as to optimize a state of life."[45] In order to optimize a healthy state of life, biocriminality—bodies that threaten the security of the population—must be controlled and eradicated. The "mechanism of the biocriminal" justifies the "death-function in the economy of biopower by appealing to the principle that the death of others makes one biologically stronger insofar as one is a member of a race or a population, insofar as one is an element in a unitary living plurality."[46]

The biopolitical can seem to imply an all-seeing surveillance/discipline/normalization society where, as Gilles Deleuze puts it, states seek to defend "precious space" from a "toxic or infectious agent, a sort of 'biological danger.' "[47] Yet states, through their attempts to optimize a state of life, create new forms of insecurity. As Foucault comments in *Society Must Be Defended*, an "excess of biopower appears when it becomes technologically and politically possible for man not only to manage life but to make it proliferate, to create living matter, to build the monster, and ultimately, to build viruses that cannot be controlled and that are universally destructive."[48]

Felix Guattari develops these concerns in *The Three Ecologies*, an essay first published in 1989. For Guattari, citizens in "integrated world capitalism" are infantilized by consumerism, mass media, and the standardization of behavior. The biopolitical governance of integrated world capitalism appears unable to respond to techno-scientific and economic advances that are creating deterioration in the three ecologies: the social ecology, mental ecology, and environmental ecology. Discussing the problems that are emerging from integrated world capitalism, Guattari observes that while attempts are being made to respond to this excess of biopower, "[p]olitical groupings and executive authorities appear to be completely incapable of understanding the full implication of these issues."[49] He goes on to comment:

> The increasing deterioration of human relations with the socius, the psyche and "nature," is due not only to environmental and objective pollution but is also the result of a certain incomprehension and fatalistic passivity towards these issues as a whole, among both individuals and governments. . . . Refusal to face up to the erosion of these three areas, as the media would have us do, verges on a strategic infantilization of opinion and a destructive neutralization of democracy.[50]

Guattari's thought leads to a recognition that it is not simply that the public sphere is infantilized by governments—and the "sedative discourse" of the media—but that we are existing within governmental powers' infantile denial of the excess of biopower, the precarious life, a denial of the violence, danger, and suffering that the desire for mastery and control of life and territory can cause. On this view, the cultural products discussed in this chapter are not designed as a "strategy for deception" for the citizenry; they are an invitation to share in the same experiment of power and mastery as those who are shaping life and death in the precarious life. For Guattari, the deterioration of the diversity of life in the three ecologies must be challenged through a new "ecosophical" aesthetic in art, media, therapy, architecture, et cetera. But, at the same time:

> [t]he ecosophical perspective does not totally exclude a definition of unifying objectives, such as the struggle against world hunger, and end to deforestation or to the blind proliferation of the nuclear industries; but it will no longer be a question of depending on reductionist, stereotypical order-words which only expropriate other more singular problematics and lead to the promotion of charismatic leaders.[51]

The state of exception that makes possible a global war on terror provides a way to avoid confronting broader issues of insecurity, focusing on a "stereotypical" problem of security and governance to the exclusion of other issues. In many ways, this politics of security requires a charismatic leader, a leader to embody military-scientific messianism, in order to individualize and moralize, as the cultural products discussed in this chapter have shown, what amounts to a condition of denial from Guattari's perspective. On this view, the excess of biopower cannot be reduced to the problems of terror and military insecurity, and problems may emerge as deterioration in the three ecologies begins to be felt in "developed" spaces where "a refusal of discourse that produces dehumanization"—and rejection of oppositional voices—is harder to maintain.

In this sense, the catastrophe in New Orleans after Hurricane Katrina in 2005 provides an example of the point Guattari is making: on one hand, the Bush administration deflected funds that could have provided protection for the population in New Orleans due to a focus on terror and homeland security; on the other, there was an immediate failure of imagination in terms of responding to this "natural" disaster. Some commentators were quick to draw the links to human-generated climate change, but as Barbara Adam observes, climate change has been denied "reality status" in the imagination of global danger because "cause is not succeeded by consequence in a simple immediate, linear way. The issue of global warming, in other words, is replete with uncertainties and the prospect of an indeterminate and indeterminable future."[52] Regardless of the issue of causality here, the disaster has shown how the state apparatus may be incapable of protecting populations from "natural" disasters and traditional approaches to security will need to be rethought in terms of the deterioration of the three ecologies and the condition of fatalistic passivity.[53] Only terror has reality status in this logic of biopower.

As the Bush administration gazed at the images of suffering in New Orleans, of the vulnerable becoming wasted life, they should have heeded the second part of the aphorism by Nietzsche mentioned above: "And when you gaze long into an abyss the abyss also gazes into you."[54] When similar events were depicted in summer 2004 in the film *The Day After Tomorrow* the absurdity of U.S. citizens fleeing to Mexico as refugees was perversely amusing; now images of citizens as refugees inside the United States had become reality, shot through in its media presentation with Ridley Scott's "fear of a black planet," *Black Hawk Down*.

The danger is that the media will continue to play down the problems of ecological deterioration, individualizing and moralizing the events in terms of the irresponsibility of the Bush administration, with government proposing reforms with the promise of a better response *next time*, rather than reflecting on the conditions of the biopolitical ordering of populations and their consumption regimes that may produce future vulnerability. The Bush administration was quick to argue for a new era of *responsible* governance with regard to race politics in a manner that gives the impression of sensitively acknowledging a failure to protect—renewing a projection toward the future and relegitimating authority—but silences questions about future ecological danger and the logic of biopower that reduces vulnerability to terror. Bush admitted:

> As all of us saw on television, there's also some deep, persistent poverty in this region, as well. That poverty has roots in a history of racial discrimination, which cut off generations from the opportunity of America. We have a duty to confront this poverty with bold action. So let us restore all that we have cherished from yesterday, and let us rise above the legacy of inequality.[55]

For Butler, our current challenge is to "to create a sense of the public in which oppositional voices are not feared, degraded or dismissed, but valued for the instigation to a sensate democracy they occasionally perform."[56] But in addition, what we are beginning to see is that if we are to survive the precarious life we are creating, where "cause is not succeeded by consequence in a simple immediate, linear way," and where governments respond to the uncertainty of global danger with fatalistic passivity, the challenge for the public sphere is far more complicated: we will have to find a means not simply to challenge what Butler refers to as the "desensitizing dream machine" but to draw out the connections between the excess of biopower and the biopolitical ordering of the three ecologies.[57]

Notes

1. Judith Butler, *Precarious Life: The Powers of Mourning and Violence* (London: Verso, 2004), p. xii.
2. Ibid.
3. For an exploration of these "other passages" see Giovanna Borradori, *Philosophy In A Time of Terror: Dialogues With Jurgen Habermas and Jacques Derrida* (Chicago: University of Chicago Press, 2003).
4. Butler (2004), p. 148.
5. Ibid., p. 4.
6. Borradori (2003), p. 105.
7. See James Der Derian, *Virtuous War: Mapping the Military-Industrial-Media-Entertainment-Network* (New York: Westview Press, 2001).
8. Butler (2004), p. 6.
9. Ibid.
10. Ibid., p. 4.
11. Ibid., p. 5.
12. Ibid.
13. Ibid., p. 15.
14. Ibid.
15. Ibid., p. 16.

16. Ibid.

17. Ibid., p. 41.

18. Borradori (2003), p. 28.

19. Jean Baudrillard, *The Spirit of Terrorism* (London: Verso, 2003), p. 47.

20. Borradori (2003), p. 87.

21. Felix Guattari, *The Three Ecologies* (London: Athlone, 2000), p. 50.

22. Douglas McGray, "The Marshall Plan," *Wired*, February 2003, http://www.wired.com/wired/archive/11.02/marshall.html. Retrieved August 14, 2006.

23. For a discussion of the existential refrain see Ian Pindar, "Translator's Introduction," in Felix Guattari (2000).

24. Annie Leibovitz and Christopher Buckley, "War and Destiny: The White House in Wartime," *Vanity Fair*, February 2002, p. 48.

25. Graydon Carter, "The War Room," *Vanity Fair*, February 2002, p. 18.

26. Roland Barthes, *Mythologies* (London: Fontana Press, 1993), p. 92.

27. Ibid.

28. *Going Upriver: The Long War of John Kerry*, directed by George Butler, Non Fiction Films, 2004.

29. Butler (2004), p. 2.

30. Ibid., p. 3.

31. Charles Krauthammer, "Voices of Moral Obtuseness," in *The Iraqi War Reader*, eds. Micah L. Sifry and Christopher Cerf (London: Touchstone, 2003), p. 218.

32. Ann Coulter, "Why We Hate Them," in Sifry and Cerf (2003), p. 235.

33. See Cynthia Weber's discussion of Moore and Liscombe in *Imagining America at War* (London: Routledge, 2005).

34. For a useful introduction to "affect" see Clare Colebrook, *Gilles Deleuze* (London: Routledge, 2001).

35. Guattari (2000), p. 50.

36. Paul Virilio, *Cinema and War: The Logistics of Perception* (London: Verso, 1998), p. 33.

37. For an introduction into superheroes and cultural theory see Scott Bukatman, *Matters of Gravity: Special Effects and Supermen in the 20th Century* (London: Duke University Press, 2003).

38. *Mighty Marvel Must Haves 2* (originally published in *Spiderman* 36, February 2002).

39. *Man on Fire*, directed by Tony Scott, Fox Home Entertainment, 2004.

40. Friedrich Nietzsche, *Beyond Good and Evil* (London: Penguin, 1998), p. 84.

41. Geoffrey McNab, "Cinema is Over," *The Guardian*, April 29, 2005, http://film.guardian.co.uk/interview/interviewpages/0,6737,1472494,00.html. Retrieved August 14, 2006.

42. Butler (2004), p. 151.

43. Ibid., p. 149.

44. Paul Virilio, "The Strategy of the Beyond," in *The Virilio Reader*, ed. James Der Derian (Cambridge: Blackwell, 1998), p. 90.

45. Michel Foucault, *Society Must Be Defended* (London: Penguin, 2004), p. 246.
46. Ibid., p. 258.
47. Gilles Deleuze, *Foucault* (London: Athlone, 1999), p. 92.
48. Foucault (2004), p. 254.
49. Guattari (2000), p. 27.
50. Ibid., p. 41.
51. Ibid., p. 34.
52. Barbara Adam, "Re-Vision: The Centrality of Time for an Ecological Social Science Perspective," in *Risk, Environment and Modernity*, eds. Scott Lash, Bronislaw Szerszynski and Brian Wynne (London: Sage, 1996), p. 97.
53. This idea is developed in Mark J. Lacy, *Security and Climate Change; International Relations and the Limits of Realism* (London: Routledge, 2005).
54. Nietzsche (1998), p. 84.
55. "President Discusses Hurricane Relief to the Nation," Office of the Press Secretary September 15, 2005, http://www.whitehouse.gov/news/releases/2005/09/20050915-8.html. Retrieved August 14, 2006.
56. Butler (2004), p. 151.
57. See, e.g., Michael Klare, *Blood and Oil: The Dangers and Consequences of America's Growing Petroleum Dependence* (London: Penguin, 2005).

CHAPTER 5

PERSISTENCE OF MEMORY? THE (NEW) SURREALISM OF AMERICAN SECURITY POLICY

Kyle Grayson

It is my hope that in the months and years ahead, life will return almost to normal. We'll go back to our lives and routines, and that is good. Even grief recedes with time and grace. But our resolve must not pass. Each of us will remember what happened that day, and to whom it happened. We'll remember the moment the news came—where we were and what we were doing. Some will remember an image of a fire, or a story of rescue. Some will carry memories of a face and a voice gone forever. I will not forget this wound to our country or those who inflicted it. I will not yield; I will not rest; I will not relent in waging this struggle for freedom and security for the American people.
—George W. Bush[1]

An interesting technology of remembrance has localized around the events of 9/11, a series of representations that is essential to understanding contemporary American security policy. The power/relations of remembrance have participated in the constitution of a series of interwoven parables that have formed particular matrices of meaning, all of which paint pictures of (geo)politics, the American Self, the American Other, and the legitimate range of policy possibility in the post-9/11 world. As such, Jenny Edkins has argued, the aesthetic contours of the dominant forms of memorialization in the United States in response to 9/11 have, in combination with the social practices of securitization and criminalization, reinserted linear narratives and previously constructed scripts of global politics, American hegemony, and the legitimate exercise of political voice.[2] Thus, the coping strategy brought about by the routinized remembrance of the trauma of 9/11 has been one that has instantiated a form of collective *anterograde* amnesia (i.e., the inability to form alternate memories) that draws meaning from one (and only one) contextual environment of interpretation.

The routinization of remembrance has taken many forms from official memorial services on the anniversary of 9/11 to collections of poetry, songs, and reflections cataloged on various Internet websites. Even the homeland defense system institutionalized by the American federal government is a type of memorial with increases in the level of alertness drawing upon the fears that the American public experienced in the aftermath of 9/11. These mechanisms that seek to provide a level of vigilance so that these forms of violence never happen again require that what must never happen again be remembered.

To this end, rather than upsetting previously dominant security discourses within the United States, we can see their reassertion through the militarized practices of the Bush Doctrine and homeland security in response to the trauma of 9/11. Thus, critical questioning of the consequences made possible by the pursuit of national security objectives and a largely unaccountable national security architecture has not yet occurred within internal American debates. Instead, there has been much discussion of "the facts" with respect to the accumulation of accurate data, both in terms of the events of 9/11 and those that followed (e.g., Operation Enduring Freedom and Operation Liberation Iraq) couched in the terms of intelligence successes and failures. Unfortunately, these debates have been frustratingly narrow with participants holding steadfast to unstated commitments to "epistemic realism," which according to David Campbell "sanctions a logic of explanation whereby it is the purpose of analysis [and 'political' argument] to identify . . . self-evident things and material causes so that actors can accommodate themselves to the realm of necessity they engender."[3] With contending sides assuming that "the facts" speak for themselves and failing to acknowledge the inherent subjectivity of narratives (in terms of the narrator, the audience, and the iterative that makes them intelligible), the range of viable critique has been disciplined so that the dominant processes of interpreting these facts through the prism of national security remains untouched.

As such, the "dissident gurus" of the populist Left, along with a growing legion of conspiracy theorists, have engaged in critiques that are based to varying extents on a series of claims that the Bush administration had prior knowledge or should have had prior knowledge of the events of 9/11.[4] Therefore the contention is that this prior knowledge and/or the capacity to have had prior knowledge has made the memorialization of the victims disingenuous and the pursuit of the "war on terror" illegitimate. However, these interpretations occlude a much larger political problem, for the logical corollary to this position is that if no prior knowledge existed for 9/11, the practices of the war on terror are without a doubt legitimate responses. Within the discourse of popular American critique, no alternative to the violence of the national security state has been provided.[5] Therefore, within the current parameters of recognized debate, to disagree with contemporary U.S. security policy, one must disagree with *the* official American governmental account of what transpired on 9/11 and the explanations for these events; within the discursive framework that has been operationalized by the Bush administration and those who have publicly positioned themselves as critics, it has become very difficult to communicate opposition to current directions in American security policy by opposing the interpretative disposition of the national security state.

Moreover, there is a disturbing pervasiveness of the belief in an underlying rationality at play with regards to the actions of the United States post-9/11. Apologists for the war on terror have made a series of arguments that the Bush administration, by striking back with ferocious violence, has strategically calculated the best way to ensure the national interests of the United States.[6] Thus mirroring the logic of neoliberal economic theory, the attainment of national security is said to "trickle down" into the provision of personal safety for American citizens. In response, mainstream critics have asserted that the depraved indifference toward preventing the events of 9/11 and the pursuit of the war on terror are nothing but cleverly produced ruses to legitimate American geopolitical aims (inter)nationally and/or to facilitate resource accumulation by petro-capitalists and the military-industrial complex.

More revealing have been critiques of the American state of exception in which the law has become the absence of law for the exercise of sovereign U.S. power.[7] Within this environment, it is argued that biopolitics (i.e., control of life) and the extension and accelerated reproduction of bare life (i.e., life that is denied political voice and agency) have depoliticized American security policy to a disturbing extent.[8] From the indefinite imprisonment of suspects at Guantánamo Bay and other secret facilities to the proposed constitutional amendments to prevent same-sex marriages, biopolitics has proliferated in the post-9/11 environment while the *political* retreats in the face of (national) security imperatives framed by hypermasculine lenses.[9]

The important concerns raised with respect to political possibility in the national security state and the paradoxes of responsible reaction to 9/11 are inextricably tied to a set of *problematiques* constituted within the security/identity nexus. The construction of the American "we" post-9/11 and what this "we" must be secured against are mutually constitutive; the label "danger" results not from drawing on the objective characteristics of the material environment "out there" but rather "from the calculation of a threat that objectifies events, disciplines relations, and sequesters an ideal of identity of the people said to be at risk."[10] But given the collective trauma experienced by the American body politic and the inability to recall context (both before and after 9/11), the nodal point around which the constructions of Self and Other have been anchored embodies a lingering dilemma.

Within this identity/threat dynamic, Maja Zehfuss has argued that

> the question is not merely how we ought to react, but more fundamentally who "we" are in the first place. This is a much more problematic question than has been acknowledged. Our invocations of memory presuppose an identity, a remembering "we," if you will. As we have already seen, this raises issues to do with our inability to remember as the "we" we were. We can remember only as who we are now.[11]

By understanding contemporary American foreign policy as a series of performatives that attempt to (re)construct the American Self by not recognizing this dilemma, one is able to draw interesting parallels with the motion picture *Memento* (2001) directed by Christopher Nolan.[12] In particular, themes that deal with the ontological security provided by the pursuit of vengeance and the interpretative role of memory in the construction of scripts through which we "read" our world(s) and our place(s) within them are echoed in post-9/11 American foreign policy practices. As such, it is my contention that *Memento* can serve as an analogy for the paradox of the American state as an unfulfilled entity that must (re)create a continuous source of threat in order to imbue itself with meaning in the post-9/11 world, while at the same time perpetuating a collective sense of amnesia to its central role in this meaning-producing project. Thus, (re)reading American security policy via *Memento* reveals spaces in which we can question the hegemonic interpretations of the American *Self* and its *Others* in order to raise the possibility that what *was* and what *is* do not necessarily have to *be*.

Moreover, this analysis also points to what Salvador Dali referred to as "the camembert of time," the impermanence and transitory characteristics of memories and their ability to shape-shift their meanings through processes of recollection and the context in which they are remembered. While memory may be persistent, its content and meaning are not permanent, regardless of the claimed accuracy of the manner in which it has been recorded. Thus, to gain a fuller appreciation of the politics of remembrance and the American security practices made possible post-9/11, it will be argued that a turn toward Dali's surrealist aesthetic is analytically beneficial. By abandoning epistemic realism's fetish toward explanatory models based on assumptions of rationality, a surrealist interpretation can provide novel insight into the arbitrariness and the cruel absurdity of American security policy post-9/11.

Reading *Memento*

Great harm has been done to us. We have suffered great loss. And in our grief and anger we have found our mission and our moment. Freedom and fear are at war. The advance of human freedom—the great achievement of our time, and the great hope of every time—now depends on us.

—George W. Bush[13]

The discipline of International Relations has become accustomed to conceptualizing identity as a relatively fixed social phenomenon at both the individual and collective levels that is reflective of the innate characteristics of agents.[14] However, theoretical contributions from nonstructuralist, feminist, and postcolonial theory have shown that the foundations of the Self or nation-state, the basis of our identities as either an individual or as a collective are unstable, always in a state of negotiation, and perpetually in need of reinforcement because they are not predetermined givens.[15] Ultimately, there is no absolute core that provides uncontested transhistorical meaning; the target of understanding is always moving and conveying a multiplicity of narratives about what it may (or can) be. Yet, within dominant frameworks of thought, uncertainty and unknowns become the ultimate types of threat to our confidence, for who or what we are can never be fully realized when facing these predicaments. For societies like the United States that are ethnically and culturally diverse, the need to be able to present a coherent national identity is particularly acute lest the American body politic lose sight/site/cite of who it is and where it should be placed in relation to the rest of the world.[16]

Fear of the effects of uncertainty and the unknown in regards to self-identity is taken up within popular culture through stories of amnesia and brainwashing, instances in which the Self loses sight of the parameters in which the core of its identities are located in opposition to the threats/dangers "out there." The motion picture *Memento* explores these themes in a manner that highlights the contingent nature of identity and its reliance on the creation of threat for foundations. It also highlights how the performative aspects of identity and threat construction must remain hidden for there to be any possibility of ontological security.

The central story of *Memento* is one that borrows its mood from the classic film noir genre. The central character Leonard Shelby, a former insurance claim investigator, is trying to track down the remaining perpetrator responsible for the rape and murder of his wife.[17] The twist in the plot is that Leonard suffered a head injury during this home invasion, leaving him with *anterograde* amnesia (i.e., the inability to form new memories). As a result, while he believes (and the audience is led to believe) that he has clear memories of events previous to the incident, he cannot remember anything subsequent for more than 15 minutes, even less if he becomes upset or distracted. Thus, like the United States, Leonard struggles with the aftereffects of trauma and develops his own processes of aestheticization to cope with his situation.

Because of his inability to store new memories, Leonard keeps notes, takes Polaroid photographs, and commissions a series of tattoos that decorate his body in attempts to stave off the constant state of disorientation when one is no longer aware of who one is. As the movie progresses, it is revealed to the audience that Leonard has collected information on his wife's killer: his name is James or John; he is a drug dealer; and he has found out his license plate number. This information serves as a discursive collage of evidence that Leonard cites in order to performatively constitute his awareness of Self. It is through these mementos that Leonard navigates and draws meaning from a world in which his mind is trapped in the experience of a perpetual present with a hazy memory of a distant past.

While the central plot itself is quite fascinating, what makes the movie unusually applicable to understanding American security policy post-9/11 as a series of performative constructs is the way in which it is presented. *Memento* is organized so that it plays against conventional narrative type; the story is revealed in backward increments of roughly five to ten minutes. These scenes that are shot in color alternate with black and white scenes that make use of a voice-over to provide some background on Leonard Shelby.

As the story works backward, each color sequence reveals "new" characters: a motel clerk; Teddy, a cop who has befriended Leonard; Natalie, a femme fatale whose connection to Leonard is initially unclear; her criminal boyfriend Jimmy; and a drug dealer named Dodd. The black and white scenes intertwine the circumstances of Leonard's present with the story of Sammy Jankis, an insurance claimant who he had to investigate in his previous life. The story of Sammy Jankis, a tale of another individual with *anterograde* amnesia, is juxtaposed with the color scenes that regress toward the beginning of the intrigue, showing how Leonard has discovered the clues that point to the identity of his wife's killer.

What the viewer learns through the black and white scenes is that Leonard investigated and denied a medical claim made by Sammy Jankis on the grounds that his amnesia was a mental problem rather than a physical one and was therefore not covered by his insurance policy. The implication is that Leonard believed that Sammy could overcome his condition if he so desired. Sammy Jankis's wife is unable to handle Leonard's decision and the implications that can be drawn from it, so she begins to doubt the sincerity of her husband's inability to cope and function as a "normal" human being.

Believing that her husband, no matter the circumstances, would never intentionally harm her, she tests Sammy by asking him to administer several shots of insulin (she is diabetic) in rapid succession. Sammy does as he is told, and his wife slips into a coma from which she will not wake; however, she does have the bittersweet satisfaction of knowing that her husband truly is suffering from a debilitating condition. The end result for Sammy Jankis is that he is placed in a mental hospital where he spends all of his waking moments waiting for the arrival of his wife, unaware that he was the coauthor of her death.

As this story is told, there are microsecond flashbacks in which the character of Sammy Jankis is replaced with Leonard and in which Jankis's wife is replaced with the image of Leonard's wife (from the color scenes). All of this deliberately creates confusion as to what story is being told here: is it the story of Sammy Jankis or is it the story of Leonard Shelby?[18] In turn, this confusion calls into doubt the basic ontological foundations under which Leonard Shelby tries to make sense of his world. Did intruders really kill his wife? Or did Leonard accidentally kill his wife and concoct a story to alleviate his own feelings of guilt and helplessness? These fundamentally different narratives, of course, have incredibly important implications in Leonard's search for justice.

As the story moves backward within the narrative that is shot in color, viewers become increasingly aware that the nodal points around which Leonard's identities are located as an avenger, as a righter of wrongs, as a husband, as a "good guy," and as a sane individual are being manipulated not only by the shady characters that surround him, but most importantly by Leonard himself. Over time, the audience discovers that Teddy, after leading Leonard to his wife's killer several months earlier, has been using him to kill drug dealers, including Jimmy. Natalie, in revenge, also attempts to use him in order to murder Teddy. Ultimately, we discover that

Leonard sets himself up to believe that Teddy is his wife's killer, all of which is facilitated by Leonard's meticulous yet cryptic record keeping. Teddy's grizzly death becomes the opening scene of the movie after a confrontation with Leonard in which he admits to manipulating him and reveals that Leonard may have actually killed his own wife. As a result, what the audience is led to believe will be a simple "whodunit" turns into a much darker and sinister exploration of the performative of self-identity, the construction of threat, and the interpretation of danger.

The inability to create new memories makes Leonard vulnerable to having memories constructed for (and by) him, while his ongoing desire for vengeance is harnessed by himself and others in order to (re)produce Leonard as a wronged man on a quest for justice.[19] At one point in the movie, Leonard, while acknowledging the difficulties of his condition, also points to the freedom that it provides him with, the freedom from doubt:

> Memory's unreliable. . . . Memory's not perfect. It's not even that good. Ask the police; eyewitness testimony is unreliable. . . . Memory can change the shape of a room or the color of a car. It's an interpretation, not a record. Memories can be changed or distorted, and they're irrelevant if you have the facts.

One critic has remarked that this treatment of memory forms the very heart of the film, for "*Memento* is a movie largely *about* memory—the ways in which it defines identity, how it's necessary to determine moral behavior and yet how terribly unreliable it is, despite its crucial role in our experience of the world."[20] Yet the irony of Leonard's statement is not so much in his recognition that memory is an interpretative act as it is in the supposed dichotomy between memory (i.e., interpretation) and "facts," a dichotomy that resonates because it is so ingrained in contemporary modes of thought. Thus, the statement is a form of dark comic relief given that, throughout the film, the audience is made painfully aware that not only can we never be sure of the facts, but that *facts* themselves are always conditioned by interpretative frameworks of varying legitimacy. *Memento* thus points to how we construct facts and shape discourses through processes of memorialization such as the written word, photography, film, and other forms of art. By making our memories into tangible items, we can fool ourselves into believing that these are *the* facts that provide *the* one accurate and true description of the world.

Moreover this dichotomy is weakened further if we acknowledge that facts are always interpreted. They do not speak for themselves; we *must* speak for them. As such, our interpretations of facts proscribe the possibilities own every single lead. . . . But the best way to secure the homeland, the best way to make sure that I do my job, is to hunt the killers down one by one and bring them to justice. And that is precisely what America is going to do. . . . And we're going to continue making sure we send a clear message: either you're with us or you're with the enemy. . . . I believe that this country is so strong, and so powerful, and so good and decent, that out of the evil done September the 11th can come some important, lasting contributions to the world, starting with peace. . . . Out of the evil done to America has come a new culture, a new sense of responsibility. The enemy thought they were hurting America, and they killed too many lives, no question about it. But they didn't realize who they were dealing with. They were dealing with the greatest nation, the most decent nation, the most compassionate nation on the face of this Earth.

Remarks by the President on Iraq in Cincinnati, October 7, 2002

We also must never forget the most vivid events of recent history. On September the 11th, 2001, America felt its vulnerability—even to threats that gather on the other side of the earth. We resolved then, and we are resolved today, to confront every threat, from any source, that could bring sudden terror and suffering to America. . . . We know that Iraq and the al Qaeda terrorist network share a common enemy—the United States of America. We know that Iraq and al Qaeda have had high-level contacts that go back a decade. . . . And we know that after September the 11th, Saddam Hussein's regime gleefully celebrated the terrorist attacks on America. Iraq could decide on any given day to provide a biological or chemical weapon to a terrorist group or individual terrorists. Alliance with terrorists could allow the Iraqi regime to attack America without leaving any fingerprints. . . . The attacks of September the 11th showed our country that vast oceans no longer protect us from danger. Before that tragic date, we had only hints of al Qaeda's plans and designs. Today in Iraq, we see a threat whose outlines are far more clearly defined, and whose consequences could be far more deadly. Saddam Hussein's actions have put us on notice, and there is no refuge from our responsibilities. We did not ask for this present challenge, but we accept it. Like other generations of Americans, we will meet the responsibility of defending human liberty against violence and aggression. By our resolve, we will give strength to others. By our courage, we will give hope to others. And by our actions, we will secure the peace, and lead the world to a better day.

President Honors Veterans of Foreign Wars at National Convention, August 22, 2005

This hour, a new generation of Americans is defending our flag and our freedom in the first war of the 21st century. The war came to our shores on and limits of social action by constructing the context within which decisions are made. The irony of course is that we often "forget" both the interpretative acts we have undertaken to establish memories as facts in discourse and alternative interpretative options that are available both at the instant when they are discursively constructed and when we draw meaning from them afterward. The tenuous distinction between *memory* and *facts*, which runs through *Memento*, is crucially relevant to American practices of securitization, criminalization, and aestheticization post-9/11. Central to these processes has been the tantric repetition of what happened on September 11, why it happened, and who poses an ongoing threat to the United States. Yet, rather than being an independent response to a "new" international security environment, the Bush administration's security mantras and this environment were mutually constitutive, a dynamic facilitated by the trauma of 9/11 which allowed for any security claims to be afforded the privileged status of "fact." Thus what was presented as fact was in turn memorialized and what was memorialized is now taken as fact, masking the (at least) two-staged process of mutually constitutive interpretation.[21]

Second, the never-ending pursuit of his wife's murderer gives Leonard significance in a life that would otherwise be unable to generate any purpose for him; this search provides him with a level of ontological security that he would otherwise not have. To admit to himself that he has accomplished his task would be to end any chance that he could go on living a meaningful life, which in his case is defined by the pursuit of vengeance. To admit to successfully avenging the murder of his wife (if she was in fact murdered) would be to condemn himself into an ongoing present with no ontological constellation in place through which to read meaning. There would be no good guys or bad guys. There would be no goal to strive for. There would be nothing to accomplish. There would be no trauma initiated by Others to confront.

It is here that we can draw a parallel with David Campbell's paradox of states as unfulfilled entities. Like Leonard, the United States must performatively (re)create ongoing problems, hazards, and threats through discourses of danger that (re)produce an evangelism of fear so that they (and their citizens) can navigate and make sense of the differences contained (or quarantined) within "external" worlds.[22] However, there is no preconstituted Self that exists prior to the performative expressions of its characteristics in discourse.[23] There is no "independent" higher authority to help define the identity characteristics of an actor and reassure subjects of the correctness of these boundaries.[24] Nor is there an objective blueprint mapping a "pure" Self that can be used as a guide for this process.

This makes the performative of identity by the Self all the more necessary because it is the performative itself that constitutes identity rather than being the product of a fixed preexisting identity that can be appealed to.[25] Therefore, within the United States, security policy is the vehicle through which discursive articulations of the nation-state (and society) as Self take place in attempts to fix the boundaries around which protective barriers must be built to prevent the intrusion of Otherness.[26] As Campbell notes, to stop these performatives and their performances would be to disrupt the ability of the state to exist as a functioning unit. The basis of the performatives that actors undertake (i.e., the characteristic a state asserts as being naturally its own) derives from choices about how one wants to see oneself, how one wishes to be seen by others, and how one wants to see its Others. Therefore, while it may be difficult to do so, we are able to shape the scripts through which we read the world and through which we want the world to read us.

In other words, the identity of being a "state" and a state's "identity" must be constantly performed through the "repeated, yet, varied" discursive articulation of these characteristics.[27] Specifically, in the speeches immediately following 9/11 and those that came later with respect to Iraq, the United States performatively constituted itself (and its Others) with strength and conviction. Consider the following examples:

Television Broadcast to the American People, September 11, 2001

Today, our fellow citizens, our way of life, our very freedom came under attack in a series of deliberate and deadly terrorist acts. . . . Thousands of lives were suddenly ended by evil, despicable acts of terror. . . . These acts of mass murder were intended to frighten our nation into chaos and retreat. But they have failed. Our country is strong. A great people have been moved to defend a great nation. . . . America was targeted for attack because we're the brightest beacon for freedom and opportunity in the world. . . . The search is underway for those who are behind these evil acts.

Presidential Address to a Joint Session of Congress and the American People, September 20, 2001

On September 11th, enemies of freedom committed an act of war against our country. . . . Who attacked our country? The evidence we have gathered all points to a collection of loosely affiliated terrorist organizations known as al Qaeda. . . . Our war on terror begins with al Qaeda, but . . . it will not end until every terrorist group of global reach has been found, stopped, and

defeated. Americans are asking, why do they hate us?
freedoms—our freedom of religion, our freedom of spee
vote and assemble and disagree with each other. . . . The
the murderous ideologies of the 20th century. By sacrif
serve their radical visions—by abandoning every value
power—they follow the path of fascism, and Nazism, and
they will follow that path all the way, to where it ends: ir
grave of discarded lies. . . . Every nation, in every region
to make. Either you are with us, or you are with the te
way to defeat terrorism as a threat to our way of life is to
and destroy it where it grows. . . . The civilized world is
side. . . . Our nation—this generation—will lift a dark th
our people and our future. We will rally the world to thi
by our courage. We will not tire, we will not falt
fail. . . . The course of this conflict is not known, yet i
Freedom and fear, justice and cruelty, have always been
that God is not neutral between them. Fellow citizens
with patient justice—assured of the rightness of our ca
the victories to come. In all that lies before us, may God
may He watch over the United States of America.

Factsheet on the Taliban, U.S. Departm
October 17, 2001

The Afghan people have been the primary victims of
the Taliban came to power in 1996. . . . The Taliban
people the unwilling hosts of foreign armed terroris
and endangered the Afghan people, and made Afgh
world community. . . . The humanitarian situation
Twenty years of internal armed conflict, and four year
have contributed to this situation, but the Taliban hav
situation much worse, holding the Afghan people l
agenda.

President Bush's Address to the Rep
of Florida Majority Dinner on Jur

We're dealing with cold-blooded killers, and that
people who hijack a great religion and kill in the na
are people who send youngsters to their death, and
I just want you to know that my main focus, and the
working people, is to do everything we can to prote

the morning of September the 11th, 2001. Since then the terrorists have continued to strike—in Bali, in Riyadh, in Istanbul, and Madrid, and Baghdad, and London, and Sharm el-Sheikh and elsewhere. The enemy, the terrorists, are ruthless and brutal. They're fighting on behalf of a hateful ideology that despises everything America stands for. Our enemies have no regard for human life. They're trying to hijack a great religion to justify a dark vision that rejects freedom and tolerance and dissent. They have a strategy, and part of that strategy is they're trying to shake our will. They kill the innocent. They kill women and children, knowing that the images of their brutality will horrify civilized peoples. Their goal is to drive nations into retreat so they can topple governments across the Middle East, establish Taliban-like regimes, and turn that region into a launching pad for more attacks against our people. In all their objectives, our enemies are trying to intimidate America and the free world. And in all their objectives, they will fail. Like the great struggles of the 20th century, the war on terror demands every element of our national power. Yet this is a different kind of war. Our enemies are not organized into battalions, or commanded by governments. They hide in shadowy networks and retreat after they strike. After September the 11th, 2001, I made a pledge, America will not be—will not wait to be attacked again. We will go on the offense and we will defend our freedom.

These speeches (as elements constitutive of practical and popular discourses) are the *notes, Polaroids,* and *tattoos* of the American body politic that shape the ways in which meaning can be drawn from the (inter)national environment and concretizes the knowledge of the American Self in the aftermath of experiencing the trauma of 9/11.[28] And it is these performatives to which the Bush administration returns with each successive securitized geopolitical performance. In key policy documents we see the entrenchment of these perceptions of the world and the United States' position within it that construct official policy as *the* only prudential response. For example, in the slew of revised national security strategy documents of the Bush administration, 9/11 is drawn upon in discussions of a range of security vulnerabilities:

Forward to National Security Strategy 2002

The gravest danger our Nation faces lies at the crossroads of radicalism and technology. Our enemies have openly declared that they are seeking weapons of mass destruction, and evidence indicates that they are doing so with determination. The United States will not allow these efforts to succeed. We will build defenses against ballistic missiles and other means of delivery. We will cooperate with other nations to deny, contain, and curtail our enemies' efforts to acquire dangerous technologies. And, as a matter of common sense and self-defense, America will act against such emerging threats before they are fully formed. We cannot defend America and our friends by hoping for the best. So we must be prepared to defeat our enemies' plans, using the best intelligence and proceeding with deliberation. History will judge harshly those who saw this coming danger but failed to act. In the new world we have entered, the only path to peace and security is the path of action.[29]

The National Security Strategy 2002

The United States of America is fighting a war against terrorists of global reach. The enemy is not a single political regime or person or religion or ideology. The enemy is terrorism—premeditated, politically motivated violence perpetrated against innocents. In many regions, legitimate grievances prevent the emergence of a lasting peace. Such grievances deserve to be, and must be, addressed within a political process. But no cause justifies terror. The United States will make no concessions to terrorist demands and strike no deals with them. We make no distinction between terrorists and those who knowingly harbor or provide aid to them. The struggle against global terrorism is different from any other war in our history. It will be fought on many fronts against a particularly elusive enemy over an extended period of time. Progress will come through the persistent accumulation of successes—some seen, some unseen. Today our enemies have seen the results of what civilized nations can, and will, do against regimes that harbor, support, and use terrorism to achieve their political goals. Afghanistan has been liberated; coalition forces continue to hunt down the Taliban and al-Qaeda. But it is not only this battlefield on which we will engage terrorists. Thousands of trained terrorists remain at large with cells in North America, South America, Europe, Africa, the Middle East, and across Asia.[30]

National Strategy to Combat Terrorism 2002

The terrorist attacks of September 11, 2001, in Washington, D.C., New York City, and Pennsylvania were acts of war against the United States of America and its allies, and against the very idea of civilized society. No cause justifies terrorism. The world must respond and fight this evil that is intent on threatening and destroying our basic freedoms and our way of life. Freedom and fear are at war. . . . The struggle against international terrorism is different from any other war in our history. We will not triumph solely or even primarily through military might. We must fight terrorist networks, and all those who support their efforts to spread fear around the world, using every instrument of national power—diplomatic, economic, law enforcement, financial, information, intelligence, and military. . . . We will never forget what we are ultimately fighting for—our fundamental democratic values and way of life. In leading the campaign against terrorism, we are forging new international relationships and redefining existing ones in terms suited to the transnational challenges of the 21st century.[31]

National Security Strategy to Combat Weapons of Mass Destruction 2002

Weapons of mass destruction (WMD)—nuclear, biological, and chemical—in the possession of hostile states and terrorists represent one of the greatest security challenges facing the United States. . . . Weapons of mass destruction could enable adversaries to inflict massive harm on the United States, our military forces at home and abroad, and our friends and allies. Some states, including several that have supported and continue to support terrorism, already possess WMD and are seeking even greater capabilities, as tools of coercion and intimidation. For them, these are not weapons of last resort, but militarily useful weapons of choice intended to overcome our nation's advantages in conventional forces and to deter us from responding to aggression against our friends and allies in regions of vital interest. In addition, terrorist groups are seeking to acquire WMD with the stated purpose of killing large numbers of our people and those of friends and allies—without compunction and without warning. We will not permit the world's most dangerous regimes and terrorists to threaten us with the world's most destructive weapons. We must accord the highest priority to the protection of the United States, our forces, and our friends and allies from the existing and growing WMD threat.[32]

The National Strategy to Secure Cyberspace 2003

The terrorist attacks against the United States that took place on September 11, 2001, had a profound impact on our Nation. The federal government and society as a whole have been forced to re-examine conceptions of security on our home soil, with many understanding only for the first time the lengths to which self-designated enemies of our country are willing to go to inflict debilitating damage. We must move forward with the understanding that there are enemies who seek to inflict damage on our way of life. They are ready to attack us on our own soil, and they have shown a willingness to use unconventional means to execute those attacks. While the attacks of September 11 were physical attacks, we are facing increasing threats from hostile adversaries in the realm of cyberspace as well.[33]

Yet, criticism is muted toward security measures such as national missile defense or the increase in panoptic networks to combat illegal migration that do not even make sense in relation to the "facts" presented as being constitutive of the events of 9/11 by the Bush administration. For example, 9/11 can be perceived as an indication that a future attack on the United States will be delivered by nontraditional military means, as well as demonstrating the ability of al Qaeda operatives to work within the legalities of the immigration system and integrate into American society.[34] Still, 9/11 is evoked to give credence to securitizing these particular issues and pursuing a narrowly constructed range of militarized policy options. Thus, the United States has shown an inability to read any contemporary issue outside of the 9/11 prism, which has combined with an unwillingness to transpose these "lessons" into policy when they conflict with the dominant understanding of what 9/11 means for the attainment of national security.

Finally, an ethos of critique can be detected through a reading of *Memento*. Above all else, this film demonstrates the importance of recalling Maja Zehfuss's questions about "how have we come to be a particular way in the present?" or perhaps more precisely "how have we come to represent ourselves in a specific fashion in the present?" Currently, within the United States, Zehfuss describes a very different gaze that fixes on 9/11 with the argument that

[in] looking to September 11 to understand recent events [it has] turn[ed] it into the root, the cause, the origin. It is as if nothing had ever happened before. The US administration wants us to see the "war against terrorism" as an effect of September 11. In other words, the events of September 11 are the "cause" of its policies today. We may not, however, ask how we got there lest we be disrespectful of the dead.[35]

Unfortunately, as Judith Butler has warned, in seeking to understand "how the global map arrived at this juncture, through asking how, in part, the US has contributed to the making of this map" one faces the danger of being defined as "complicitous with an assumed enemy."[36]

However, this may be a risk worth taking for as Butler argues:

[I]f we paralyze our thinking in this way [i.e., by not asking the "how possible" question], we will fail morality in a different way. . . . We will fail to take collective responsibility for a thorough understanding of the history which brings us to this juncture. We will, as a result, deprive ourselves of the very critical and historical resources we need to imagine and practice another future, one which will move beyond the current cycle of revenge.[37]

Thus, by being prepared to ask "how possible" questions, we can avoid the pitfalls of Leonard Shelby/Sammy Jankis and expose the inherently subjective nature [*sic*] of identity and security. "How possible" questions also bring to light the inherent instability of identity by allowing us to examine how the foundations of the Self may shift over time, thereby opening the possibility that both what *was* and what *is* do not necessarily have to *be*. In this way, responsibility can be recognized as extending beyond previously perceived boundaries, and sources of vulnerability can be reassessed. But, in recognizing the performative element within the security/identity nexus, how can we understand the manner in which this dynamic has manifested itself in contemporary American security practices? By turning to surrealism, a compelling but ultimately troubling narrative emerges.

The Surrealism of (American) Security Policy

The simplest surrealist act consists of going out into the street revolver in hand and firing at random into the crowd as often as possible. A man who has not had, at least once, the longing to be finished in this fashion with the petty system of corruption and cretinization now rampant has his place reserved for him in that crowd, belly at pistol point.

—Andre Breton[38]

Surrealism has become one of those terms within popular discourse that is associated with elements of the irrational (i.e., anything weird, extraordinary, or deranged), an imprecision that allows it to be used to describe everything and yet nothing.[39] However, by deploying the notion of surrealism to the contemporary study of security, one can move beyond the pervasive assumptions of rationality and teleology that are indigenous to contemporary affirmations and critiques of American security policy to reveal the arbitrariness and brutal absurdity of these (re)actions. The surrealist movement that officially formed in Paris in 1924 was a broadly based and often loose coalition of artists and intellectuals who were strongly influenced by Dada, Sigmund Freud, and Karl Marx. What is often forgotten today is that the surrealists identified themselves as both political agitators and artists. Thus, Breton described the surrealist artistic ethos as one in which "authentic art goes hand in hand with revolutionary social activity: like the latter it leads to the confusion and destruction of capitalist society."[40] Contemporary American security policy is surreal not by embracing this transformative ethos but rather in how its method of drawing upon the irrational to read, navigate, and react to the details of a geopolitical painting of its own creation has been central in maintaining the hegemony of capitalism, neoliberalism, sovereignty, and militarism; these are the surrealist acts of American global politics.[41] In teasing out elements of the new surrealism, I will necessarily be limiting the exploration to draw exclusively on the aesthetic methods of Salvador Dali.[42]

Dali painted with what he called "the most imperialist fury of precision," a technique that can be discerned in the fine details of his paintings. In the post-9/11 era, the United States has also engaged in its own attempts at an "imperialist fury of precision" through an ongoing devotion to the global panopticon, its products of surveillance and intelligence, in both real and virtual worlds. While Dali's goal was to "systematize the confusion and to contribute to the total discrediting of reality," the United States has adopted these practices for the purposes of concretizing its own mental images of the geopolitical and its associated dangers. Thus, the American body politic is flooded with the "facts" about what they need to fear, who must bear responsibility for the events of 9/11, and what the United States *must* do to secure itself against these "evildoers." But the disclosure is rarely ever "total" as terror alerts increase and subside; individuals are named, hunted, sometimes found, and detained; rogues are created without the mention of context; and invasions are planned, announced, and launched. By calling upon the American body politic to "trust" that the Bush admin- istration has *the* monopoly on truth and information that cannot be publicly shared for security risks, the absence of clearly identifiable "evidence" is no more than a temporary inconvenience with future revelations serving to justify actions after the "fact."

Thus, given the guardedness with which the United States looks out into the world and the fierceness of its imaginings, one can see the expro- priation of Dali's "paranoia-critical method," which produces spectacular results from harnessing the interpretative powers of madness.[43] In *La Femme Visible*, Dali argued,

> Paranoia makes use of the external world to impose the obsessive notion with the disturbing particularity of making valid the reality of this notion for others. The reality of the external world serves as an illustration and a proof, and is put in the service of the reality of our mind.[44]

Thus, in contemporary American security policy, there is a "spontaneous method of irrational knowledge based on the critical and systematic objec- tivation of delirious associations and interpretations."[45]

As such, absolutely nothing is beyond suspicion, for in utilizing an inter- pretative framework influenced by paranoia, the Bush administration reveals the double significance of things that otherwise may have not reg- istered within standard threat matrices.[46] This has made it possible for even those elements that have been the referent objects of post-9/11 securitization to be treated as dangers. For example, it has been asserted that

> as a modern liberal democracy Canada possesses a number of features that make it hospitable to terrorists and international criminals. The Canadian Constitution guarantees rights such as the right to life, liberty, freedom of movement, freedom of speech, protection against unreasonable search and seizure, and protection against arbitrary detention or imprisonment that make it easier for terrorists and international criminals to operate. In addition, a technologically advanced economy and infrastructure facilitate operations and activities as well as providing a myriad of opportunities for abuse.[47]

Within this formulation of threat, it is precisely the characteristics that define membership in the grouping of "civilized" states in dominant American geopolitical discourses that are being used to construct Canada as a security vulnerability. Thus the spectrum of threat expands beyond what are presented as the contemporary incarnation of totalitarianism (e.g., "terrorists," the "Axis of Evil") to subsume anything that at a particular moment in time is seized upon by paranoiac imagination as constituting a threat to the American national security state.

To build upon the interpretative fervor of paranoia-criticism, we can see American security policy applying what Dali referred to as the "psychic anamorph," a process defined as "the instantaneous reconstitution of the desire by its refraction in a cycle of memories."[48] For example, Dali described the psychic anamorph as "the instantaneous reconstitution of the desire of thirst by its refraction in a cycle of masochistic memories."[49] In this way, one can see the American desire for revenge playing through ongoing processes of memorialization post-9/11 from the meticulous record keeping of the dead found at Ground Zero (including statistics on race, gender, citizenship) to federal encouragement (and suggested guidelines) for conducting remembrance ceremonies by the White House Commission on Remembrance.[50]

What is most remarkable about the American psychic anamorph has been the high levels of management of its interpretative possibilities and the delegitimation within popular discourses of "how possible" questions. Moreover, through the scope of the psychic anamorph, the absence of discussion of American casualties in the multipronged war on terror, the prohibition on the broadcasting or pictorial representation of the body bags returning from Afghanistan and Iraq, and the lack of discussion of civilian casualties become not merely strategies to deflect responsibility for the consequences of the U.S. administration's actions but also a means by which to keep the cycle of masochistic memories that constitute the desire for revenge focused on 9/11.[51] Thus, rather than becoming satiated by the toppling of a regime or the imposition of democracy, the uncertainty of what needs to done perpetuates that something must continually be done if the United States is to be avenged and made secure.[52] With the national security state firmly entrenched as the interpreter of legitimacy and guided by the infinite vulnerabilities constructed through the processes of paranoia–criticism, the limits of securitized action may only be found in the eventual realization of the material constraints of the United States.

Some Conclusions?

The only difference between a madman and me, is that I am not mad.

—Salvador Dali

Emboldened by a moral clarity not seen since the cold war, the United States has shown an unwillingness or lack of capacity to remember what happened prior to the traumatic events of 9/11 and seek out connections that might give a fuller (but ultimately less clear) understanding of Self and Other. The current (a)political context is one where the possibility that muted versions of today's policies contributed to an international environment in which 9/11 became possible is incapable of penetrating the psyche of the American body politic. Yet, all hope is not lost, for like Leonard Shelby, one can still discern faint echoes of confusion over what the American body politic has been traumatized by, and the articulation of uncertainties and lingering suspicions about what the United States can claim to be. To this point, the "success" of the Bush Doctrine has not been so much in its clear and decisive policy prescriptions (as admirers contend) but in its persistent masking of the possibility of alternative remembering(s) of whatever 9/11 might have been through the promotion of its own vision of what 9/11 was/is, and depoliticizing this memorialization by appealing to "facts" produced by this dynamic. As such, the frame of debate remains distant to questioning the legitimacy of responding to unforeseen violence with violence.

Indications of the madness that constitutes this position can be found in the United States as a global actor both in terms of its aesthetic method and the outcomes that these methods make possible. For those who stand slightly outside of the performative imaginings of the United States, the performances of national security bear an uneasy resemblance to those who are condemned as being confined to the repertoire of terrorists and rogue states. Most starkly, thousands of Afghani and Iraqi civilians perish, thousands of casualties are suffered by "coalitions of the willing," and civil liberties become economized in conditions made possible from the direct application of American power and the extension of bare life in the name of political voice. But the United States does not serve as the sole author in this surrealist project; many other states contribute to surrealist readings of the world and perpetuate the pathology of representing militarism as a mode of being that brings peace. Thus, to gain an understanding of the new geopolitics, there must be a turn toward the irrational impulses that constitute the performatives and performances of contemporary security policy and a renewed attention paid to how these become accepted in various body politics as "facts." Finally, what this analysis also reveals is the surrealist manner in which these "facts" are interpreted and expressed in security policy performance. By turning to Dali's paranoiac-critical method and the psychic anamorph, the inherent irrationality and pathology of state security policy can be understood, questioned, and transformed so that the capricious constitution of bare life ceases as an acceptable security practice.

Notes

1. Address to a Joint Session of Congress and the American People, September 20, 2001.
2. Jenny Edkins, "Forget Trauma? Responses to September 11," *International Relations*, 16:2 (2002): 252–253.
3. David Campbell, *Politics Without Principle: Sovereignty, Ethics, and the Narratives of the Gulf War* (Boulder: Lynne Rienner, 1993), pp. 7–8. "Political" is being used pejoratively here to indicate its "problem solving" and partisan nature in this deployment. Within this paper, political is designated in terms of the arena in which particular systems of power are established, maintained, and challenged. See ibid., p. 256.
4. For a sustained discussion of the ways in which the political imaginary of the Bush Administration coheres around preemptive desires, see Cynthia Weber's contribution to this volume.
5. Related to this observation, Maja Zehfuss has argued that "what is, or indeed what was, isn't actually the point. The point is what is done, to be doing something. The actionism of the high-tech war effort nicely covers up the fact that we are at a complete loss as to how to respond to 'the events of September 11.' " See Maja Zehfuss, "Forget September 11th," *Third World Quarterly*, 24:3 (2003): 522.
6. For example see Michael Hirsh, "Bush and the World," *Foreign Affairs*, 81:5 (2002): 18; Michael Howard, "What's in a Name?: How to Fight Terrorism," *Foreign Affairs*, 81:1 (2002): 8; Morton I. Abramowitz, "Dear Dubya: FP Asks One of America's Most Seasoned Former Diplomats to

Rate Bush Foreign Policy," *Foreign Policy* (May 2002): 78–79; and Kenneth M. Pollack, "Next Stop Baghdad?" *Foreign Affairs*, 81:2 (2002): 32.

7. See Giorgio Agamben, *Homo Sacer: Sovereign Power and Bare Life* (Stanford: Stanford University Press, 1998).

8. Edkins (2002), p. 247. Paul Rabinow and Nikolas Rose have (in relation to the work on governmentality by Michel Foucault) defined biopolitics as those endeavours which attempted to rationalize the problems presented to governmental practice by the phenomena characteristics of living human beings constituted as a population. See "Introduction: Foucault Today," in *The Essential Foucault: Selections from Essential Works of Foucault 1954–1984*, ed. Paul Rabinow and Nikolas Rose (New York: New Press, 2003), p. xxix.

9. In the aftermath of 9/11 Muneer Ahmed has argued that "the hate violence [within the United States], our national fervour, and our over-reliance on military solutions are all unquestionably gendered male." See Muneer Ahmed, "Homeland Insecurities: Racial Violence the Day After September 11," *Social Text*, 20:3 (2002): 108–109.

10. David Campbell, *Writing Security: United States Foreign Policy and the Politics of Identity*, 2nd ed. (Minneapolis: University of Minnesota Press, 1998), p. 3. Objectification here refers to instances in which the dominant interpretation of an event is naturalized within a particular social context so that it is no longer seen as an interpretation but rather as an objective truth.

11. Zehfuss (2003), pp. 519–520.

12. Performatives refer to "the reiterative and citational practice[s] by which discourse[s] produce the effects that [they] name" and should not be confused with performance which is "a singular or deliberate act." From Judith Butler quoted in Cynthia Weber, "Performative States," *Millennium*, 27:1 (1998): 81.

13. Address to a Joint Session of Congress and the American People, September 20, 2001.

14. For example, see Barry Buzan, Ole Waever, and Japp de Wilde, *Security: A New Framework for Analysis*. (Boulder: Lynne Rienner, 1998) and Alexander Wendt, *Social Theory of International Politics* (Cambridge: Cambridge University Press, 1999). The popularity of this approach within the discipline has greatly contributed to the view of identity as dynamic (in some near past) but contemporarily fixed. Mainstream constructivists give units to be studied a preexisting identity which in essence refuses to acknowledge that it is the agency of actors that gives rise to these identities and that these actors are not necessarily states. When identity is not taken as a given and is denaturalized, we can see it as the tenuous political outcome of performativity rather than as an innate characteristic(s) of an agent. The failure of the *via media* approaches to ask the kinds of questions that seek to discover how particular identities have been socially constructed has given rise to a very limited vision of the role

of ideas (and discourse) in International Relations. In essence, the influence of ideas is confined to interactions between already existing actors in an already existing system, where identities are depoliticized and potentially ahistorical.

15. David Campbell argues that "identity is an inescapable dimension of being. No body could be without it . . . it is not fixed by nature, given by God, or planned by intentional behaviour. Rather identity is constituted in relation to difference. But neither is difference fixed by nature, given by God, or planned by intentional behaviour. Difference is constituted in relation to identity." See Campbell (1998), p. 9.

16. Sight/site/cite refers to the subjects, objects, and texts that are constitutive of identity. See Gearoid O'Tuathail, *Critical Geopolitics* (Minneapolis: University of Minnesota Press, 1996), pp. 43 and 71.

17. One attacker was killed by Leonard mid-ordeal.

18. The official *Memento* website further blurs any distinction between Leonard Shelby and Sammy Jankis. See http://otnemem.com/index.html.

19. By hiring a prostitute to reenact what he considers to be the final moments with his wife before the attack, we see Leonard trying to shore up his own sense of who is and where he has come from, even if for a brief period of time.

20. For an excellent review of *Memento*, see Andy Klein, *Everything You Wanted to Know About "Memento,"* Salon.com (2001), http:// archive.salon.com/ent/movies/feature/2001/06/28/memento_analysis/ (accessed March 1, 2003).

21. This is not to argue that there is some ultimate meaning to 9/11 that could be discerned if a more accurate process of recollection was in place. Rather, the point is that there never is one discernable meaning inherent in an event and that, as a dynamic phenomenon, meaning is always transforming at the instant before it becomes fully concretized. Thus, a "true" comprehension of meaning as "fact" is impossible.

22. Campbell (1998), p. 48.

23. Weber (1998), p. 80.

24. This is not to say that hegemonic actors do not try and play this role. See Roxanne Lynn Doty, *Imperial Encounters: The Politics of Representation in North-South Relations* (Minneapolis: University of Minnesota Press, 1996).

25. Lene Hansen, "The Little Mermaid's Silent Security Dilemma and the Absence of Gender in the Copenhagen School," *Millennium*, 29:2 (2000): 301–302.

26. For Campbell, drawing out the implications of performativity means that we should see the state as having "no ontological status apart from the various acts which constitute its reality"; rather, its status as a sovereign presence in world politics is produced by a "discourse of primary and stable identity"; and that the identity of any particular state should be

understood as "tenuously constituted in time . . . through a *stylized repetition of acts*," and achieved, "*not* [through] *a founding act, but rather a regulated process of repetition*," See Campbell (1998), p. 10.

27. Weber (1998), p. 80.
28. Performatives of the American Self have been operationalized and reaffirmed through the enactment of specific policies that are set to respond to terrorism. But as Butler reminds us, "performativity is . . . not a single act for it is always a reiteration of a norm or set of norms, and to the extent that it acquires an act-like status in the present, it conceals or dissimulates the conventions of which it is a repetition." Thus, to understand how current U.S. discourses and policies have become possible, one must look from where they have been derived and what makes them able to be reiterated, understood, and accepted. See Judith Butler, "Bodies that Matter," in *Feminist Theory and the Body*, eds. Janet Price and Margrit Shildrick. (London: Routledge, 1999), p. 241. Such a project extends far beyond the scope of this exploratory chapter, but must be undertaken to gain a contextual understanding the American reaction to 9/11.
29. Office of the President of the United States, The National Security Strategy of the United States of America (Washington, D.C.: Office of the President of the United States, 2002).
30. National Security Strategy (2002), p. 5.
31. Office of the President of the United States, National Strategy for Combating Terrorism (Washington, D.C.: Office of the President of the United States, 2003), pp. 1–2.
32. Office of the President of the United States, The National Strategy to Combat Weapons of Mass Destruction (Washington, D.C.: Office of the President of the United States, 2002), p. 1.
33. Office of the President of the United States, The National Strategy To Secure Cyberspace, (Washington, D.C.: Office of the President of the United States, 2003), p. 5.
34. This of course makes terrorism appear as something that is external to the United States in origin and forgets the acts of uncoded Americans (i.e., white Christian males) like the Unibomber and Timothy McVeigh.
35. Zehfuss (2003), p. 520.
36. Judith Butler, "Explanation and Exoneration, or What We Can Hear," *Theory and Event*, 5:4 (2002): 8.
37. Butler (2002), p. 11.
38. Deuxième Manifeste du surréalisme (1929). Quoted in Maurice Nadeau, *The History of Surrealism* (Cambridge: Belknap Press of Harvard University Press, 1989), p. 54.
39. In this way, surrealism is similar to those threats said to emerge from terrorist aims and activities.
40. Quoted in Maurice Nadeau, *The History of Surrealism* (Cambridge: Belknap Press of Harvard University Press, 1989), p. 117.
41. Rationality and irrationality are very problematic terms to be using here. I am aware of the inherent subjectivity of the terms and the ways in which

they have been constitutive of specific power relations (including gender binaries) that have made numerous forms of discipline and oppression possible. More importantly, I understand that in making use of this terminology I may (even in critique) be contributing to the shoring up of their foundations. Thus, I think this is a move that must be taken with great caution and reflexivity in order to avoid being complicit in the reproduction of hierarchy. Thus, the argument being made here is that social analysis should proceed under the assumption that no actor can be rational and therefore, the irrational is central to all actors in making sense of and responding to their particular social environments.

42. The irony is that Dali was chastized by other members of the surrealist movement for lacking political sensibilities and being overly concerned with commercial success.

43. Again, I am very reticent to be deploying loaded language like "madness" in this discussion because of the inextricable ties with the concept to a history of power and oppression. However, given the general dismissal of applying individual ethical standards to the behavior of states, I want to push against the barrier of inculpability by applying current medical norms to these actions. Thus, the desire is to pathologize the behavior of *all* states. This strategy is open to reconsideration.

44. Quoted in Nadeau (1989), p. 184.

45. Ibid., p. 184. While the assumption of a clear demarcation between internal and external worlds (and meanings found within each) is highly problematic for reasons discussed previously, both Dali and the United States have operated with this belief.

46. For further discussion of the paranoiac-critical method, see Sarane Alexandrian, *Surrealist Art* (London: Thames and Hudson, Ltd., 1991), p. 100 and ibid., pp. 183–190.

47. Federal Research Division Library of Congress, *Nations Hospitable to Organized Crime and Terrorism* (Washington, D.C.: Library of Congress, 2003), p. 145. For further discussion, see David Mutimer in this volume.

48. Alexandrian (1991), p. 103.

49. Ibid.

50. See http://www.remember.gov/ for officially suggested ways to remember 9/11.

51. For further elaboration on the ways in which deaths in Iraq constitute particular imagined memory, see Cristina Masters in this volume.

52. This is compounded by what might be diagnosed as the Attention Deficit Disorder of the American body politic and its appointed leaders; even in the "war on terror" there is a pronounced inability to remember what has been done and what is being done with respect to security practice. For example, Afghanistan has quickly fallen off the radar screen of the American general public as the focus shifts to the quagmire in Iraq. The inattention of the American security policy community was foreshadowed with the embarrassing exclusion of publicly pledged funds toward the rebuilding of Afghanistan in the *Fiscal Year 2004 Budget Request* delivered early in 2003.

CHAPTER 6

SECURITIZING THE UNCONSCIOUS: THE BUSH DOCTRINE OF PREEMPTION AND *MINORITY REPORT*

Cynthia Weber

On June 1, 2002, President George W. Bush articulated his administration's primary justification for Gulf War II, what become known as the Bush Doctrine of Preemption. This doctrine holds that it is politically, legally, and morally defensible for the United States to use force against a perceived foreign foe in order to prevent future harm against itself, even though that perceived foreign foe has not yet attacked the United States. In his speech to graduating West Point cadets, Bush claimed that "our security will require all Americans to be forward-looking and resolute, to be ready for *preemptive action* when necessary to defend our liberty and to defend our lives."[1] Later that month, the forward-looking film *Minority Report* was released in U.S. cinemas. Based on Philip K. Dick's short story of the same name, *Minority Report* is a futuristic tale that critically explores a U.S. domestically applied system of preemptive justice through the fictitious Department of PreCrime.[2] Not surprisingly, the film was read by critics as an eerie allegory of the Bush Doctrine of Preemption, even though the film's director Steven Spielberg publicly declared his support for the president's policies in the so-called "war on terror."[3]

   The Bush Doctrine of Preemption and *Minority Report*'s Department of PreCrime not only institutionally reorder U.S. relationships to justice and security. They also remap what Michael Shapiro calls "moral geographies," "a set of silent ethical assertions that preorganize explicit ethicopolitical discourses" and what John Agnew calls the "modern geopolitical imagination," which consists of structuring "practices based on a set of understandings about 'the way the world works.' "[4] They do so in what is the most silent (yet screaming) space of all, the unconsciousness. What both the Bush administration and the Department of PreCrime claim is that securing "being"—whether of the individual or of the individual state—is a matter of securitizing the unconscious (i.e., of rendering the unconscious an additional domain of U.S. security practices). It is a matter, in other words, of extending the moral geographies of which Shapiro writes from that which goes without saying to that which *must* go without thinking and extending the modern geopolitical imagination of which Agnew writes from the outer earth to the inner individual. In so doing, they articulate a specific (pre)vision of American morality and what I call "U.S. moral grammars of war"—codes and contexts that structure the meaning of U.S. morality tales about war by grounding them in a specific articulation of the U.S. "we." Whether by intention (as in the case of the Bush administration) or by inference (in the case of *Minority Report*), the U.S. moral grammar of war and the moral American U.S. "we" who ground it are firmly figured within the Bush administration's discourse on the war on terror.

Using *Minority Report* as its interpretive guide, this chapter considers how the securitization of the unconscious is performed in primarily fiction (film) but also "fact" (U.S. foreign policy). It does so by considering three themes— the relationship between embodied subjects (I) and the unconsciousness (the mind's eye, represented in *Minority Report* by "I"s and "eyes"), the relationship between subjects (I/eyes) and the state (the I/eyes to we/nation relationship), and the relationship of both of these to the feminine. The chapter makes two general arguments. Implicitly, it argues that American moralities and U.S. moral grammars of war are not only formulated in traditional realms of politics but also in geopolitical moral imaginaries in which U.S. foreign policy intersects with popular (often filmic) imaginaries as well as with narratives about the family.[5] Elaborating on this final point about the family, the chapter explicitly argues that the feminine is the keystone of the U.S. moral grammar of war in the war on terror because it is the foundational figure upon whom a specific articulation of a moral U.S. "we" is constructed. What this means is that, as the U.S. "we" looks ahead to who a future moral American "we" might become (which is the theme of *Minority Report* and a theme in everyday post-9/11 American life), it ought to begin by understanding how the feminine both secures and insecures the complex relationship between justice and security, particularly as it functions in relation to the present-day Bush administration's policies of securitizing the unconscious.

Minority Report

Minority Report combines futuristic film noir with Spielberg sentimentality to tell a tale about preemptive justice. Set in the District of Columbia in 2054, the film stars Tom Cruise as Chief Inspector John Anderton of the Police Department's Division of PreCrime. PreCrime, as its name suggests, is designed to catch criminals before they commit their crimes. What makes PreCrime function is the "precogs" (the precognitives)—twin brothers Arthur and Dashiell and the girl Agatha (Samantha Morton)— whose exposure in the womb to their mother's hallucinogenic drugs endowed them with the "gift" to see the future. But their gift is actually a curse, for the future they see is that of murders that are about to happen. By downloading the precogs' visions and then artfully interpreting them, the Division of PreCrime, whose most talented man in the field is Anderton, is able to catch the criminals before they actually murder their intended victims.

The film's opening sequence not only illustrates how PreCrime works (in this case, by preventing the death of Sarah Marks and her lover Donald Dubin at the hand of her husband Howard), but it also establishes the film's central motif: the relationship between the "I" and the "eye" and the relationship between the "I/eye" and the "we/nation." The film opens to ominous sounds of cymbals, reminiscent of both the thunder of an approaching storm and the quickening of the human heart. These sounds foreshadow not only the action that is about to take place but its pace. For the images we are about to see come in quick flashes, never lasting more than a few seconds and sometimes lasting only a few frames. Over a black screen, the credits and the film's title fade in and out; they fade in overlit, blue-tinted lava lamp-like shapes. As the soundtrack continues, the shapes form into a close-up image of a man and a woman kissing. Faded in over this image is a pair of scissors. To a cymbal crash, the scissors violently slide off the screen, seemingly pushed. Cut to an image of the male lover struggling in a bathtub. Cut to a different man in a suit walking upstairs, with scissors in his hand, to the woman and her lover kissing, viewed through a pair of eye glasses sitting on a bedside table, to the couple in bed with the suited man standing over them. The male lover rushes off the bed toward the bathroom when the suited man confronts the woman, slashing down at her with the scissors in his hand. Cut to the bathtub, where the suited man's arm is drowning the male lover.

Up to this point, all of the action has been shown in a forward linear progression, even though it is jumpy, partial, and dreamlike. From this point onward in the dreamlike sequence, the action jumps between forward and backward temporalities. Cut to a backward action shot of bloody water rushing back into the bathtub, then a forward action shot of the male lover running from the bed to the bathroom as the suited man chases him with the scissors. Cut to the face of President Abraham Lincoln with one eye poked out, scissors protruding through the opening. A small boy is holding the president's paper head in one hand and a pair of scissors in the other. Return to the suited man standing in the upstairs bedroom. As he raises his glasses to put them on, he says to the woman (in bed with her lover), "You know how blind I am without them." In this same hand that holds his glasses, the suited man also holds the scissors. We see this action from various views, with the horrified woman in the background. "Howard, don't cry," she tells him. At this, the suited man/Howard turns around and violently slashes the woman with the scissors.

Cut to the scissors in water from the overflowed bathtub, with the water moving backward, to the wounded woman in bed struggling to breathe, to water flowing back into the bathtub, with the terrified male lover sitting in it. Water then falls onto the floor. Cut to a close-up of the female victim. Fade to a close-up of another woman's eye, then to an extreme close-up of the vivid blue eye of the precog Agatha. In a rapid zoom-out shot, the camera retreats from Agatha's eye to show all of Agatha's pale white face. She is wearing what appear to be large headphones, and her head is surrounded by a hazy, milky, bluish background.

Agatha (very slowly, overenunciating): "Mur-der." As she speaks, her face is submerged a few inches below the surface of the milky blue liquid. Air bubbles escape her lips. Her eyes remain wide open. This is the end of the dreamlike sequence, which from the time we see the first image until we cut away from the submerged Agatha runs for a mere 60 seconds. The ending of this sequence is marked not only by Agatha's close-up (which seems to establish that she is author of the dream/premonition) but also by replacing the hazy, partial, rapid succession of dream shots with crisper, more predictable images (albeit still blue-washed and overlit) presented though linear progressive, real time-like editing and in the absence of the clash-filled soundtrack.

Cut to a laser machine cutting grainy wood into two round, reddish balls. The machine releases the balls into a maze of clear tubes. The camera follows the balls as the first comes to rest at an exit labeled "VICTIM." The ball is inscribed with two names—Sarah Marks (the woman) and Donald Dubin (her lover). Cut to John Anderton (Tom Cruise) entering the futuristic PreCrime building. As Anderton enters the building, situating subtitles fade in and out on the screen, "Department of PreCrime," "Washington, D.C.," "The year 2054." Cut back to Agatha receding deeper into the water, eyes and mouth open, wearing a distressed expression. Cut to the second ball as it lands at the exit labeled "PERPETRATOR." It reads "Howard Marks" (the suited man).

In view of "remote witnesses" who we see on separate screens in the background, Chief Inspector Anderton prepares to review the evidence generated from the precogs' premonitions. Donning electronic gloves that allow him to manipulate images on the clear screen before him, Anderton artfully conducts the precog-generated images to his selected music, Schubert's "Unfinished Symphony." As Anderton tries to piece together the predicted crime, the film cuts back and forth between his assembly of predicted events and real-time events in the Marks' household. As Howard looks for his eye glasses, Sarah helps their young son memorize the Gettysburg Address. The son makes an Abraham Lincoln mask by cutting out Lincoln's eyes as Anderton and his men draw closer and closer to the soon-to-be crime scene, finally descending from the sky like jet-packed angels just in time to rescue the would-be victims. For his premeditated (but not yet committed) crime, Howard is "haloed." He is forced to wear an electronic headband that incapacitates him physically while securing his unconscious. Once haloed, he will be shipped to the Hall of Containment (a kind of purgatory between thought and thoughtlessness) where he will be held indefinitely. This is the end of the opening sequence.

What we have in this opening sequence is not just the seeds of a moral dilemma—arresting a man for a crime he thought about but did not (yet) commit means the man is not (yet) a criminal—but a particular way to think about this moral dilemma, that is, through a complex series of "I" to "eye" and "I/eye" to "we/nation" relationships. To unpack these relationships, it is helpful to consider how *Minority Report* plays on (and with) vision.

Even though the film is obsessed with eyes, one of the first things the film establishes is that eyes do not provide us with the clearest insights. Howard Marks (our would-be murderer in the opening sequence) "sees" that his wife is having an affair even though he is not wearing his glasses and claims to be blind without them. Marks' physical lack of visual clarity is mirrored by the experience of the film's viewers, who use their eyes to scan the film's first 60-second sequence without being able to make proper sense of it. It is only once these images are understood not as visions but as previsions that they begin to make sense. Visions are made by the eye; previsions are made by the unconscious, by the mind's eye. And while the eye is always linked to an "I"—to a human subject—the mind's eye might well be subjectless.

This, the film tells us, is how we should think about the precogs. As Anderton explains the precogs to a Detective Witwer (Colin Farrell) who has come to investigate the workings of the Department of PreCrime before the DC-wide program becomes a national program, "It's best not to think of them as human." The precogs—three drugged, twenty-something human bodies suspended in a milky, amniotic-like fluid with electrodes downloading their mental images—are regarded by the public not as humans but as deities. They appeared to the state as a miracle six years earlier and ever since have become a holy trinity allowing the state to uphold justice. Even the PreCrime investigators play on these ideas, calling the room that houses the precogs "the temple" and referring to themselves as more like priests than police.

If the precogs are the holy trinity who seem to see one collective vision with their one collective unconscious eye (itself a symbol of deification), then it is the priestly police who (like any priests) are the human interpreters of this vision.[6] It is they who connect the subjectless single "eye" of the precogs to the subjective "I" of the state (which, because it is a collective subjectivity, is always also a "we"). This is Anderton's job, for he is the "eyes" and the "I" of the state. Using his physical eyes and his conscious mind, he interprets the precogs' visions of the evil unconscious of would-be murderers to enable and enforce state justice.

From the perspective of the Department of PreCrime and the many U.S. citizens who end up voting for PreCrime to go national, this system of literally blind justice (blind because the precogs see with their minds, not with their eyes) is perfect. If there is an error in the system, it could not rest with the deified precogs but only with their human interpreters. In other words, prevision (the unconscious subjectless "eye") is perfect whereas vision (the conscious subjective "I") is imperfect. The task of Detective Witwer, who works for the U.S. Attorney General and represents "the eyes of the nation now upon us" (as the Head of PreCrime puts it), is to check for human error in the PreCrime system before it goes national. But, of course, things are more complicated than this. *Minority Report*'s opening sequence does not just establish the benefits of prevision over vision, but it also suggests that prevision, like vision, might suffer from limitations. The film does this in at least two ways.

First, the opening sequence contains not two violent stabbings, but three. It is not only Sarah Marks and her lover who are stabbed but also President Abraham Lincoln whose eyes are cut out by the Marks' young son. Lincoln is a complex U.S. president who is revered by many Americans for guiding the Northern states to a victory in the Civil War and thereby becoming the father of a new nation, one that was premised upon and promised to uphold the ideals of liberty and freedom for all men regardless of race. As such, Lincoln stands as a president who could see beyond the turmoil of his present situation and recover and more broadly interpret America's founding ideals of justice for all in a materializing, reconfigured nation. Yet to achieve this ideal prevision of America, to arrive at this moral U.S. "we" of who "we" might become, Lincoln was also the first U.S. president to suspend the right of habeas corpus (the right not to be held indefinitely without charge). Lincoln, then, denied individual civil liberties to Americans as a means toward ensuring his vision of collective liberty—of justice for all—by providing security for all. This was how Lincoln domestically solved the problem of the relationship between justice and security during the Civil War.

Almost a century and a half later, President George W. Bush seems to harken back to Lincoln's domestic solution to solve America's international problem of balancing justice and security in its war on terror.[7] In the U.S.-led war in Afghanistan in 2001, the Bush administration distinguished between enemy soldiers and "enemy combatants," the latter suspected of being terrorists somehow linked to the al Qaeda network. These enemy combatants were not treated as prisoners of war but instead shipped to the U.S. military base at Guantánamo Bay, Cuba, where the majority of them have been held without charge ever since. U.S. treatment of these suspected terrorists violates not only the Geneva Convention but also the U.S. constitutional requirement of habeas corpus. But the Bush administration maintains that the suspension of the civil liberties of these terrorist suspects is necessary for the security of the United States in its war against terror.

Over the next three years, the Bush administration extended the scope of its preemptive justice measures from deeds to (pre)thoughts. The U.S. Department of Justice did so domestically by claiming that U.S. citizen Jose Padilla (also known as Abdulla al-Muharjir) was involved in the initial stages of a plan to explode a dirty bomb somewhere in the United States, labeling him an enemy combatant which enabled his transfer from the criminal justice system to the military justice system, and holding him indefinitely without charge since May 2002.[8] Defending the Bush administration's handling of Padilla, Deputy Defense Secretary Paul Wolfowitz explained, "There was not an actual plan. We stopped this man in the initial planning stages," meaning that a conviction in criminal court would have been virtually impossible to attain.[9] Padilla, then, is being held for what the Bush administration thinks he thought, not for what the Bush administration can prove he was about to do, much less did. The criminal act here has not just moved from the deed to the thought; it has moved from the conscious thought to the unconscious one. For, as Wolfowitz puts it, "There was not an actual plan." To the extent that consciousness comes into play here at all, it relates not to Padilla's prethought plan but to the Bush administration's moral geography of terror as the consciousness through which all acts and now thoughts and prethoughts must be first securitized and then and only then formally judged.

The Bush administration mobilized its moral geography of terror to securitize the unconscious not only domestically but also internationally. President Bush extended the scope of preemptive justice internationally when, on June 1, 2002, he announced what has come to be called the Bush Doctrine of Preemption. Claiming that America's cold war practices of deterrence are insufficient in America's new war on terror and making a veiled reference to Iraqi President Saddam Hussein, the president explained,

> Containment is not possible when unbalanced dictators with weapons of mass destruction can deliver those weapons on missiles or secretly provide them to terrorist allies. We cannot defend America and our friends by hoping for the best. We cannot put our faith in the word of tyrants, who solemnly sign non-proliferation treaties, and then systematically break them. If we wait for threats to fully materialize, we will have waited too long. . . . [O]ur security will require all Americans to be forward-looking and resolute, to be ready for *preemptive action* when necessary to defend our liberty and to defend our lives.[10]

By March 2003, the Bush Doctrine of Preemption became the principle justification for the U.S.-led war in Iraq, known as Operation Iraqi Freedom. As the president explained in his March 19, 2003 address to the nation,

> The people of the United States and our friends and allies will not live at the mercy of an outlaw regime that threatens the peace with weapons of mass murder. We will meet that threat now, with our Army, Air Force, Navy, Coast Guard and Marines, so that we do not have to meet it later with armies of fire fighters and police and doctors on the streets of our cities.[11]

President Bush's justification for his war in Iraq, then, rests not only in his claim that Saddam Hussein had weapons of mass destruction but in an accompanying claim about the unthinkable distress Saddam's presumed (pre)thoughts of using such weapons against the United States causes to Americans. As such, Operation Iraqi Freedom seems to be less about securing the freedom of the Iraqi people from Saddam's brutal regime than it is about securing the freedom of the American people from the horrific previsions of what their government imagined Saddam had in store for them in the not-too-distant future.

Lincoln's and Bush's beliefs are eerily echoed in the PreCrime slogan, "To insure that that which keeps us safe also keeps us free." That the Marks' young son is stabbing Lincoln through the eyes suggests that Lincoln's (and PreCrime's and now maybe Bush's) vision and prevision of America as a land of liberty achieved through the suspension of individual civil rights needs to be reenvisioned. That Lincoln's eyeless face becomes this now fatherless son's mask for his school recitation of the Gettysburg Address confirms that this change in perspective is imminent.

The second way the opening sequence implies the limitations of prevision is in its naming of the precogs. Viewers learn that the precogs are named Arthur, Dashiell, and Agatha. Because the blue-washed film of *Minority Report* constantly reminds viewers of the film noir genre, it doesn't take much thought to realize where the precogs' names came from: Sir Arthur Conan Doyle, Dashiell Hammett, and Agatha Christie. What is striking about the precogs' names is that they are not the names of famous detectives but of famous detective writers. They are the authors of stories rather than the assemblers of facts. This makes perfect sense when we consider the relationship between the precogs and the police in which the precogs generate images that Chief Inspector Anderton scans for clues and assembles into a coherent timeline that predicts future injustices. But by naming the precogs after authors rather than detectives, the film suggests two things. First, it suggests that, like good detective novels, precog visions are (potentially) fictitious in nature. Second, it suggests that, just as these three detective writers use different styles to tell distinct stories, so too might the three individual precogs tell the same story in different ways. Indeed, they might even tell different stories.

It is this possibility that the precogs might disagree, that they might generate conflicting previsions, that Anderton discovers when the precogs predict that Anderton himself will commit murder in three days' time. As Anderton learns from the cocreator of the PreCrime system, the eccentric Iris Hineman (Lois Smith), while the precogs are never collectively wrong, Agatha sometimes sees things differently, producing a *minority report* of the predicted crime. If Anderton, who is predicted to kill a man he has never even heard of much less met, can prove that Agatha sees his future differently, then he might be able to clear his name and escape eternity in the Hall of Containment.

Of course, all this presents problems for Anderton. Anderton is a true believer in the PreCrime system, a system to which he has devoted himself since the disappearance and presumed murder of his young son, Sean. Had PreCrime existed when Sean was taken, Anderton convinces himself, Sean would be alive today. Sean's disappearance and presumed death not only led to Anderton's devotion to PreCrime but also to the breakup of his marriage and his addiction to narcotics. Instead of enjoying his white, happy, heterosexual nuclear family as he did in the past, Anderton now revisits them as homemade holographic movies that he interacts with in his drug-induced state. Now that Anderton stands accused by the only thing he has left in the world to believe in and the only legal channel for this mourning father's vigilante impulses—the justice of PreCrime—he will either end up losing his (un)conscious life (by being haloed for his crime) or losing his faith in PreCrime (because if Anderton doesn't commit the predicted murder, then this means the system is not perfect).

As a criminal on the run, Anderton ceases to be the "I" and "eyes" of the state and instead comes under the constant surveillance of other state eyes. There are those of Anderton's fellow officers and Detective Witwer. But more menacing is the constant mechanical surveillance of Anderton's eyes: routine public transportation ID scans, billboard scans leading to personally directed advertisements, shop scans that lead to sales pitches based on his purchasing history. But most disturbing of all are the mechanical spiders used by the police to ID all warm bodies in dangerous locations, like the tenement Anderton hides out in.

John Anderton's only hope of evading detection by the state is to stop being John Anderton. And to do that, John Anderton must "swap" his "I" and his "eyes" for those of another. In a sleazy backstreet operation, this is precisely what Anderton does. It is while Anderton is blindfolded, shielding his new eyes from light so that he does not go blind, that the spiders invade his building to check all I's/eyes. When Anderton's clever attempts to evade them ultimately fail, the spiders shine a bright light into his left eye. This not only confirms that, to the state, Anderton is a new/another man; it fulfills an earlier prophesy told to Anderton by his eyeless drug dealer, "In the land of the blind, the one-eyed man is king." When Anderton (who has kept his old eyes so he can use them to break into the temple and steal Agatha to download his minority report) loses one of his old eyes down a drain, the prophesy's fulfillment is repeated. But in repeating it, this means that the new Anderton is a mix of his old vision and his new vision, allowing him to see what he needs to see in the past, albeit differently. Indeed, Agatha's persistent question to Anderton is "Can you see?" With these eyes, Anderton ultimately does.

But before Anderton can see what Agatha wants him to see, he must settle his own fate. Anderton ultimately succeeds in downloading Agatha's previsions about his predicted crime. But to his bitter disappointment, Agatha did not see events in Anderton's future any differently than did Arthur and Dashiell. Agatha does not provide Anderton with a minority report, or at least not the sort of minority report Anderton expected. Instead of offering an alternative vision of Anderton's crime (for she has none), Agatha repeatedly tells Anderton, "You can choose," which amounts to a minority report on predestination itself and raises the question, "If you know your future, are you doomed to fulfill it?"

Mindful of his future, Anderton does choose. When Anderton discovers that his intended victim is the abductor of his missing son Sean, Anderton tells Agatha, "I *am* going to kill this man." But when he comes face to face with his intended victim, a tearful Anderton instead chooses to arrest the man, only then to discover that the whole thing was a setup. Anderton's intended victim was promised money for his family in exchange for his own death at Anderton's hand. Desperate for the money, the man grabs Anderton's gun, still in Anderton's hand, and shoots himself. This suicide looks exactly like the murder the precogs predicted. And for this "crime," Anderton is eventually arrested, haloed, and contained.

What we have at this point, then, are two failures in the PreCrime system that are both located on the side of prevision rather than vision. On the one hand, because the precogs produce only images but no text, they either cannot always distinguish between or cannot communicate the distinction between murder and suicide, thereby leading to the conviction of an innocent man like John Anderton. But even more importantly, prevision fails because when would-be criminals know their own future, they can choose to act differently. In Anderton's case, this means deciding not to kill his son's killer; in Saddam's case, this means not stockpiling and/or using weapons of mass destruction. Overall, what this means is that, under particular circumstances, previsions are not the same thing as predestination.

Thus, using prevision, even the precogs cannot always answer in the affirmative to Agatha's insistent question, "Can you see?" Through his encounters with Agatha, eye swaps, and lost faith in PreCrime, Anderton finally does see what Agatha hoped he would—that his boss Lamar Burgess (Max von Sydow) murdered her mother Ann Lively who threatened the future of PreCrime because she wanted Agatha back. Anderton solves the mystery of Ann Lively's disappearance (which is really a death) because, this time, Agatha does have a minority report. But it is a minority report that can only be understood when looked at through a different "eye/I."

Agatha's question to Anderton, "Can you see?," then, might be restated as "Can you become someone who can see otherwise?" Anderton does so only when he is forced to, when this would-be criminal must swap out his original eyes to avoid detection by the state. Even so, this one-eyed man of *Minority Report* is never quite king, especially an enlightened one. For while Anderton may be our action hero—our man on the run throughout most of the film—he isn't really much of a detective. He was wrong about PreCrime, he was wrong about his boss (whom he trusted) and Detective Witwer (whom he mistrusted), and he was initially wrong about Ann Lively's death.

Minority Report isn't about this clever man saving the day; it is about his repeated failure to see things clearly and his search for clarity in all the wrong places (PreCrime, drugs, memories of his lost family). Strikingly, every time Anderton loses the trail, it is a woman who sets him straight. Agatha pleads with him to see her prevision about her mother's death properly. Iris Hineman informs Anderton that there is such a thing as a minority report and that it is always held by the most gifted of the precogs, the girl. And Anderton's ex-wife Laura (Kathryn Morris) takes no time to figure out that Lamar Burgess has betrayed Anderton, at which point she rescues him from prison and convinces Anderton's ex-colleagues to cooperate in a plot to expose Burgess. *Minority Report*, then, locates invention (Iris), knowledge (Agatha), and meaningful action (Laura) not in our male hero but in the feminine. For without the feminine guiding Anderton at every turn, one-eyed or not, he wouldn't see a thing. Instead, Anderton would be more like the one-eyed soldier in the final shot of the haunting Vietnam War film *The Quiet American*, a figure who symbolizes a loss of (international) perspective rather than a reenvisioning of the world through the knowledge that vision and prevision ultimately fail.

Minority Report tells us that the choice between these two very different ways of seeing and these two very different previsions of a future moral America(n) is "ours." "We" (as a U.S. "we") can choose. "We" can be moral America(ns) not just by refusing to commit crimes but, more importantly, by insisting on seeing the world—including our own world—differently. To do this, we must begin by reconsidering the relationship between justice and security. "We" must admit not only that vision (surveillance of what people do: e.g., intelligence that claimed to show Saddam Hussein stockpiling weapons of mass destruction) and prevision (surveillance of what people [should not] think: e.g., Jose Padilla's not-yet plan to explode a dirty bomb in the United States or Saddam's unissued threat to use weapons of mass destruction against the United States) fundamentally fail to provide security, they also fundamentally fail to provide justice. "We" must see that the PreCrime dream of securing the body by securing the unconscious always leads to dehumanization, whether through the deification of troubled "children" (like the precogs) or the detention of "I"s whose "eyes/windows to the soul" may have been misread (be these of the detainees of Camp X-Ray or Jose Padilla).

In making its case against equating "I"s with "eyes"—identity with the unconscious—the film implies yet another way the state might act immorally. When the state accuses someone of a future crime, might it not set in motion a chain of events that actually leads to the fulfillment of that accusation? Is this not what happened to Anderton, a man who literally ran into his victim because he was running away from the state? As one reviewer put it, "Take away the accusation, and there would be no question of him [Anderton] committing a criminal act. The prediction drives the act—a self-fulfilling prophesy."[12] Even though Anderton did not fulfill this prophesy (he arrested his intended victim, who then committed suicide), the point remains. Accusations based upon an equation of identity with the unconscious are dangerous. In Bush's war on terror, more than anything else it is the administration's exercise of preemptive justice that seems to cement the sympathies of at least some of the accused with the terrorists they are purported to sympathize with. If we can see this, then who "we" might become is not only a moral America(n) but a more secure one.

Overall, *Minority Report*'s moral grammar of war is one that demands a reenvisioning of who "we" think we were and who "we" think we are. It is in the visions and previsions of Abraham Lincoln and now George W. Bush through their questionable decision to attain state freedom by suspending individual freedoms—including freedom of (pre)thought—that "we" need to look at again. On this, the film is clear. What it is less clear on is the role the feminine plays in making this reworking of the relationship between justice and security possible.

As pointed out earlier, it seems to be Agatha's insistent question, "Can you see?" that enables the change in Anderton's and ultimately America's perspective. It is the feminine that makes America's moral reenvisioning of itself, the world, and itself in the world possible. The film implies that to become a moral America(n), the U.S. "we" would be well advised to take careful note of what the feminine is showing it.

Yet even as it portrays the feminine as innovative, intelligent, and active, *Minority Report* caricatures each of its female characters though gender stereotypes so much so that the film at best sends mixed messages about the feminine and what it wants "us" to see. Iris, the coinventor of PreCrime, is not just cast as an innovative scientist and (as her name implies) a messenger to the gods (for it is she who tells Anderton of the minority reports). Pictured as she is living in her secluded home protected by killer plants, Iris is not so much colorful as dangerously eccentric. Furthermore, we learn that it was never Iris's intention to use the precogs to create the perfect justice system. Her eye/iris was not meant to link the unconscious to criminality. Instead, looking through her eye/iris of compassion, Iris's desire was to save these children who became precogs. Iris, then, is less a scientist than she is motherly humanist, which adds to her disruptive character.

Agatha, the seer of the future and the keeper of past knowledge, is portrayed as innocence itself. She is a troubled child who through no fault of her own sees a troubling future. But in her characterization, Agatha's innocence is taken to the extreme. For more than anything else, Agatha resembles an infant. She lives in the temple with the other precogs, cradled in a womb-like pool of what might be amniotic fluid or mother's milk, dressed in what the film's costume designer referred to as "an embryonic kind of covering."[13] Even though it is Agatha whose minority reports have the capacity to destroy the state's system of justice, this disruptive potential is downplayed by casting her as utterly dependent, inside and outside the temple. On the inside, she is nurtured on a mix of mother's milk (drugs) and motherly love (by her caretaker). On the outside, she is dressed and walked by her abductor Anderton and, after the demise of PreCrime, cocooned in a remote island home with the twins. Nor is it Agatha's intention to bring down PreCrime. Rather, her repeated question to Anderton, "Can you see?" is a plea for his help in bringing her mother's murderer to justice, not a desire to dismantle the justice system itself.

Finally, Anderton's wife Laura, who is the feminine embodiment of meaningful action, is always first and foremost characterized as wife and mother. She first appears in Anderton's home movie holograms as his wife, after establishing that she is also the mother of his child. Later, the present Laura, ex-wife to John, explains that she left her husband because every time she looked at him she saw their dead son. The final shot of the film shows the future Laura reunited with her husband John and pregnant with their future child. As these cameos of Laura illustrate, regardless of how pivotal Laura is to bringing down the PreCrime system, she is always tied historically, narratively, and visually to reproduction. Reproduction—and indeed, rebirth—is her most meaningful act.

Taken together, the three main female characters of *Minority Report* are all stereotypically feminine. They are all introduced to viewers first in a home setting. Their desires are all familial: to help troubled children, to get justice for a mother, to get justice for a husband. And their ambitions are private, not public. What this means is that no matter how much they privately assist Anderton in his public quest to dismantle PreCrime, and they enable America(ns) to rethink the relationship between justice and security, what is always brought to our attention about these women is that they secure what is traditionally domestic—the white, happy heterosexual domestic family.

This is no small contribution to the state. For it is upon this foundation that the literal and figurative rebirth of the nation is made possible.[14] But by functioning as homebodies, don't the women of *Minority Report* resemble women of World War II, animating traditional U.S. imaginaries of women relegated to the role of homefront, however much this role fails to capture what they are really up to?[15] As such, don't these women ultimately lack credit for undertaking meaningful moral action and find themselves cast as stagehands, marginalized to the wings in the patriarchal performance of the nation's rebirth? This is, after all, John Anderton's/Tom Cruise's movie about a father's desperate search for his lost son/fatherhood.

These concerns seem to be all the more convincing when we note that *Minority Report* ends for John Anderton very much where it began—with a happy holographic image of family come to life, first technically and then biologically. It is a sentimental ending, with Anderton lovingly stroking Laura's pregnant belly. Doesn't this mean that in *Minority Report* who "we" might become is merely a future echo of who we think "we" were—the foundational family of World War II, a family firmly (believed to be) controlled through patriarchal relationships?

The answers to these questions are both "yes" and "no." For what we find in *Minority Report* is that the feminine is cast in not just one role, but two. Through the film's use of stereotypes, the feminine functions as we have long grown accustomed to feminine functioning—as that which secures the home. But by making the feminine more innovative, intelligent, and meaningfully active than its male lead, the film makes a claim to the disruptive potential of the feminine to insecure the state.[16] However seemingly contradictory this dual casting of the feminine may seem to be, I would argue that it is utterly consistent. For what this future feminine does is combine what we think we knew about the feminine in the past (a traditional figure who always fought for home and family) and what we think we know about the contemporary feminine (a feminist backlash caricature of the feminine as a figure who seems to only fight for herself, albeit under the guise of fighting for her family; think about *Fatal Attraction*). By combining the stereotypical role of the past feminine with its stereotypical disruptive potential in its contemporary role, *Minority Report* directs this disruptive potential away from its own seeming selfish private aims to more collective and ultimately public/national aims. What this means in *Minority Report* is that the feminine functions to secure the home/nation while insecuring state policies (like homeland security domestically and preemptive justice internationally) that might insecure it. In so doing, it is not only itself safely contained in the home(land); the feminine also contains rather than fuels the vigilante impulses of the masculine (the U.S. "we's" desire for payback expressed in films like *Collateral Damage* or even *In the Bedroom*).

Thanks to this dual function of the feminine, for the home and (as the moral force of the homeland) against anything that might insecure home/nation (including state policies), "our" U.S. character is transformed.

The U.S. "we" emerges as a subject very much like the new John Anderton, who can see differently not because he relies on previsions to see the future or to secure the unconscious for the state. The U.S. "we" can see differently because, like Anderton, it has one eye on the past (one old eye) and one eye on the present (one new eye). This, *Minority Report* tells us, is what it takes to become a moral America(n). And this, it promises, is who "we" might become in the future.

Conclusion

Minority Report draws a devastating picture of the Bush administration's moral geography of terror, its practices of securitizing the unconscious through its policies of preemptive "justice," and its construction of a so-called moral American "we." As such, it stands as a warning to all Americans that justice and security both in the United States and as it is projected by the United States abroad are dangerously out of balance. Who the U.S. "we" might become—and indeed, who it must become—is a nation willing to get this balance right.

How the U.S. "we" can do that is first by reconsidering the relationship between crime and the unconsciousness. It is not possible, *Minority Report* tells us, to police the unconscious by drawing an equivalence between (not) thinking about doing something bad and actually doing something bad. No matter how many times we might be right in our suspicions, preemptive justice is unjust if we are wrong even once. What this means is that while both Lincoln and Bush for a time had the extralegal authority to suspend the individual civil rights of suspected, would-be criminals, neither of them had the moral authority to do so, however well intentioned they claim to have been.

Whether articulated as a failure of the system or a failure of the morally certain (and therefore morally blind) servant of the state, *Minority Report* tells the U.S. "we" that it chose badly when it chose either a system (PreCrime) or a leader (Bush) who believed more firmly in security than in justice. But, as the film tells us, "we" can choose. If the first four years of the Bush administration were a prevision of what was to come, then because "we" already know our future, "we" are/were not condemned to repeat it. The choice is/was "ours." The trajectory for becoming a moral America(n) lies in choosing to live with increased physical insecurity if that means living with increased justice (although at the moment U.S. security policies create more insecurity than they do security). By making this choice, future stories about who "we" might become can sustain a positive image of moral America(ns) in ways we failed to sustain in Lincoln's time or in Bush's war on terror.

But at what cost? As articulated in *Minority Report*, there are serious constraints on our moral choices because there are serious constraints on who this U.S. "we" is allowed to be. *Minority Report* always constrains the feminine. For while the feminine is depicted as intelligent, innovative, and active, it is also always somehow domesticated/contained/constrained. This occurs in *Minority Report* by resorting to feminine stereotypes that construct Iris, Agatha, and Laura as an unruly U.S. home(front) while keeping them firmly within a discourse of home.

It is surely a step forward that *Minority Report* portrays the feminine as active and inventive rather than as erased (as it appears in other post-9/11 films linked to the war on terror like *Behind Enemy Lines* and *Black Hawk Down*) or discredited (as in *Collateral Damage* and *In the Bedroom*). But how it reactivates the feminine is utterly problematic. For this reactivation is never an end in itself; it is always a means toward reenabling masculine authority in the name of reestablishing justice—to allow John Anderton to finally figure things out so he can save "us" from the system of PreCrime.

By mixing the domesticated feminine who secures the U.S. home(front) with the public feminine who insecures the U.S. state, *Minority Report* does succeed in curbing the vigilante impulses of its male hero. But by constraining the feminine within this domestic space, *Minority Report* also denies the feminine a reliable foundation for political resistance. For this political resistance must always be activated by and seen through (at least one eye of) the masculine, the figure who ultimately rules the home(land).

Agatha's treatment by Anderton in the film serves as our fictitious example of contained political resistance; Colin Powell's treatment by the Bush administration serves as our example of contained political resistance in the war on terror. Think about it. Reading the script of *Minority Report* onto the Bush administration's war on terror, we find three precogs in Bush's first term—the always-in-agreement twins Secretary of Defense Donald Rumsfeld and Deputy Secretary of Defense Paul Wolfowitz and the often-dissenting Secretary of State Colin Powell. It is Powell who holds the minority report on the Bush administration not (only) because of his over-coded minority status as both an American racial minority and as an intelligent and innovative thinker but also because he has consistently been located in the outsider, feminized position in that administration. First overruled when trying to build more genuine international support and a worldwide coalition against al Qaeda in the run-up to the bombing of Afghanistan and then in the run-up to Gulf War II, and made to recant his assessment that Saddam Hussein had no weapons of mass destruction that could pose a threat to the United States, Powell's minority report has always been firmly contained/constrained/domesticated by the hegemonic narrative of the Bush administration. And we can all see where that has gotten us.

The case of Colin Powell is but one example. But the general point here is clear. For what all of this means is that if the U.S. "we" is to redress the Bush administration's dubious balance between justice and security and rewrite its moral geography of terror so that the securitization of the unconscious is politically, legally, and morally impermissible, it had better entertain as many minority reports as it can get its I's/eyes on. And that will require the U.S. "we" to decouple the Bush administration's prevision of U.S. security from its strategy of securitizing unruly bodies—be they unlikely terrorist, underrated officials, or otherwise feminized characters—by containing them in a hegemonic logic of home.

Notes

Thanks to Annette Davison, Mick Dillon, Anne-Marie Fortier, Mark Lacy, Sasha Roseneil, Jackie Stacey, Charles Weber, and two anonymous reviewers for their comments on this essay, and to Alana Chazan, Maya Joseph, Anne Kirkham, Evan Rowe, Amy Sodaro, Masha Spaic, and Roberto Trad for discussing this material with me in my "Moral Grammars of War" course at the New School University, Spring 2003.

1. George W. Bush, "President Bush Delivers Graduate Speech at West Point," June 1, 2002, http://www.whitehouse.gov/news/releases/2002/06/2002061-3.html (my italics).

2. Philip K. Dick, *Selected Stories* (New York: Pantheon, 2002).

3. That the timing and implications of Spielberg's film seem to go against what the director intended is supported by Spielberg's comments to *The New York Times*. As Jeremy Lott reported on June 17, 2002, "According to a recent Matt Drudge leak of a *New York Times* story, Spielberg has declared himself 'on the president's side' in Bush's efforts to 'root out those individuals who are a danger to our way of living.'" See Jeremy Lott, "Prophecy and Paranoia," June 17, 2002, http://reason.com/hod/j1061702.shtml, accessed August 4, 2006. Also see David Edelstein, "Blame Runner: *Minority Report* is a Fabulous, Witty Totalitarian Nightmare," June 21, 2002, http://slate.msn.com/toolbar.aspx?action= print&id+2067225 August 4, 2006; and Dahlia Lithwick, "Hiding the Dirty Bomber from the US Constitution: The Bush administration establishes a Department of Precrime," June 11, 2002, http://slate.msn.com/toolbar.aspx?action= print&id=2066866 (accessed August 4, 2006).

4. Michael Shapiro, *Violent Cartographies: Mapping Cultures of War* (Minneapolis: University of Minnesota Press, 1997), p. 16 and John Agnew, *Geopolitics: Re-Visioning World Politics*, 2nd ed. (New York: Routledge, 2003), p. 9.

5. Agnew (2003) and Cynthia Weber, *Moral America: Contemporary Politics and Film from 9/11 to Gulf War II* (New York: New York University Press, 2005).

6. Thanks to Alana Chazon for this point.

7. First Lady Laura Bush explicitly drew a parallel between her husband and President Lincoln and their efforts to achieve both security and freedom when she addressed the 2004 Republican National Convention in New York City. Making a link to both the Civil War and to the Second World War, Mrs. Bush told delegates, "No American President ever wants to go to war. Abraham Lincoln didn't want to go to war, but he knew saving the Union required it. Franklin Roosevelt didn't want to go to war—but he knew defeating tyranny demanded it. And my husband didn't want to go to war, but he knew the safety and security of America and the world depended on it. . . . And I was there when my husband had to decide. Once again, as in our parents' generation, America had to make the tough choices, the hard decisions, and lead the world toward greater security and freedom." Laura Bush, "Remarks by First Lady Laura Bush to the Republican National Convention," (2004), http://www.whitehouse. gove.news/releases/2004/08/print/20040831-15. html, August 4, 2006.

8. For further discussion of the implications of the shift from civil to military tribunals, see Engin F. Isin and Kim Rygiel in this volume.

9. Lithwick (2002).

10. Bush (2002), my italics.

11. George W. Bush, "President Bush Addresses the Nation," March 19, 2003, http://www.whitehouse.gov/news/release/2003/03/20030219-17.html.

12. James Berardinelli, "*Minority Report*," June 21, 2002, http://movie-reviews.colossus.net/movies/m/minority_report.html, accessed August 4, 2006.

13. *Minority Report*, directed by Steven Spielberg, Twentieth Century Fox (2002).

14. Sonya Michel, "American Women and the Discourse of the Democratic Family in World War II," in *Behind Enemy Lines: Gender and the Two World Wars*, ed. Margaret Randolph Higonnet et al. (New Haven: Yale University Press, 1989), pp. 154–167; Lauren Berlant, *The Queen of America Goes to Washington City: Essays on Sex and Citizenship* (Durham: Duke University Press, 1997); Stephanie Coontz, *The Way We Never Were: American Families and the Nostalgia Trap* (New York: Basic Books, 2000).

15. Cynthia Weber, "Flying Planes Can Be Dangerous," *Millennium*, 31: 1 (2002): 129–147.

16. On the disruptive potential of the feminine, see Luce Irigaray, *Speculum of the Other Woman*, trans. Gillian C. Gill (Ithaca, NY: Cornell University Press, 1985).

CHAPTER 7

THE BIOPOLITICS OF SECURITY: OIL, EMPIRE, AND THE SPORTS UTILITY VEHICLE

David Campbell

"Others" at Home and Abroad Post-9/11

In the wake of 9/11 the Bush administration has called upon established foreign policy discourses to cement the idea of a nation at war.[1] Given the amorphous and often virtual nature of the "war on terror," in which the adversary is by definition largely unseen, the association of other resistant elements with terrorism has become a mechanism for materializing the threat. Notorious in this regard was the Bush administration's linking of internal and external threats by aligning individual drug use at home with support for terrorism abroad. In itself, this is not a new argument, with alleged links to terrorism having been featured in previous episodes of the U.S. "war on drugs."[2] However, the Bush administration went one step further by making a causal connection between individual behavior and international danger. The Office for National Drug Control Policy (ONDCP) launched hard-hitting advertisements in which the social choices of hedonistic youngsters were said to directly enrich and enable terrorists threatening the United States.[3]

This argument sought to discipline domestic behavior by linking it to external danger and was controversial. One ironic response, first made by conservative columnist Arianna Huffington, was to argue that if funding terrorism was the concern then "soccer moms" driving sports utility vehicles (SUVs) were more easily linked to the problem through the increased revenues for Middle East oil producers their reliance on an uneconomical family vehicle generated. Huffington described how two Hollywood producers had written spoof scripts for advertisements that parodied the ONDCP campaign. Linking one's consumer choice with the international threat of the moment, one of these scripts declared the SUV parked in a family's driveway was "the biggest weapon of mass destruction."[4]

Huffington's column generated considerable debate, and a new lobby group—the Detroit Project—was launched so the advertisements could be made and broadcast as part of a campaign to link improved fuel efficiency with national security. Although most television stations refused to air the commercials (demonstrating a corporate fear of controversy that compromises free speech claims), they garnered much attention, and came to highlight the cultural clash between SUV manufacturers and users and those concerned about the vehicles' communal effects.[5]

This controversy raged in the run-up to the U.S.-led invasion of Iraq in 2003 and was part of a larger discourse about the relationship between oil and security. While the ONDCP campaign targeted the casual narcotic user, the Detroit Project advertisements in effect saw the United States as an addict whose oil habit could only be satisfied by an act of international crime. Both arguments sought to individualize responsibility by positing a tight causal connection between personal choice and political effect, thereby following in a long line of issues whose social and political context have been subsumed by the politics of individualization. While the Detroit Project advertisements simplified issues in a manner akin to the ONDCP campaign, in the context of an attempt to understand the relationship between oil and security, they raise more difficult issues with respect to the relationship between the internal and external.

While individual SUV owner-drivers cannot be said to directly endorse terrorism simply as a result of automotive choice, it is the case (as will be demonstrated below) that the SUV has come to underpin U.S. dependence on imported oil. In turn, this dependence underpins the U.S. strategic interest in global oil supply, especially in the Middle East, where the American military presence has generated such animus. As a result, the SUV symbolizes the need for the United States to maintain its global military reach. Given the dangers this global military presence provokes, it might therefore be possible to say the SUV is one of America's greatest national security threats. This chapter seeks to explore the validity of those connections and claims as part of a critical examination and retheorization of the relationship between oil and security. Its aim is to conceptualize the relationship between individual choices and geopolitical effects without adopting or endorsing the moral leveling and individualization of responsibility in the crude arguments that demonize certain behaviors in the correlation of drugs, oil, and terror.

The starting point for this rethinking is that the interconnections between what appear as individual consumer preferences for certain vehicles and their geopolitical effects should be regarded as part of a complex called "automobility." In John Urry's assessment, "automobility can be conceptualized as a self-organizing autopoietic, non-linear system that spreads worldwide, and includes cars, car-drivers, roads, petroleum supplies and many novel objects, technologies and signs."[6] As a complex system, automobility has profoundly affected the social and geographical structure of daily life. In the environment it has spawned, the territorialities of home, leisure, and work have been "unbundled" such that urbanism has been "splintered."[7]

While automobility is recognized as a world wide system, and notwithstanding the occasional references to oil rich states, petroleum supplies, and import dependence, the focus of the literature is principally domestic with relatively little attention to the global security context.[8] The theme of this chapter is that such a concern is conceptually limited, and that in conjunction with the unbundling of domestic territorialities we need to appreciate the way (especially though not exclusively in the United States) the "unbounded" consumption of automobility produces an "unbordered" sense of the state in which security interests extend well beyond the national homeland.

At the same time, this deterritorialization of the space of automobility and its security effects does not mean we exist above and beyond territory. To the contrary, the globalization of automobility and its security implications results in the creation of new borderlands with uneven consequences. These borderlands are conventionally understood as distant, wild places of insecurity where foreign intervention will be necessary to ensure domestic interests are secured. They include zones of exploration and the spaces traversed by pipelines, both of which involve the further marginalization of impoverished indigenous communities. The fate of these people and places is subsumed by the privilege accorded a resource central to the American way of life, the security of which is regarded as a fundamental strategic issue.[9]

However, if we understand borderlands as spatially disparate contact zones where practices intersect, actors and issues meld into one another, and conflicts potentially arise, then the translocal borderlands of automobility encompass networks that connect cultures of individual consumption with practices of global security through multiple sits of materialization and territorialization at "home" and "abroad." As a consequence, the argument here wants not only to supplement the automobility literature's focus on the "inside," but also to overcome the way arguments about resource conflicts emphasize the "outside." Instead of there being two parallel approaches, each understanding their concerns as driving one way, this article brings the question of security into the heart of the concern with automobility to demonstrate how these practices contribute to the production of national identity.

The first step in the argument is to reconceptualize the relationship between foreign policy, security, and identity so we can appreciate what is at stake in linking internal behaviors with external threats at this juncture in American politics and set the grounds for a spatial understanding that goes beyond "the domestic" versus "the foreign." The second step is to consider how the domain of the cultural, social, and political can be conceptualized so that the complexity of the interconnections can be appreciated. Central to this is an understanding of the way "domestic" law, regulation, and policy work to create the geopolitics of identity in the new borderlands of automobility. This will be illustrated in the chapter's third and fourth sections that tell the story of oil consumption, automobility, and regulation in the United States. Regulation refers to more than governmental policy and encompasses the question of the production of desire. As such, the questions of geopolitics and identity are linked to a cultural politics of desire that exists beyond the institutionalized sites of the state, and the account of the SUV's rise to popularity as family transport in the United States will show this. The SUV is the icon through which the role of security to automobility can be best understood because it can be appreciated as a cultural site that transgresses the inside and outside and—through conceptualizations of security it both embodies and invokes—because the SUV folds the foreign back into the domestic thereby rendering each problematic.

Together these elements will demonstrate that the predominant representation of oil as simply an external, material cause of insecurity is insufficient for a more comprehensive and nuanced understanding of contemporary geopolitics. However, while this chapter was prompted by and written in the context of the U.S.-led invasion of Iraq and its aftermath, the argument is not seeking to explain the causes of and reasons for that invasion.[10] Instead, it seeks to articulate an understanding of the conditions of possibility for the specific decisions that led to the invasion as a particular moment of U.S. (and allied) global strategy. The effect of that strategy is to "reborder" the state in a multitude of cultural and political sites as a way of negotiating the social forces that have splintered both conventional locales and frames of reference.

Foreign Policy, Security, and Identity:
From Geopolitics to Biopolitics

As an imagined community, the identity of a state is the effect of formalized practices and ritualized acts that operate in its name or in the service of its ideals. Enabled by shifting our theoretical commitments from a belief in pre-given subjects to a concern with the problematic of subjectivity, this understanding renders foreign policy as a boundary-producing political performance in which the spatial domains of inside/outside, self/other, and domestic/foreign are constituted through the writing of threats as externalized dangers.

The narratives of primary and stable identities that continue to govern much of the social sciences obscure such an understanding. They limit analysis to a concern with the domestic influences on foreign policy, which allows for the influence of the internal but assumes that the external remains a realm of necessity that presents itself to the pre-given state and its agents. In contrast, by assuming that the identity of the state is performatively constituted, we can argue that there are no foundations prior to the operation of the problematic of identity/difference in the determination of inside/outside and self/other. Identity is constituted in relation to difference and difference is constituted in relation to identity, which means that the "state," the "international system," and the "dangers" to each are coeval in their construction.

Over time, of course, ambiguity comes to be disciplined, contingency is fixed, and dominant meanings are established. In the history of U.S. foreign policy—regardless of the radically different contexts in which it has operated—the formalized practices and ritualized acts of security discourse have worked to produce a conception of the United States in which freedom, liberty, law, democracy, individualism, faith, order, prosperity, and civilization are claimed to exist because of the constant struggle with and often violent overcoming of opponents said to embody tyranny, oppression, anarchy, totalitarianism, collectivism, atheism, and barbarism.

This record demonstrates that the boundary-producing political performance of foreign policy does more than inscribe a geopolitical marker on a map. The construction of social space also involves an axiological dimension in which the delineation of an inside from an outside also gives rise to a moral hierarchy that renders the domestic superior and the foreign inferior. Foreign policy thus incorporates an ethical power of segregation in its performance of identity/difference. While this produces a geography of "foreign" (even "evil") others in conventional terms, it also requires a disciplining of "domestic" elements on the inside that challenge the sense of self being produced. This is achieved through exclusionary practices in which resistant elements to a secure identity on the "inside" are linked through a discourse of "danger" with threats identified and located on the "outside." Though global in scope these effects are national in their legitimation.[11]

The ONDCP drugs and terror campaign was an overt example of this sort of exclusionary practice. However, the boundary-producing political performances of foreign policy operate within a global context where relations of sovereignty are changing. Although Michael Hardt and Antonio Negri have overplayed the transition from modern sovereignty to imperial sovereignty in *Empire*, there is little doubt that new relations of power and identity are present. According to Hardt and Negri, in our current condition:

> Empire establishes no territorial center of power and does not rely on fixed boundaries or barriers. It is a decentered and deterritorializing apparatus of rule that progressively incorporates the entire global realm within its open, expanding frontiers. Empire manages hybrid identities, flexible hierarchies, and plural exchanges through modulating networks of command. The distinct national colors of the imperialist map of the world have merged and blended in the imperial global rainbow.[12]

As shall be argued here, the sense of fading national colors is being resisted by the reassertion of national identity boundaries through foreign policy's writing of danger in a range of cultural sites. Nonetheless, this takes place within the context of flow, flexibility, and reterritorialization summarized by Hardt and Negri. Moreover, these transformations are part and parcel of change in the relations of production. As Hardt and Negri declare, "in the postmodernization of the global economy, the creation of wealth tends ever more toward what we will call biopolitical production, the production of social life itself, in which the economic, the political, and the cultural increasingly overlap and invest one another."[13] While the implied periodization of the term "postmodernization" renders it problematic, the notion of biopolitics, with its connecting and penetrative networks across and through all domains of life, opens up new possibilities for conceptualizing the complex relationships that embrace oil, security, U. S. policy, and the SUV. In Todd Gitlin's words, "the SUV is the place where foreign policy meets the road."[14] It is also the place where the road affects foreign policy. Biopolitics is the concept that best lets us understand how those meetings take place.

Michel Foucault argues biopolitics arrives with the transformation in waging war from the defense of the sovereign to securing the existence of a population. In Foucault's argument, this historical shift means that decisions to fight are made in terms of collective survival, and killing is justified by the necessity of preserving life.[15] It is this centering of the life of the population rather than the safety of the sovereign or the security of territory that is the hallmark of biopolitical power which distinguishes it from sovereign power. Giorgio Agamben has extended the notion through the concept of the administration of life and argues that the defense of life often takes place in a zone of indistinction between violence and the law such that sovereignty can be violated in the name of life.[16] Indeed, the biopolitical privileging of life has provided the rationale for some of the worst cases of mass death, with genocide "understandable" as one group's life violently secured through the demise of another group.[17]

However, the role of biopolitical power in the administration of life is equally obvious and ubiquitous in domains other than the extreme cases of violence or war. The difference between the sovereign and the biopolitical can be understood in terms of the contrast between Foucault's notion of "disciplinary society" and Gilles Deleuze's conception of "the society of control," a distinction that plays an important role in Hardt and Negri's *Empire*. According to Hardt and Negri, in the disciplinary society, "social command is constructed through a diffuse network of *dispositifs* or apparatuses that produce and regulate customs, habits, and productive practices." In the society of control, "mechanisms of command become ever more democratic, ever more immanent to the social field, distributed throughout the brains and bodies of the citizens." This means that the society of control is "characterized by an intensification and generalization of the normalizing apparatuses of disciplinarity that internally animate our common and daily practices, but in contrast to discipline, this control extends well outside the structured sites of social institutions through flexible and fluctuating networks."[18]

Network is, therefore, the prevailing metaphor for social organization in the era of biopolitical power, and it is a conception that permits us to understand how the effects of our actions, choices, and life are propagated beyond the boundaries of our time-space location.[19] It is also a conception that allows us to appreciate how war has come to have a special prominence in producing the political order of liberal societies. Networks, through their extensive connectivity, function in terms of their strategic interactions. This means, "social relations become suffused with considerations of power, calculation, security and threat."[20] As a result, "global biopolitics operates as a strategic game in which the principle of war is assimilated into the very weft and warp of the socio-economic and cultural networks of biopolitical relations."[21]

This concern with biopolitical relations of power in the context of net-worked societies is consistent with the analytical shift to the problematic of subjectivity central to understanding the relationship between foreign policy and identity. That is because both are concerned with "a shift from a preoccupation with physical and isolated entities, whose relations are described largely in terms of interactive exchange, to beings-in-relation, whose structures [are] decisively influenced by patterns of connectivity."[22] At the same time, while we are moving away from physical and isolated entities, the structures that are produced by these network patterns of con-nectivity often appear to be physical and isolated. As Lieven de Cauter argues, we don't live in networks, we live in capsules. Capsules are enclaves and envelopes which function as nodes, hubs, and termini in the various networks and contain a multitude of spaces and scales. These enclaves can include states, gated communities, or vehicles. Though they appear physical and isolated, there is "no network without capsules. The more networking, the more capsules. Ergo: the degree of capsularisation is directly propor-tional to the growth of networks."[23] The result is that biopolitical relations of power will produce new borderlands that transgress conventional under-standings of inside/outside and isolated/connected.

Together these shifts pose a major theoretical challenge to much of the social sciences, which have adhered ontologically to a distinction between the ideal and the material which privileges economistic renderings of complex social assemblages.[24] As we shall see, overcoming this does not mean denying the importance of materialism but, rather, moving beyond the simple con-sideration of objects by reconceptualizing materialism so it is understood as interwoven with cultural, social, and political networks. This means "paying increased attention to the material actually requires a more expan-sive engagement with the immaterial."[25]

The Biopolitics of Oil and Security

Most accounts of the role of oil in U.S. foreign policy embody economistic assumptions, rendering oil in materialistic terms as an independent variable that causes states to behave in particular ways. In the prelude to the inva-sion of Iraq, even the best commentaries represented oil as the real reason motivating the build up to war.[26] Similarly, a Greenpeace campaign pic-tured the (oil) "drums of war" and invited people to read about "what's really behind the war on Iraq."[27] In addition to manifesting specific epis-temological assumptions, these views regard resource geopolitics as pri-marily a question of supply. Before we move beyond this frame of reference to explore what goes unexplained by this focus, we need to nergy security is likely to produce new and intensive forms of insecu- for those in the new resource zones, which are located in some of the t strategically unstable global locations.[34] As a result of this, the United es has been providing increased military support to governments in the pian Basin area, Latin America, and sub-Saharan Africa—regardless of r ideological complexion or human rights record.[35]

A geopolitical understanding of these developments is necessary but not cient. That is because the geopolitical frame focuses solely on the sup- of oil without interrogating the demand for this resource that makes it valuable. Possession of a material resource is meaningless unless social works value that resource. As such, including the demand side, and pay- attention to the politics of consumption as much as the problem of pro- ction, is a first step toward understanding the biopolitics of security.

The Production and Regulation of Oil Consumption in the United States

e value of oil comes from its centrality to one of the defining characteristics U.S. society—mobility. It is mobility that drives U.S. oil consumption as transportation sector accounts for two-thirds of petroleum use. In turn, ssenger vehicles are the largest consumers of oil in the transportation sec- , using 40 percent of the 20 million barrels of oil consumed each day. eir central role in the consumption of oil is only going to expand, as creases in the number, size, and usage of vehicles propel America's petro- um appetite. Of the additional 8.7 million barrels of oil that will be quired each day by 2025, 7.1 million barrels (over 80 percent) is needed fuel the growth in automobility. In global terms this appetite is stagger- g, with the U.S. passenger vehicle fleet alone responsible for one-tenth of petroleum consumption.[36]

There is a regulatory regime designed to address the consumption of oil d the foreign dependence it produces, which, over time, has produced w borders of identity at home and abroad. In response to the oil price hikes the early 1970s, Congress passed the Energy Policy Conservation Act of 975 which, in part, established fuel economy guidelines for vehicles.[37] The overnance of fuel economy is centered on the Corporate Average Fuel conomy (CAFE) standards which establish a target figure for the combined utput of a particular manufacturer. The objective was to double the 1974 eet fuel economy average by 1985, with a graded series of improvements up o 27.5 miles per gallon, where it has remained since 1990.[38]

At the heart of the CAFE standards is the distinction between a car" and a "light truck." Cars are defined simply as "4-wheel vehicle[s]

appreciate the infrastructure of oil resource geopolit
issue so important.

Securing global oil supplies has been a tenet of U.S. f
post World War II era. Because the Middle East hold
known reserves of oil, this objective has made the regi
concern for successive U.S. administrations. As the larg
nomical supplier of Middle East oil Saudi Arabia has ha
this strategic calculation, with the United States agreein;
nally and externally) the Saudi regime in return for p
Saudi oil. Over the years this arrangement has cost the
of billions of dollars in military assistance.[28] This strategy
the Carter Doctrine of 1980, which, in the wake of the
Afghanistan, declared that any power that threatened to c
Gulf area would be directly challenging fundamental U.S.
interests and would be seen as engaged in an assault on th

None of this would be required if the United States
imported oil for its economic well-being. However, in
fueled 53 percent of domestic consumption, and the U.S
Energy forecasts only increasing dependence. By 2025 oi
dence is expected to rise to around 70 percent of domesti
percentages mean the United States will consume an additi
barrels of oil per day by 2025. Given that total petroleum
were 11.4 million barrels per day, this is a very substantial

In recent years, faced with increased dependence on
United States has been seeking to diversify supply, with so
outcomes. As the country was preparing to go to war with I
States was importing half of all Iraqi exports (which satisfied
of America's needs), even though this indirectly funded
Saddam Hussein.[30] Some Republicans in Congress used this
Democratic Senate leader Tom Daschle as an Iraqi sympat
that the Democrat's failure to support drilling in the A
Wildlife Refuge (ANWR)—as the Bush administration de
America into unholy commercial alliances.[31] While this
overlooked the fact that ANWR's 3 billion barrels of reserv
ever supply six months of the United States' total oil needs, it
how the internalization of a cleavage between business and e
interests is sustained through an association with external thre

The drive for diversification is now a major security obje
2001 review of energy policy chaired by Vice President Dick
final chapter focused exclusively on strengthening global al
energy producers to achieve that goal.[33] However, the geopol

not designed for off-road use" while light trucks are four-wheel vehicles

> designed for off-road operation (has 4-wheel drive or is more than 6,000 lbs
> GVWR and has physical features consistent with those of a truck); *or* which is
> designed to perform at least one of the following functions: (1) transport more
> than 10 people; (2) provide temporary living quarters; (3) transport property in
> an open bed; (4) permit greater cargo-carrying capacity than passenger-carrying
> volume; *or* (5) can be converted to an open bed vehicle by removal of rear
> seats to form a flat continuous floor with the use of simple tools.[39]

This distinction is significant because when the CAFE regime was established, in contrast to its treatment of cars, Congress did not set a target for the improvement of light truck fuel economy. The first standard came in 1979 (15.8 mpg) and rose to 20.7 mpg in 1996 with a marginal increase to 22.2 mpg required by 2007.[40] These standards fall well short of what is technologically possible in automotive efficiency with 20.7 mpg being no more than what had been achieved on the road in 1983.[41]

It was a consumer politics of identity that motivated the distinction between cars and light trucks. Automotive manufacturers, industry groups, and their political allies in Congress argued that light trucks were the "workhorses of America," and "commercially vital" for the blue-collar businessmen and farmers who needed cheap transport for their materials. However, by the late 1960s manufacturers had started to stress the family and leisure benefits in advertisements for light trucks, and by the time Congress was creating the distinction between cars and light trucks on the grounds of commercial utility, more than two-thirds of the light trucks on the road were being used as family transport, with nearly three quarters carrying no freight whatsoever.[42] Moreover, each time the regulations changed, automakers altered their models so they could escape CAFE standards limited restrictions. When the weight limit for light trucks subject to CAFE standards rose from 6,000 lbs to 8,500 lbs, automakers kept their products free from the standards by increasing the size of their models to 8,550 lbs or more. As a result, the regulatory regime turned many light trucks into the heaviest passenger vehicles on the road.[43]

Light trucks did not only benefit from more lenient fuel economy standards. They were granted less restrictive environmental standards, exempted from "gas guzzler" and luxury taxes, and their purchase can be written off against income tax.[44] These benefits were granted because light trucks were a market sector U.S. automakers had almost exclusively to themselves following the imposition in 1964 of a 25 percent tariff on imports. In place for nearly thirty years (and still in place for pick-up trucks), this gave U.S. automakers comparative advantage in an under regulated sector of the market, and policy makers have been lobbied incessantly about the need to protect this valuable sector.[45] It is this dynamic that has led the automotive industry to be one of the principal opponents to international climate control agreements. Faced with pressure to improve fuel efficiency in order to reduce emissions, the major manufacturers argued such requirements would harm their economic position, a claim that was pivotal in the Bush administration's decision to withdraw U.S. support for the Kyoto protocol.[46]

Creating Inefficiency and the SUV

The CAFE regulatory regime has helped reduce American oil imports—without these minimal standards the United States would be currently using an additional 2.8 million barrels of oil per day.[47] However, overall this legal framework has failed to curb import dependence. Indeed, the CAFE regulatory regime has had two profoundly negative effects. The first has been to permit an overall *decline* in U.S. automotive efficiency in the last twenty years. While the original goal of the 1975 legislation was achieved in its first decade, fuel economy has been getting worse ever since. Because of the popularity of light trucks, the U.S. vehicle fleet is currently six percent less efficient than the peak achieved in 1987–1988.[48]

The second consequence of the CAFE regulatory regime is that it has *created* the market position of light trucks that in turn have undermined the original gains in automotive fuel efficiency. The distinction between cars and light trucks created a market niche where the automakers could profitably produce heavy, inefficient, polluting, and unsafe vehicles. And as the policy makers have made incremental steps toward tightening the regulations, the automakers' drive to escape these controls has meant the production of even larger and less efficient vehicles. According to the Union of Concerned Scientists, this regulatory induced expansion is "almost like an arms race."[49] This interplay in the network connecting policy makers, auto manufacturers, and consumers is, therefore, a classic example of the strategic interactions that define social relations in a biopolitical context.

Given the favorable regulatory regime, the auto manufacturers have exploited the opportunities afforded light trucks to such a degree they have changed the character of the new vehicle market. With the weak regulatory regime permitting old technology as the basis for light trucks, their low production costs mean they are particularly profitable. As a result, the big three American automakers now make more light trucks than cars, and light trucks (a category including pick-ups, minivans, and SUVs) outsold cars for the first time in 2001.[50] In particular, it is the boom in SUV sales (which increased by a factor of 10 to 25 percent in this time) that has seen light trucks overtake the car as the favored form of passenger vehicle in the United States.[51] With light trucks constituting 54 percent of the new vehicle market in 2003–2004, large pick-up trucks increasingly popular, and automakers ensuring their new "luxury crossover vehicles" are officially classified as light trucks, this sector looks set to dominate family motoring in the United States for some time.[52]

SUVs and the Politics of Desire

While the regulatory regime has constructed the market position of the "light truck," and while the automakers have developed and exploited this market development to profitable ends, it nonetheless takes consumers to purchase these products in large numbers before light trucks could have surpassed the car as the favored passenger vehicle. What, then, is it about light trucks, especially the SUV, which appeals to American consumer desire?

The genealogy of the SUV can be traced to the Jeep, a small vehicle that came to prominence in World War II. The U.S. Army wanted a light four-wheel drive truck that could transport troops and a heavy machine gun, and more than half a million were produced. Highly successful in all its tasks, "the Jeep became a sign, the emblem, the alter ego of the American fighting machine."[53] From the outset, then, the SUV has been marked by the military. Once the war had been won, Jeep traded on its military background and attempted to modify and sell its vehicles to the family market. Never very successful, given the U.S. market then favored stylish and comfortable station wagons for large families, the company stumbled along and was sold to the American Motors Corporation (AMC) in 1969.[54]

When AMC undertook to revitalize the Jeep brand it noticed that its Wagoneer model was sold mostly to affluent families in urban areas who respected Jeep's military heritage and wanted to be associated with its outdoor image. On the back of this assessment, Jeep sales expanded rapidly in the early 1970s with *Time* magazine calling the basic model a "macho-chic machine." However, as a basically primitive piece of technology, being built on the same World War II truck chassis that made it famous, the Jeep was a vehicle swimming against the tide of environmental consciousness and safety regulation in 1970s America. But Washington policy makers were very reluctant to regulate a weak mid-West auto producer out of business, so Jeep executives successfully lobbied to have Jeep classified as a truck and thus free from new legislation, such as the Clean Air Act of

1970.[55] This established the precedent for differentiating light trucks from cars that the CAFE standards enshrined to such devastating effect.

The military background of the Jeep was part of the heritage that played a role in the development of the model that launched the boom in SUVs— the Ford Explorer. In 1986 when Ford designers began the process of developing a new model line for the 1990s their methods were more anthropological than automotive:

> They started by trying to take the cultural pulse of the time, paying special attention to the evolving values of the baby boomer generation. They watched some of the most popular movies of the time: *Rambo First Blood Part II*, *Rocky IV*, and *Top Gun*. The clipped photographs from magazines and arranged them into a series of large collages, each for a different period of a few years, and were struck by how many people were wearing cowboy hats and other Western attire in their collage of contemporary photos. They took note of the wide media attention give[n] to the two Jeeps that Reagan kept at his ranch near Santa Barbara, California.[56]

The most important SUV was conceived in a time dominated by the paramilitary culture that emerged after, and in response to, America's defeat in Vietnam. Obvious in the Hollywood movies the Ford designers watched, it was manifested also in "techno-thriller" novels by the likes of Tom Clancy and the emergence of paintball as a popular national game. In this energetic cultural militarism, which saw the remasculinization of American identity, heroes are those individuals who overcome the bureaucratic constraints of daily life, braved abnormal environments to fight America's enemies, and often traveled in exotic vehicles.[57]

Incorporating some of the codes of cultural militarism, the Explorer also embodied elements of the classic rhetoric of American identity, thus demonstrating the way in which vehicles are part of the imaginaries, geographies, and practices of national identity.[58] Baby boomers did not want vehicles akin to the old-fashioned station wagons that had dominated the family vehicle market until the 1990s. Instead, they wanted to use their increasing affluence to express a rugged individualism by purchasing vehicles that allowed them to "to feel a bond with the great outdoors and the American frontier."[59] Central to this was four-wheel drive technology. Prospective buyers told consumer researchers they almost never used this capacity but wanted it anyway. The fact that 80 percent of SUV owners live in urban areas and no more than 13 percent of their vehicles have been off road does not diminish this desire.[60] The reasoning behind this paradox was that four-wheel drive

offered the promise of unfettered freedom to drive anywhere during vacations. These customers might have given up their childhood dreams of becoming firefighters, police officers or superheroes, and had instead become parents with desk jobs and oversized mortgages. But they told Ford researchers that SUVs made them feel like they were still carefree, adventurous spirits who could drop everything and head for the great outdoors at a moment's notice if they really wanted to do so.[61]

Combined with this fantasy of vehicular freedom, SUV owners manifest a concern with social insecurity. French medical anthropologist turned marketing consultant Claude Rapaille, argues that SUVs offer the physical embodiment of Americans' concern with "survival and reproduction." According to Rapaille, the United States is a society riven with the fear of crime and other insecurities (even in the period prior to September 11). The same conditions that have led to the private security guard industry and the growth in gated communities are behind the consumer's desire to ensure that their family vehicle offers a high level of personal security. Amidst this neo-medievalization of society, as we retreat to our fortified enclaves (or capsules) secure against others, SUVs become "armored cars for the battlefield."[62]

With high front ends, towering driving positions, fenders designed to replicate the haunches of wild animals and grilles intentionally designed to evoke snarling jungle cats, SUVs give their owners an aggressively panoptic disposition to the world.[63] With names like Tracker, Equinox, Freestyle, Escape, Defender, Trail Blazer, Navigator, Pathfinder, and Warrior—or designations that come from American Indians (Cherokee, Navajo) or places in the American West (Tahoe, Yukon)—SUVs populate the crowded urban routes of daily life with representations of the militarized frontier.[64] In the words of one marketing consultant, they say to the outside world: "America, we're risk takers, America, we're rugged."[65] This comes across in interviews with SUV owners in California who, while acknowledging the problems caused by the motoring choice, explain it in terms of security: "The world is becoming a harder and more violent place to live, so we wrap ourselves with the big vehicles." In the words of another: "It gives you a barrier, makes you feel less threatened."[66] Crucially, both those voices are from mothers, and indicate how SUVs find particular favor amongst women. Keen on the high riding position for maximum visibility, the large ground clearance of their four-wheel drive vehicles also intersects with their concerns about security. In one study, respondents surprised researchers by telling them this feature meant "it's easier to see if someone is hiding underneath or lurking behind it."[67] Together these desires coalesce into a sense of the SUV being an "urban assault vehicle" for the homeland city at war—albeit with the expected comforts that also make it a form of "portable civilization"—with the driver as a military figure confronting but safe from an insecure world.[68]

Nowhere do the vectors of security, war, and the SUV intersect more clearly than in the production of the Humvee and Hummer. In 1981 the U.S. military determined that a larger vehicle was required to replace the Jeep. The resulting High Mobility Multipurpose Wheeled Vehicle (or Humvee) came to prominence during the first Gulf War in 1990–1991, carrying forward the place of these four-wheel drive vehicles in the global construction of American identity.[69] The Hummer gained notoriety when Arnold Schwarzenegger purchased one for civilian use, provoking the manufacturers to see how they could benefit from the then emerging SUV boom. As with early Jeeps, the first Humvee was a crude vehicle, so in 2001 the company produced a more refined but still gargantuan Hummer H2. Said to be infused with "military-derived DNA," H2 owners regarded them as embodying "testosterone."[70] In the wake of the September 11 attacks the already favorable consumer ratings for the Hummer soared as people prioritized personal security at a time of permanent and unconventional war.

With televised coverage of the invasion of Iraq once again foregrounding the Humvee, the Hummer H2 became the best-selling large luxury SUV in America (with women accounting for one-third of all purchases). Hummer owners have exhibited a profound patriotism and the vehicles have come to occupy a special cultural place (as the featured vehicle on the popular TV show *CSI: Miami* for example). As one H2 owner declared, "When I turn on the TV, I see wall-to-wall Humvees, and I'm proud. . . . They're not out there in Audi A4's . . . I'm proud of my country, and I'm proud to be driving a product that is making a significant contribution." [71] Advertisements for the Hummer have called up all the reasons people favor SUVs and leavened with some measure of self-parody. Alongside images of the H2, the tag lines include "When the asteroid hits and civilization crumbles, you'll be ready"; "It only looks like this because it is badass"; and—with special appeal to the prospective female customer—"A new way to threaten men." One Hummer poster, for which the copywriters might not have appreciated the contemporary geopolitical significance of their statement, inadvertently encapsulated the H2's meaning: "Excessive. In a Rome at the height of its power sort of way."[72]

Unsurprisingly, the in-your-face attitude of the Hummer (part of "the axles of evil") has made it a favorite target of protest groups campaigning against SUVs, ranging from web sites abusing H2 owners, to the satire of Bill Maher and Micah Ian Wright, the evangelical "What Would Jesus Drive?" campaign, and the Earth Liberation Front's (ELF) arson against the vehicles.[73] Responding to what the FBI regards as "domestic terrorism" by the ELF, Hummer owners have wrapped the flag ever more tightly around their vehicle. According to the founder of the International Hummer Owners Group (IHOG [sic]), "the H2 is an American icon . . . it's a symbol of what we all hold so dearly above all else, the fact we have the freedom of choice, the freedom of happiness, the freedom of adventure and discovery, and the ultimate freedom of expression. Those who deface a Hummer in words or deeds . . . deface the American flag and what it stands for."[74]

Excess in the automotive world is not restricted to the Hummer, however. In many ways it has been only the most obvious manifestation of a recent trend. At the 2003 Detroit motor show, on the eve of war with Iraq, many new models with vast engines and enhanced power were displayed. With styling cues taken from the muscle cars of the 1960s (which were produced prior to the onset of the "Vietnam syndrome"), these new designs were read as bold assertions of "American technological virtuosity" and "American self-confidence." At the same time, this bravado—what Claude Rapaille labeled a "return to pride and power"—was seen as a response to the political climate of crisis and fear.[75]

This trend was epitomized when Ford unveiled its new concept vehicle, the SYN^US (a name derived from "synthesis" and "urban sanctuary" to emphasize that the outside is about security while the inside is about a high-tech life) at the 2005 Detroit motor show.[76] Although a small SUV, it demonstrates how the foreign is folded back into the domestic by reference to the border zones of contemporary urban life. The promotional blurb argues, "as the population shifts back to the big cities, you'll need a rolling urban command center. Enter the SYN^US concept vehicle, a mobile techno sanctuary sculpted in urban armor and inspired by the popular B-cars of congested international hotspots." The styling is "intimidating," it deploys protective shutters when parked, has bullet-resistant windows, all designed to make "any mission possible." At the same time as it takes the notion of urban assault vehicle to its logical conclusion, it also parades a fine sense of portable civilization, with an interior that can be "a mini-home theater with multi-configuration seating and multi-media work station. . . . Plus, you can monitor your surroundings in real time as seen by the rear-mounted cameras."[77]

What these developments indicate is the extent to which the discourses of homeland security are being materialized in automotive form. As De Cauter argues, the fear produced by networks unbundling and splintering our locales means we retreat to capsules, but this increased capsularization only enhances fear which, in turn drives further capsularization. By addressing cultural anxieties with embodiments of material power, the U.S. auto industry is therefore pursuing a path familiar to national security policy. But this response is also paradoxical, because in meeting insecurities founded on oil dependence with products that will consume ever more petroleum is simply to promote the conditions of crisis.

Paradoxes of the SUV

Much about the rise of the SUV appears paradoxical. Given the centrality of security to the appeal of the SUV the foremost paradox concerns safety. SUV owners are convinced the size of their vehicles is synonymous with their safety, while accident records show SUVs are more dangerous than cars. The occupant death rate per million SUVs is some 6 percent higher than the equivalent for cars, meaning that an additional 3,000 people die annually because they are in SUVs rather than cars, thereby replicating the death toll of September 11 every year.[78] The principal reason for the SUV's poor safety record is their tendency to rollover in accidents. The vehicle height that owners cherish for its ground clearance and visibility makes SUVs prone to tip easily. Rollovers account for one-third of all road deaths in the United States, and the fatality rate for rollovers in SUVs is three times higher than in cars, but neither the industry nor the regulators have addressed this problem.[79]

In collisions that do not result in rollovers, SUVs do offer their occupants greater safety when compared with those in the other vehicle. However, the safety of SUV occupants comes at the cost of substantially higher death rates for those they collide with. When SUVs hit a car from the side, the occupant of the car is twenty-nine times more likely to be killed than their SUV riding brethren.[80] What this means is that in collisions that do not result in rollovers SUVs achieve their relative safety by externalizing danger. As Keith Bradsher has concluded, "for each [Ford] Explorer driver whose life is saved in a two-vehicle collision by choosing an Explorer instead of a large car, an extra five drivers are killed in vehicles struck by Explorers."[81] This has led the current Head of the NHTSA to lament that "the theory that I am going to protect myself and my family even if it costs other people's lives has been the operative incentive for the design of these vehicles, and that's just wrong."[82] But in the absence of regulation individuals faced with growing numbers of SUVs on the road are going to opt for these vehicles even though this will increase the collective danger. The result, in Bradsher's words, is a "highway arms race."[83]

Other paradoxes in the rise of the SUV also involve the relationship between the individual and the collective. The SUV's popularity is drawn from its association with the freedom and rugged individuality of the frontier, but the dominant market position of the light truck sector would not have been possible without the regulatory designs of Washington bureaucrats and politicians. The SUV invokes notions of wilderness and adventure, even though its owners, who rarely if ever venture beyond the urban, are driving a vehicle that is highly damaging to the environment. And SUV owners defend their vehicle choice against criticisms of these kinds by invoking an American's right to be free of government and regulation, even though the entire infrastructure of motoring that makes it possible to choose one model over another—road construction, maintenance, law enforcement, and the like—requires a state subsidy upwards of $2.4 trillion annually.[84] The pervasiveness of these paradoxes stems from the way individual choices are part of a biopolitical whole with geopolitical consequences, something signaled by the concept of automobility.

The Auto Social Formation of Automobility

The concept of automobility—or that of the "auto social formation" or "car culture"—calls attention to the hybrid assemblage or machinic complex that the apparently autonomous entities of car and driver comprise.[85] In the "automobilized time-space" of contemporary society we can observe a networked, sociotechnical infrastructure that is in process, an infrastructure in which there is "the ceaseless and mobile interplay between many different scales, from the body to the globe."[86] As such, automobility is one dimension of empire, in the sense proposed by Hardt and Negri.

The relationship between the auto and the urban has always been at its strongest in the United States. The beautification of cities through the construction of avenues, malls, and parkways in the early twentieth century coincided with and furthered the rise of the automobile.[87] While the development of technology was obviously important, a transformation in American urban culture—wherein streets came to be viewed as traffic ways rather than recreational social spaces—was fundamental to the creation of the auto social formation.[88] Most obvious in the urban planning of Robert Moses, whose bridges, expressways, and parkways transformed New York City and its environs, these infrastructural developments came to be the leitmotif of modernity.[89] National highway systems became the centerpieces of utopian plans—as in General Motors, "Futurama" in the 1939 World's Fair in New York—and were realized in the cold war years as a consequence of the Interstate Highways and Defense Act of 1956.[90]

Although constructed as a means to achieve the unification of social life, the web of traffic routes that permeate urban space have in practice furthered the fragmentation of the urban and its peri-urban and suburban spaces, creating in the process new borderlands (which in turn require new capsules of security).[91] The distanciation of life elements (home from work, family from friends, haves from have nots) that are part of this urban fissure in turn promotes further reliance on automobility as people seek to overcome, traverse, or bypass these divisions. Importantly, this partitioning of the urban world has been codified in and encouraged by planning legislation. Embodying a functionalist view of the city as an organized machine, American urban planners from the 1920s onward relied on a system of zoning controls that separated uses and imposed homogenous criteria on specified areas. Hostile to mixed usage or hybrid formations, these uniform zoning codes (known as Euclidean zoning after a 1926 Supreme Court decision in favor of the village of Euclid) have produced urban sprawl and the elongation of travel routes.[92] In the absence of public transport systems, these urban forms have further increased reliance on the car. For residents of the border zones known as "edge cities" there is little choice but to rely on private transport for mobility. Contemporary urban life is both sustained by oil in the form of the car and requires increasing oil consumption through the use of the car urban life promotes. Citizens are thus coerced into a limited flexibility, creating a situation that is "a wonderful testament to the ability of a sociomaterial structure to serve its own reproduction."[93]

Not that this is exclusive to America. The United States remains the archetypical case of the auto social formation, with more automobiles than registered drivers, and a per capita fuel consumption rate that is ten times the rate of Japan's and twenty times as much as European city dwellers.[94] Nonetheless, the social forces behind automobility are global, and societies other than the United States (China, for example) are witnessing profound growth in private vehicle usage. SUVs are growing in popularity—while equally attracting opprobrium—in Australia, New Zealand, South Africa, the United Kingdom, and other EU states.[95] As the icon of automobility, the SUV is imperial.

Concluding Themes

The SUV is a vehicle of singular importance. It is a node in a series of networks that range from the body to the globe which when combined establish the conditions of possibility for U.S. strategic policy, and demonstrate that geopolitics needs to be understood in the context of biopolitics. In the story outlined here, it is the central role of mobility in American society that grants oil its social value. This chapter has outlined the key moments of connectivity in those networks that have given rise to the American auto social formation—the way the transport sector dominates petroleum use, the importance of passenger vehicles as the major consumers of oil in the transport sector, how light trucks have come to be the auto manufacturers' dominant product overtaking the car as the choice for the majority of families, who find themselves with little choice other than the private vehicle as they move through the domains of their life. All this—the auto social formation of automobility—has resulted in a situation where energy efficiency declines and dependence on oil from unstable regions increases as Americans drive further in less economical vehicles. Pivotal in this account is the role played by various laws and regulations— including fuel economy standards, exemptions for light trucks, tax rebates, trade tariffs, international environmental agreements, and zoning codes—in enabling and supporting automobility. Indeed, the story is tragic in so far as the regulatory regime designed to increase energy efficiency and reduce oil dependence (the CAFE standards) has in fact created inefficiency and given rise to a class of vehicles (SUVs) that undermine the overall objective.

The SUV's importance goes well beyond these instrumentalized concerns, because a renewed emphasis on the material requires an extended engagement with the immaterial. As such, the SUV is the icon of automobility in contemporary America, invested with codes drawn from the militarized frontier culture of post-Vietnam America and manifesting the strategic game animating social and cultural networks in contemporary liberal society. The SUV is the vehicle of empire, when empire is understood as the deterritorialized apparatus of rule that is global in scope but national and local in its effects. The SUV is a materialization of America's global security attitude, functioning as a gargantuan capsule of excess consumption in an uncertain world. With its military genealogy and its claim to provide personal security through the externalization of danger, the SUV is itself a boundary-producing political performance inscribing new geopolitical borderlands at home and abroad through social relations of security, threat, and war. The SUV draws the understanding of security as sizable enclosure into daily life, folds the foreign into the domestic, and links the inside to the outside, thereby simultaneously transgressing bounded domains while enacting the performative rebordering of American identity.

Because of its cultural power and pivotal place in the constitution of contemporary America, challenging the encoded performances of the SUV is a difficult proposition. Instrumentally, rectification could begin with changes in the regulatory regime to increase economy standards (perhaps via efforts to reduce greenhouse gas emissions, as the state of California proposes) and a political recognition that energy conservation is itself "the first and cheapest rapid-deployment energy resource."[96] But bringing about change involves something more incisive than fine-tuning public policy. As this chapter makes clear, a biopolitical understanding of automobility is necessary because we are dealing with dispositions and practices that exceed the structured sites of social institutions. As such, transformation requires so much more than the individualization of responsibility proposed in the advertisements encouraged by the Detroit Project. Can the politics of desire be remodeled to make the SUV an "unpatriotic relic?"[97] Only if America's security attitude can resist the reinscription of the homeland at war and begin to work with the networks of the biopolitical that exceed yet effect the borders of our communities.

Notes

This chapter has been a long time in the making and incurred many debts along the way. The argument was first tried out in a roundtable on Hardt and Negri's *Empire* at the 2002 American Political Science Association annual meeting in Chicago, where the conversation included William Connolly and Michael Hardt. Since then audiences in Politics and International Relations departments at the Universities of Birmingham, Durham, Leeds, Newcastle, St. Andrews, Sussex, the Open University, Sun Yat Sen University and the National University of Taiwan have been helpful interlocutors. Thanks for comments, citations, and encouragement are due to Steve Graham, Jef Huysmans, Kate Manzo, Gordon MacLeod, Mat Paterson, Simon Philpott, Robert Warren, and Geoff Vigar. Special mention needs to be made of the participants at the "Legal Borderlands" symposium at Pomona College in September 2004 for their contributions. In particular, the comments of Mary Dudziak, Inderpal Grewal, Letti Volpp and two anonymous readers for *American Quarterly* were of great benefit. All, however, are absolved of responsibility for the final version. This chapter originally appeared in *American Quarterly* 57: 3, 2005, pp. 943–972.

1. David Campbell, "Time is Broken: The Return of the Past in the Response to September 11," *Theory and Event*, 5:4 (2001), http://muse.jhu.edu/journals/theory_&_event/toc/archive.html#5.4.
2. David Campbell, *Writing Security: United States Foreign Policy and the Politics of Identity*, rev. ed. (Minneapolis: University of Minnesota Press, 1998), chapter 7.
3. "Bush Tars Drug Takers with Aiding Terrorists," *The Guardian*, August 8, 2002, p. 15, http://www.guardian.co.uk/international/story/0,3604, 770783, 00. html (accessed August 18, 2002). The ONDCP web pages— http://www.theantidrug.com/drugs_terror/index.html (accessed August 18, 2002)—outline the administration argument and host copies of the advertisements.
4. Arianna Huffington, "An Ad George Bush Would Love," October 22, 2002, *Salon.com*, http://www.salon.com/news/col/huff/2002/10/22/oil/print.html (accessed October 22, 2002).
5. See http://www.detroitproject.com (accessed June 30, 2003) for the advertisements and Woody Hochswender, "Did My Car Join Al Qaeda?"

The New York Times, February 16, 2003, www.nytimes.com/ 2003/02/16/16HOCH.html (accessed February 23, 2003) for a critical response.

6. John Urry, "The 'System' of Automobility," *Theory, Culture and Society*, 21: 4 (2004): 27.

7. Ibid., p. 28; Stephen Graham and Simon Marvin, *Splintering Urbanism: Networked Infrastructures, Technological Mobilities and the Urban Condition* (London and New York: Routledge, 2001).

8. Urry (2004), pp. 26, 27, 33.

9. Michael Klare, *Blood and Oil: How America's Thirst for Petrol is Killing Us* (London: Hamish Hamilton, 2004); Catholic Relief Services, *Bottom of the Barrel: Africa's Oil Boom and the Poor*, June 2003, http://www. catholicrelief.org/get_involved/advocacy/policy_and_strategic_issues/ oil_report_one.cfm (accessed March 23, 2005).

10. For an argument that does see domestic oil consumption as the reason for the war, see Ian Rutledge, *Addicted to Oil: America's Relentless Drive for Energy Security* (London: I. B. Tauris, 2005).

11. Campbell (1998).

12. Michael Hardt and Antonio Negri, *Empire* (Cambridge, MA: Harvard University Press, 2002), pp. xii–xiii.

13. Ibid., p. xiii.

14. Quoted in "In California, S.U.V. Owners Have Guilt, but Will Travel," *The New York Times*, February 8, 2003, www.nytimes.com/2003/ 02/08/automobiles/08SUV.html (accessed February 12, 2003).

15. Michel Foucault, *Society Must Be Defended: Lectures at the Collège de France 1975–76*, trans. David Macey (London: Allen Lane, 2003), lecture 11.

16. Giorgio Agamben, *Homo Sacer: Sovereign Power and Bare Life* (Stanford: Stanford University Press, 1998).

17. Foucault (2003), lecture 11.

18. Hardt and Negri (2002), p. 23. It would be incorrect, however, to argue that this conception was radically different to Foucault's articulation of the role practices of governmentality played in constructing a "society of security." See my discussion of this in *Writing Security* (1998): 151-52, 199-200.

19. William J. Mitchell, *Me++: The Cyborg Self and the Networked City* (Cambridge, MA: MIT Press, 2003), p. 5. For an argument that network is an insufficiently fluid understanding, see Mimi Sheller, "Mobile Publics: Beyond the Network Perspective," *Environment and Planning D: Society and Space*, 22 (2004): 39–52.

20. Julian Reid, "War, Liberalism, and Modernity: The Biopolitical Provocations of 'Empire,' " *Cambridge Review of International Affairs*, 17: 1 (April 2004): 74.

21. Michael Dillon and Julian Reid, "Global Liberal Governance: Biopolitics, Security and War," *Millennium: Journal of International Studies*, 30: 1 (2001): 42.

22. Ibid., p. 55.

23. Lieven De Cauter, *The Capsular Civilization: On the City in the Age of Fear* (Rotterdam: NAi Publishers, 2004), p. 85.

24. See Marieke de Goede, "Beyond Economism in International Political Economy," *Review of International Studies*, 29: 1 (2003): 79–97.

25. Alan Latham and Derek P. McCormack, "Moving Cities: Rethinking the Materialities of Urban Geographies," *Progress in Human Geography*, 28: 6 (2004): 701. This is complementary to, but different from, the sense that objects like cars are material expressions of cultural life. See David Miller, ed. *Car Cultures* (London: Berg, 2001).

26. See, e.g., Michael T. Klare, "Bush's Real Casus Belli," *AlterNet.org*, January 27, 2003, www.alternet.org/story.html?StoryID=15036 (accessed January 29, 2003).

27. Advertisement in *The Guardian*, February 26, 2003, p. 13.

28. Patricia S. Hu, *Estimates of 1996 U.S. Military Expenditures on Defending Oil Supplies from the Middle East: Literature Review* (Oak Ridge TN: Oak Ridge National Laboratory for the Office of Transportation Technologies, US Department of Energy, revised August 1997).

29. Energy Information Administration, *Annual Energy Outlook 2004* ("Market Trends—Oil and Natural Gas"), http://www.eia.doe.gov/oiaf/archive/aeo04/index.html (accessed March 23, 2005).

30. "US Companies Slash Imports of Iraqi Oil," *Washington Post*, August 20, 2002, p. A1.

31. "Republicans Aim to Smear Tom Daschle," *CNN.com*, December 23, 2001, www.cnn.com/2001/ALLPOLITICS/12/23/column.press/ (accessed September 26, 2002).

32. Thomas L. Friedman, "Drilling In the Cathedral," *The New York Times*, March 2, 2001, www.nytimes.com/2001/03/02/opinion/02FRIE.html (accessed September 26, 2002).

33. "National Energy Policy Development Group," *National Energy Policy*, May 2001, http://www.whitehouse.gov/energy/ (accessed August 18, 2002).

34. Michael T. Klare, *Resource Wars: The New Landscape of Global Conflict* (New York: Henry Holt and Co., 2001) and Klare (2004).

35. For a sample of reports touching on these developments, see Ken Silverstein, "U.S. Oil Politics in the 'Kuwait of Africa,' " *The Nation*, April 22, 2002, www.thenation.com/doc.mhtml?i=20020422&s=silverstein (accessed September 27, 2002) and "US Sidles Up to Well-Oiled Autocracy," *The Guardian*, July 2, 2004, p. 20.

36. Energy Information Administration, *Annual Energy Outlook 2004*; and Natural Resources Defense Council, *Reducing America's Energy Dependence*, July 2004, http://www.nrdc.org/air/transportation/gasprices.asp (accessed March 23, 2005).

37. National Highway Transport Safety Administration (NHTSA), "Corporate Average Fuel Economy (CAFE)," http://www.nhtsa.dot.gov/cars/rules/cafe/ (accessed August 12, 2002a).

38. NHTSA, "CAFE Overview and Frequently Asked Questions," http://www.nhtsa.dot.gov/cars/rules/cafe/overview.htm (accessed August 12, 2002b).

39. Ibid.

40. Energy Information Administration, *Annual Energy Outlook 2004*.

41. Jack Doyle, *Taken for a Ride: Detroit's Big Three and the Politics of Pollution* (New York: Four Walls Eight Windows, 2001), p. 406.

42. Ibid., pp. 399–402.

43. Keith Bradsher, *High and Mighty: SUVs—the World's Most Dangerous Vehicles and How They Got That Way* (New York: Public Affairs, 2002), pp. 29–30.

44. Doyle (2001), pp. 398–399; Union of Concerned Scientists, "Tax Incentives: SUV Loophole Widens, Clean Vehicle Credits Face Uncertain Future," November 2003, http://www.ucsusa.org/clean_vehicles/cars_and_suvs/page.cfm?pageID=1280 (accessed August 10, 2004).

45. Bradsher (2002), pp. 11–13.

46. Doyle (2001), pp. 373–394.

47. Natural Resources Defense Council, "Reducing America's Energy Dependence," July 1, 2004, http://www.nrdc.org/air/transportation/gasprices.asp

48. *Light-Duty Automotive Technology and Fuel Economy Trends: 1975 through 2004* (EPA420-R-O4-001), April 2004, i, http://www.epa.gov/otaq/cert/mpg/fetrends/420s04002.pdf (accessed August 10, 2004).

49. Doyle (2001), p. 418.

50. Ibid., pp. 405–406; "The Station Wagon is Back, But Not as a Car," *The New York Times*, March 19, 2002, http://query.nytimes.com/search/advanced (accessed September 26, 2002).

51. *Light-Duty Automotive Technology and Fuel Economy Trends* (2004), p. iv.

52. "Sales of Big S.U.V.'s Rebounded in May," *The New York Times*, June 3, 2004, http://query.nytimes.com/search/advanced (accessed July 21, 2004); "Big and Fancy, More Pickups Displace Cars," *The New York Times*, July 31, 2003, http://query.nytimes.com/search/advanced (accessed July 21, 2004); "Bumper-to-Bumper Details of the Crossover Era," *The New York Times*, October 22, 2002, www.nytimes.com/2002/10/22/automobiles/23PATTON.html (accessed October 23, 2002).

53. Manuel A. Conley, "The Legendary Jeep," *American History Illustrated* (June 1981): 27, quoted in Michael VanderPloeg, "The Jeep, a Real American Hero," www.off-road.com/jeep/jeephist.html (accessed August 6, 2004). The Jeep also inspired the British Land Rover, which first went into production in 1947 and has furthered the SUV phenomenon beyond the US by combining post–World War II military heritage with upper class cultural values. Bradsher (2002), pp. 385–387.

54. Bradsher (2002), chapter 1.

55. Ibid., pp. 20–25.

56. Ibid., p. 50.

57. James William Gibson, *Warrior Dreams: Paramilitary Culture in Post-Vietnam America* (New York: Hill and Wang, 1994); Susan Jeffords, *The Remasculinization of America: Gender and the Vietnam War* (Bloomington: Indiana University Press, 1989).

58. Tim Edensor, "Automobility and National Identity: Representation, Geography and Driving Practice," *Theory, Culture and Society*, 21: 4/5 (2004): 101–120.

59. Bradsher (2002), p. 51. Similar valences are evident in other locales; for the way four wheel drive vehicles have played a part in Australian national identity, see Peter Bishop, "Off Road: Four Wheel Drive and the Sense of Place," *Environment and Planning D: Society and Space*, 14 (1996): 257–271.

60. Stacy C. Davis and Lorena F. Truett, *An Analysis of the Impact of the Sport Utility Vehicles in the United States*, Oak Ridge National Laboratory, Oak Ridge Tennessee, ORNL/TM-2000/147, prepared for the Office of Transportation Technologies, U.S. Department of Energy, August 2000.

61. Bradsher (2002), p. 51.

62. Ibid., pp. 95 and 97. For a compelling analysis of gated communities, see Setha Low, *Behind the Gates: Life, Security, and the Pursuit of Happiness in Fortress America* (New York: Routledge, 2003).

63. Bradsher (2002), pp. 98–99.

64. "The Shifting Geography of Car Names: Go West, Young Van," *The New York Times*, October 22, 2003, http://query.nytimes.com/search/advanced (accessed July 21, 2004).

65. "Rollover: the Hidden History of the SUV," *Frontline*, Public Broadcasting Service, February 21, 2002, http://www.pbs.org/wgbh/pages/frontline/shows/rollover/unsafe/theme.html   (accessed January 22, 2004).

66. "In California, S.U.V. Owners Have Guilt, but Will Travel" (2003).

67. Bradsher (2002), p. 150. Although the majoritarian popularity of SUVs suggest their cultural codes resonate across class, gender and racial lines, further study is needed to see which "Americans" are most attracted to these vehicles.

68. Andrew Garnar, "Portable Civilizations and Urban Assault Vehicles," *Techné: Journal of the Society for Philosophy and Technology*, 5: 2 (Winter 2000): 1–7; Stephen Graham, "Constructing 'Homeland' and 'Target': Cities in the 'War on Terror,' " unpublished paper, http://eprints.dur.ac.uk/archive/00000048/01/Graham_constructing.pdf.

69. The U.S. Army is developing a larger and heavier replacement for the Hummer, the "Smart Truck 3." "Just What America Needs—A Car Even Bigger than the Hummer," *The Independent*, November 10, 2004, p. 30.

70. The description comes from the General Motors Hummer media site at http://media.gm.com/division/hummer/index.html (accessed July 21, 2004); the owners quote from "IN OUR SUVS: Guilt-tripping, Pittsburgh

Post-Gazette (January 19, 2003)," http://www.americansforfuelefficientcars. org/readmore/ppg_011903.htm (accessed January 22, 2004).

71. "In Their Hummers, Right Beside Uncle Sam," *The New York Times*, April 5, 2003, www.nytimes.com/2003/04/05/business/05AUTO.html (accessed April 6, 2003).

72. Modernista [the Hummer advertising agency], http://www.modernista.com/ (accessed March 23, 2005); and "Spinning the Axles of Evil," *The New York Times*, January 19, 2003, http://www. nytimes.com/2003/01/19/ weekinreview/19HAR.html (accessed January 19, 2003).

73. "Spinning the Axles of Evil" (2003). Anti-SUV web sites include *Stop SUVs.org* (www.stopsuvs.org) and *FUH2.com* (http://www.fuh2.com/); Bill Maher, *When You Ride ALONE You Ride with Bin Laden* (Beverley Hills: New Millennium Press, 2002); and Micah Ian Wright's site http://www.micahwright.com/index3.htm; "Now, Add God to the List of Enemies of the S.U.V.," *The New York Times*, November 24, 2002, at http://www.nytimes.com/2002/11/24/weekinreview/24HAKI.html (accessed November 25, 2002).

74. "In Their Hummers, Right Beside Uncle Sam," (2003).

75. "A Proud and Primal Roar," *The New York Times*, January 12, 2003, at www.nytimes.com/2003/01/12/fashion/12CULT.html (accessed January 13, 2003).

76. "Synus ignites a Gen-Y debate," *Detroit Free Press*, January 19, 2005, at http://www.freep.com/money/autoshow/2005/synus19e_20050119.htm (accessed March 22, 2005).

77. Ford SYN[US], at http://www.fordvehicles.com/autoshow/concept/ synus/ (accessed January 31, 2005). While the SYN [US] is a concept vehicle, those with US$300,000 plus can purchase the "Bad Boy Truck," a nuclear-biological-chemical safe super truck based on the US Army's Medium Tactical Vehicle, being sold by Homeland Defense Vehicles of Texas. See http://www.badboytrucks.com (accessed March 22, 2005).

78. Bradsher (2002), p. xvii.

79. "The Nation: By the Numbers; S.U.V.'s Take a Hit, as Traffic Deaths Rise," *The New York Times*, April 27, 2003, at http:// query.nytimes.com/ search/advanced (accessed July 21, 2004); "Regulator Reaffirms Focus on S.U.V.'s," *The New York Times*, January 15, 2003, at www.nytimes.com/ 2003/01/15/business/ 15AUTO.html (accessed January 16, 2003). The story of this negligence is told in "Rollover: the Hidden History of the SUV." The offices of the Attorney General and consumer protection agencies across the US have a public service campaign offering driving advice to prevent rollovers (see www.esuvee.com, accessed February 22, 2005) which represents the SUV as a mammoth-like creature.

80. "Regulators Seek Ways to Make S.U.V.'s Safer," *The New York Times*, January 30, 2003, www.nytimes.com/2003/01/30/automobiles/ 30AUTO. html (accessed January 30, 2003).

81. Bradsher (2002), p. 198.

82. "Regulators Seek Ways to Make S.U.V.'s Safer," (2003).

83. Bradsher (2002), p. xix.

84. Robert Cervero, *The Transit Metropolis: A Global Inquiry* (Washington, DC and Covelo, CA: Island Press, 1998), p. 35.

85. George Martin, "Grounding Social Ecology: Landscape, Settlement, and Right of Way," *Capitalism, Nature, Socialism*, 13: 1 (March 2002): 3–30; Matthew Patterson, "Car Culture and Global Environmental Politics," *Review of International Studies*, 26: 2 (April 2000): 253–270; Mimi Sheller and John Urry, "The City and the Car," *International Journal of Urban and Regional Research*, 24: 4 (December 2000) and Urry (2004).

86. Sheller and Urry (2000), p. 738; Graham and Marvin (2001), p. 8.

87. Jane Holtz Kay, *Asphalt Nation* (Berkeley: University of California Press, 1998), pp. 144–145.

88. Clay McShane, *Down the Asphalt Path: The Automobile and the American City* (New York: Columbia University Press, 1994).

89. Marshall Berman, *All That is Solid Melts Into Air: the Experience of Modernity* (Penguin: New York, 1988), pp. 290–312.

90. Roland Marchand, "The Designers go to the Fair II: Norman Bel Geddes, The General Motors 'Futurama,' and the Visit to the Factory Transformed," *Design Issues*, 8: 2 (Spring 1992): 29; Tom Lewis, *Divided Highways: Building the Interstate Highways, Transforming American Life* (New York: Viking, 1997).

91. Graham and Marvin (2001), pp. 118–121.

92. Jay Wickersham, "Jane Jacob's Critique of Zoning: From *Euclid* to Portland and Beyond," *Boston College Environmental Affairs Law Review*, 28: 4 (2001): 547–564.

93. Sheller and Urry (2000), p. 744; Martin (2002), p. 27.

94. Cervero (1998), pp. 33 and 46.

95. See "The Cars that Ate Cities," Background Briefing, Radio National, Australian Broadcasting Corporation, June 15, 2003, http://www.abc.net.au/rn/talks/bbing/stories/s881845.htm (accessed July 21, 2004); and George Monbiot, "Driving into the Abyss," *The Guardian*, July 6, 2004, http://www.guardian.co.uk/comment/story/01254763,00.html (accessed July 21, 2004).

96. R. James Woolsey, Amory B. Lovins, and L. Hunter Lovins, "Energy Security: It Takes More than Drilling," *Christian Science Monitor*, March 29, 2002, www.csmonitor.com/2002/0329/p11s02-coop.htm (accessed August 13, 2002).

97. Rob Nixon, "A Dangerous Appetite for Oil," *The New York Times*, October 29, 2001, http://www.peterussell.com/WTC/NYTimes.html (accessed September 6, 2002).

PART III

REGULA
SECURI'
PREEMP

CHAPTER 8

SOVEREIGN CONTRADICTIONS: MAHER ARAR AND THE INDEFINITE FUTURE

David Mutimer

In the past decade air travel has become more and more widely accessible. This is the result, at least in part, of two related developments. The first is the reorganization of major air carriers into "hubs and spokes," and the second is the emergence of point-to-point low cost airlines making use of the space at small airports that major carriers no longer have any interest in exploiting—if they ever did. The combined result of these developments has been a dramatic increase in air travel as costs have fallen in both sectors of the market. As a result of this transformation it is likely that most of you reading this chapter have experienced a spoke and hub flight, being flown from wherever you begin to one of the increasingly immense airports that then serve other hubs around the world. If you are reading this in Europe, you have likely passed in this way through London, Amsterdam, or Frankfurt; in Asia through Singapore or Hong Kong. If you are based in North America, it is likely you have passed through one or more of the large U.S. airports, Los Angeles to fly over the Pacific, JFK in New York for transatlantic travel.

With a small number of differences (which do, to be sure, change how unpleasant the overall experience is) the trip through one of these hubs is largely standard. You are unloaded from your arriving plane, either by bus or through a mobile tunnel adorned with advertisements for some global business service. Then, depending on the local regulations and your ultimate destination, you either are or are not required to retrieve and recheck your baggage; you either are or are not required to clear some form of passport control. If you make these sorts of flights often enough, you may then be fortunate enough to have access to one of the ever-growing number of executive and business lounges found in most airports. There, you can have a glass of wine—perhaps even a shower—to make yourself feel a bit more human, because even with access to these lounges, the passage through these airports is profoundly dehumanizing.

It was likely an experience somewhat like this that Maher Arar was expecting when he arrived at JFK on September 26, 2002 on his way home to Ottawa after a holiday in Tunisia. Because his hub was in the United States and his travel after September 11, 2001, Maher Arar did have to clear passport control in the airport before boarding his flight home to Canada. It was at this point that his passage through the airport hub departed from the standard through which we all have passed, and in ways that render the dehumanization of that standard passage little more than the mildest affront to our personal dignity—Maher Arar was "rendered extraordinarily."[1]

While passing through screening at JFK, Maher Arar was pulled aside and sent to be interrogated as a suspected terrorist. What happened from there should beggar belief. Arar was held for almost two weeks in the United States, the first six days of which without having any access to the outside world.[2] Canadian consular officials were eventually advised of his arrest, although they were not provided with the sort of access they should have been. It later became clear that this may be in part because the information that led to his detention came from the Canadian police.

Despite the fact that Maher Arar was traveling on a Canadian passport, and despite his demands that he be returned to Canada, he was deported to Syria. Arar was born in Syria but had lived in Canada since he was a teenager, was married with a young family and a job as a software developer in the high-tech economy that has grown up in Ottawa in the past ten years. He had absolutely no record of any form of wrongdoing. He was held in Syria for almost a year, most of that time out of contact with the Canadian consular officials, once they had even been able to find out that he was there. He had been flown to Syria without the United States informing Canada of the fact. On his return, he had harrowing stories to tell. For ten months he was held in a cell he has described as

a "grave." It is three feet wide, six feet deep and seven feet high. It has a metal door, with a small opening which does not let in light because of a piece of metal on the outside for sliding things into the cell. There is a one by two foot opening in the ceiling with iron bars. This opening is below another ceiling and lets in just a tiny shaft of light. Cats urinate through the ceiling traps of these cells, often onto the prisoners. Rats wander there too.

There is no light source in the cell. The only things in the cell are two blankets, two plastic bowls and two bottles. Arar later uses two small empty boxes—one as a toilet when he is not allowed to the washroom, and one for prayer water.[3]

As if this was not enough, he was subjected to physical torture as officials tried to extract information, although not as severely as others held at the same facility whose screams, in a well-established form of psychological torture, Arar was forced to hear.

What had he done to warrant the attention of first the Canadian police, then the United States' antiterror squads, and finally the Syrian "corrections officials?" A rental application he had made in 1997 when he moved to Ottawa was cosigned by a man named Abdullah Amalki. Abdullah Amalki's brother Nazih Amalki was a colleague of Maher Arar who had asked Abdullah to witness Arar's lease as he was unable to come.[4] Adbullah Amalki was suspected of a connection to al Qaeda; Nazih Amalki never has been. This is a link so tenuous that guilt by association even seems to be an overstatement; perhaps we could term it "guilt by passing acquaintance." And yet, for that link, Maher Arar was flown to a country he barely remembered, held in a dungeon, and tortured.

We must ask why the Canadian police felt it necessary to hand Maher Arar to the United States. It seems probable that it enabled them to circumvent the human rights guarantees that should have been absolute for citizens under the Canadian Charter of Rights and Freedoms. Similarly, we must ask why the United States felt it necessary to deport him to Syria when they received the initial information from Canada and he was a Canadian citizen and resident.[5] The only answer that readily suggests itself is that the U.S. officials knew that in Canada Maher Arar was unlikely to be tortured and by extension that they were fairly certain that in Syria he would be.[6] Indeed, since the Arar case first came to public attention, it has become clear that it is only one instance of a much more extensive U.S. government program called "extraordinary rendition," which Jane Mayer in the article making the program public, aptly describes as "outsourcing torture."[7]

As disturbing as Maher Arar's story is, perhaps even more disturbing is that it is not unique. For instance, the United Kingdom has been detaining foreign terrorist suspects without charge in a practice ruled illegal only in December 2004.[8] Perhaps most infamously, the United States has constructed a new prison in the neverland of Guantánamo Bay, Cuba, to hold those

who might be suspected of being terrorists.[9] Amnesty International sums up
the position of those in this facility as follows:

> Despite a major international outcry and expert condemnation of US
> government policy, hundreds of people of around 35 different nationalities
> remain held in a legal black hole at the US Naval Base in Guantánamo Bay in
> Cuba, many without access to any court, legal counsel or family visits. Denied
> their rights under international law and held in conditions which may amount
> to cruel, inhuman or degrading treatment, the detainees face severe psycho-
> logical distress. There have been numerous suicide attempts.[10]

In a recent report, Amnesty also points out that while Guantánamo Bay is
the most widely known extraterritorial detention center, it is by no means
alone, and estimates that 70,000 people have been detained outside the
United States in pursuit of the "war on terror."[11] In addition, Amnesty
reports on growing evidence of torture:

> Interrogation techniques authorized for use in Guantánamo have included
> stress positions, isolation, hooding, sensory deprivation, and the use of dogs.
> Among the abuses reported by FBI agents are the cruel and prolonged use of
> shackling, and the use of loud music and strobe lights. They have also
> reported witnessing the use of dogs to intimidate detainees in Guantánamo.
> Yet military officials, including those involved in earlier investigations, have
> previously given assurances that no dogs have been used in this way in the
> naval base. A full independent commission of inquiry, as called for by
> Amnesty International since last May, is clearly required.[12]

These are the actions of avowedly liberal democratic states, openly committed to the rule of law, and all signatories to the Convention against Torture.[13]
Of course, these are also times of "war." We are, we are told, in a war on terror, and this type of war demands extraordinary means. At the same time, this
is not a war as are other wars we are presently fighting, such as those in
Afghanistan or Iraq.[14] This is a war rather more akin to the metaphorical wars
we have fought in the past half century: the war on poverty, the war on
drugs, and, most notably of course, the cold war. Maher Arar's story, and the
wider programs of "extraordinary rendition" and Camp Delta, demand an
interrogation of the practices that are made possible by this war. How does
the war on terror make these outrages possible, and what does the answer tell
us of the possibilities for global politics in an era conditioned by such war?

Rendering Bare Life Precarious

Among many other things, what we find shocking about Maher Arar's
story is the arbitrary way that the rights we expect apply to us all were

denied to him. The particularities of those rights stem from his Canadian citizenship: the right to Canadian consular representation, the right to be extradited to Canada, and the various rights enshrined in the Canadian Charter of Rights and Freedoms. However, the shock is more universal: we generally think we hold rights against the kind of arbitrary detention that Maher Arar suffered, and we certainly think we have a right not to be tortured. Maher Arar's story shocks us because he was rendered exceptional, that is, excepted from the rights that we expect to protect us, and in the process was stripped of most of what we consider renders us human. He was reduced, in Giorgio Agamben's evocative phrase, to "bare life."

Agamben inquires into the nature of sovereign power in contemporary politics, beginning with Carl Schmitt's noted definition of the sovereign: "Sovereign is he who decides on the state of exception." The exception that Agamben is most concerned with is the production of bare life, which he theorizes in terms of the Roman conception of *homo sacer*: life that can be killed (without committing homicide) but that cannot be sacrificed. In other words, the person rendered exceptional by sovereignty, placed under the sovereign ban, is stripped of everything other than the most basic biological fact of her life.[15] The life that remains under the sovereign ban is of so little value that it can be freely taken and cannot be presented to God or any other by way of sacrifice as there is nothing there that is sacrificed in taking the life. By extension, of course, anything is permissible against this bare life, including torture.

This account of the power of sovereignty to render human life as bare life seems to accord with Maher Arar's story. The sovereign power of the United States was exercised to render Arar exceptional, banned from the usual protections of both municipal and international law. On this account, however, while Maher Arar is rendered as the exception, his story is not exceptional in the more widely recognized sense, nor is it the expression of anything particular to the war on terror. Agamben argues:

> And if in modernity life is more and more clearly placed at the centre of State politics (which now becomes, in Foucault's terms, biopolitics), in our age all citizens can be said, in a specific but extremely real sense, to appear virtually as *homines sacri*, this is possible only because the relation of the ban has constituted the essential structure of sovereign power from the beginning.[16]

Sovereignty places all its subjects in the jeopardy of being rendered exceptional, of being reduced to bare life, and indeed Agamben shows quite persuasively how that jeopardy is necessary to the constitution of modern sovereignty. To the degree that this is so, we should not be shocked by Mr. Arar's treatment, and yet it is entirely shocking. It is shocking because it seems to us that something has changed to put Mr. Arar in this particular jeopardy. Agamben exposes the power of the modern sovereign that enables the brutal production of bare life, both for Maher Arar and for the detainees at Guantánamo Bay, but he does not allow us purchase on what has changed to allow these particular brutalities at this moment in history.

The question that Agamben does not allow us to answer is one Judith Butler has posed in relation to those held in Guantánamo Bay:

> With the publication of the new regulations, the US government holds that a number of detainees at Guantánamo will not be given trials at all, but will rather be detained indefinitely. It is crucial to ask under what conditions some human lives cease to become eligible for basic, if not universal, human rights. How does the US government construe these conditions? And to what extent is there a racial and ethnic frame through which these imprisoned lives are viewed and judged such that they are deemed less than human, or as having departed from the recognizable human community?[17]

The beginning of the answer Butler provides is that of the emergency, that is, that there are extraordinary conditions that permit extraordinary action. Butler considers the conditions for and consequences of the *indefinite* detention of the Guantánamo prisoners, an indeterminacy shared by most of those rendered extraordinarily. Maher Arar was, in this sense alone, fortunate. His story was trumpeted loudly and from the earliest days of his rendition; even the others who are known have not necessarily had the same fortune, and then there are those who have simply vanished. Indefinite detention is a stark violation of the rule of law, it is a denial of the most basic of the rights the individual holds against the state. It is, in this way, a marker of the sovereign ban, rendering those under indefinite detention as bare life.

For Butler the indefinite detentions at Guantánamo Bay are qualitatively different from previous exercises of sovereign power, at least in the latter part of the twentieth century. There are two elements to this difference that are relevant to my questions, the first is that openly detaining indefinitely renders the emergency that enables detention as indefinite in its turn:

> If detention may be indefinite, and such detentions are presumably justified on the basis of a state of emergency, then the US government can protract an indefinite state of emergency. It would seem that the state, in its executive function, now extends conditions of national emergency so that the state will now have recourse to extra-legal detention and the suspension of established law, both domestic and international, for the foreseeable future. Indefinite detention thus extends lawless power indefinitely. Indeed, the indefinite

detention of the untried prisoner—or the prisoner tried by military tribunal detained regardless of the outcome of the trial—is a practice that presupposes the indefinite extension of the war on terrorism.[18]

Such a formulation recognizes what seemed insufficient in Agamben's account. The exercise of sovereign power, the issuing of the sovereign ban, in response to the war on terror is not the same as the previous expressions of the sovereign ban, even if there are important continuities. For example, the program of extraordinary rendition predates the war on terror, but the present state of emergency transformed it: "Rendition was originally carried out on a limited basis, but after September 11th, when President Bush declared a global war on terrorism, the program expanded beyond recognition— becoming, according to a former C.I.A. official, 'an abomination.' "[19]

The second element of Butler's account echoes Agamben in his evocation of Foucault's later writings on governmentality and biopolitics:

> The future becomes a lawless future, not anarchical, but given over to the discretionary decisions of a set of designated sovereigns—a perfect paradox that shows how sovereigns emerge within governmentality—who are beholden to nothing and to no one except the performative power of their own decisions. They are instrumentalized, deployed by tactics of power they do not control, but this does not stop them from using power, and using it to reanimate a sovereignty that the governmentalized constellation of power appeared to have foreclosed.[20]

The problem is that governmental power is legitimized by biopolitics, by the capacity of the state to make live, rather than the sovereign capacity to kill or to render as bare life fit to be killed. Because of this, Butler sees the renewed virulence of the sovereign in indefinite detention as an anachronism: with the emergence of the governmental state. "Sovereignty . . . no longer operates to support or vitalize the state, but this does not foreclose the possibility that it might emerge as a reanimated anachronism within the political field unmoored from its traditional anchors."[21] Both Agamben and Butler, therefore, see a problem in the contradiction between the state's sovereign power, expressed through the sovereign ban and its ability to render as bare life, and its claim to legitimacy on the basis of the biopolitical capacity to make live. For Agamben, sovereign power is the precondition of the governmental state, but while this is difficult to contest, it also does not provide much purchase on our present problem: without access to sovereign power the state would not be the state we know, but this does not make evident how to manage the contradiction of biopolitical sovereignty. For Butler, sovereignty is an ugly reminder of our past, a position similarly difficult to contest, and similarly unhelpful in developing our understanding of the present. Indeed, Butler recognizes the lacuna, for she concludes her essay on indefinite detention with a call for new theoretical thinking:

> This new configuration of power requires a new theoretical framework, or, at least, a revision of the models of thinking power that we already have at our disposal. The fact of extra-legal power is not new, but the mechanism by which it achieves its goals under the present circumstances is singular. Indeed, it may be that this singularity consists in the way the "present circumstance" is transformed into a reality indefinitely extended into the future, controlling not only the lives of prisoners and the fate of constitutional and international law, but also the very ways in which the future may or may not be thought.[22]

Butler's questions here echo those I have posed to the case of Maher Arar, in asking us to theorize the present circumstances, that is, the war on terror, in such a way as to recognize both the continuity with past circumstances, as Agamben's account does, and its novelty, which it does not. In order to advance a little along that path, I will follow Agamben and Butler's markers and return to Foucault, and in particular to his 1976 lecture series, *Society Must Be Defended*.

Managing the Sovereignty/Biopolitics Contradiction

In the series of lectures that comprise *Society Must Be Defended*, Foucault sets out a history of a discourse he ultimately comes to call "race war." He argues that this discourse emerged in the sixteenth century among opponents of the absolutist states that were then marking the terminal phase of medieval Europe. Those states based their claims to legitimacy on a particular rendering of history, a history in which the monarch was the heir to a military victory that had forged a single people with the sovereign at its head, a people from which all traces of the vanquished had been removed either by victory or assimilation.[23] What comes to be the race war discourse contested the legitimacy of conquest. It argued, in opposition to the official history, that the invaded had never stopped resisting, that there was, in fact, a continual war being waged between the dominant invaders and the subordinate invaded, and that the right rested not with the sovereign invaders, but with those, in the parlance of the time the "race," who had consistently resisted.[24]

The social analysis that is at the heart of the race war discourse is that society is comprised of two races that are permanently at war with one another. This war forged the state in medieval invasions, but even when the invaded territory was "pacified" the war continued, though by other means, by the means of politics.[25] It was, however, still war. The fact of the state's founding in this historical, originary war destroyed the state's claim to the sovereign right, and launched a political project of revolution. The variety of these revolutions is one of the startling features of Foucault's account of the race war discourse. It was articulated as a variety of political projects in opposition to the state, as varied as the anarchist Levellers and Diggers in England to the aristocratic opponents of the Sun King in France, and ultimately gave rise to the Glorious Revolution in England and the Republican Revolution in France.[26]

The conception of race, initially at least, was not the modern conception of a biological division of the human species.[27] That conception of race was developed in the nineteenth century and transformed the race war discourse in important ways. Initially, the races were opposed groups that are enunciated at times in ways that sound to our ears like "nations" and at others in ways that we would tend to interpret as "classes." With the development in the nineteenth century of, on the one hand, Hegelian (and then Marxist) dialectics and, on the other, the biological sciences, of which Darwin's is the centerpiece, the race war discourse was bifurcated. The first variant found expression in the historical-materialist conception of history; the second in the state racism that characterized colonialism and found its ultimate expression in Nazi Germany.[28] It is this second development that is the more significant for Foucault: the articulation of the race war discourse to the new biological sciences and from there to the discourse of the sovereign right. This pair of moves transforms the discourse from an oppositional one to part of the supportive apparatus of the contemporary state.

Initially, race war argued that society was split, the state represented but one side of that split and it was an instrument of oppression, therefore it had to be overthrown by the oppressed race. This form of the argument survives in Marx, where the subordinated, now class, seeks to overthrow the ruling class in control of the state.[29] The introduction of biological racism changed that argument, so that the state became the expression of the dominant race (now understood largely as we would understand it), and its primary function was to protect the (biological) security of that race from its (biological) enemies:

At this point the discourse whose history I would like to trace abandons the initial basic formulation, which was "We have to defend ourselves against our enemies because the State apparatuses, the law, and the power structures not only do not defend us against our enemies; they are the instruments our

enemies are using to pursue and subjugate us." That discourse now disappears.
It is no longer: "We have to defend ourselves against society," but "We have
to defend society against all the biological threats posed by the other race,
the subrace, the counterrace that we are, despite ourselves, bringing into
existence."[30]

The central point is that in the late nineteenth century, the race war
discourse became articulated to sovereignty as part of the defense of the
state. Now society must be defended. It was initially, at least, overtly
"racist" in the sense we commonly understand, as it was deployed to produce the genocidal wars of nineteenth century colonialism. It finds further
expression in the violent racism of Nazi Germany, in which an extreme
version of the security apparatus of the state is deployed against the race
enemy within.[31] What is perhaps most important for my purposes is that
Foucault provides a solution to managing the contradiction raised by both
Agamben and Butler. The race war discourse is essential to maintaining the
regulatory functions of the normalizing society—it is this discourse that makes
possible the continued expression of sovereignty in an era of biopolitics.[32]

The ultimate expression of the sovereign power is the power to kill.
Returning to the Hobbesian theory of sovereignty, we find that the sovereign is the only one to retain the right to kill under the terms of the contract. More concretely, the sovereign state claims the right to kill its
enemies, whether by execution or war, and, moreover, the right to
demand its citizens be killed as part of the state's army.[33] Foucault argues
that in the nineteenth century the basis of state power was fundamentally
altered as the state began to operate biopolitically. Biopolitical society
operates on populations as a whole, with the goal of regulating those populations so as to make people live. The object is a healthy, long-lived, and,
of course, economically productive population. There is, therefore, an
important contradiction between sovereignty and biopolitics, the contradiction noted by both Agamben and Butler. Sovereignty enables the state
to kill its people, and even demands that they be killed, at least for the
defense of the state. Biopolitics, by contrast, demands that those same
people be supported, maintained, and kept undamaged: be made to live.[34]

The crucial feature of the race war discourse is that it enables the state
to retain its right to kill, or place its citizens under the sovereign ban (and
to send its own people to be killed in war) while regulating society so as to
"make live."[35] The population must be made to live and, precisely because
of that, it must be defended against the biological enemies that threaten it.
It is because of the importance of this defense to the very possibility of
biopolitics that the sovereign can still order people to their deaths to

provide for that defense, and to render them as bare life and subject to the vagaries of death and torture. Sovereignty and biopolitics are conjoined through the means of the race war discourse. Race war, as it was reformulated through the nineteenth century, is now central to the functioning of sovereignty in contemporary politics, despite initially contradicting the sovereign right in important ways. What I want to suggest is that the war on terror is the most recent expression of that discourse and is, in turn, among its most virulent articulations.

"Race War" in Contemporary Global Politics

Foucault argues that the race war discourse became biological in the late nineteenth century and was then articulated to sovereignty in terms of the need to defend society against a biologically characterized enemy.[36] In some instances this enemy was racial in the way we commonly use the term. The paradigmatic case is, of course, the Nazi state, but, by and large, the modern state produced a race war discourse with an enemy that was not characterized in overtly racial terms. The discourse did not disappear with the defeat of the Nazi state, but was, rather, reconfigured by both the United States and Soviet Union into the two legitimating discourses of the cold war.

In the United States, the discourse posited communism as a social contagion—a disease to which anyone could potentially succumb. My use of biomedical terminology is both precisely chosen and revealing. Communism was seen as a disease, a contagion that could infect society, and thus was informed by the biological turn that reconfigured race in the nineteenth century. Consider Campbell's characterization of the coding of communism and its relation to the cold war understanding of the USSR:

> 1) the well-developed antipathy toward communism in the United States stems from the way in which the danger to the private ownership of property it embodies is a code for distinguishing the "civilized" from the "barbaric" (or the normal from the pathological); and 2) this is the basis for the interpretive framework that constitutes the Soviet Union as a danger independent of any military capacity.[37]

The cold war discourse in the United States, then, stands as an exemplar of the state-race discourse, connecting sovereignty to a binary division of, now, the world and also the society of the United States, and casting the state in the role of "defender" of that society.

If this is the way in which the United States and the (western) world more generally was constituted at the time of the collapse of the Soviet

Union, and I think there would be few who would argue it was not, then the question of what to do when the Soviet Union imploded was quite profound. For the sovereignty of the biopolitical state to continue to function, society must be defended. The cold war discourse claims that defense must be mounted against an internal/external enemy that found its primary expression in the USSR, but suddenly there was no more USSR. Seen through the lens of Foucault's "race war," the end of the USSR denied the west more than just its military enemy, it denied the basis of its claim to sovereignty. It is not surprising, then, that one of the most potent responses is Francis Fukuyama's argument that history has itself come to an end.[38] Within the binary constituted by the cold war discourse, it may seem that history has indeed ended, for the underlying race war has been represented in terms of capitalism versus communism, and capitalism seems to win handily. If we accept a binary constitution of the world, and do not see that binary as something produced in something larger, then the defeat of one side produces the eternal victory of the other. There are no other options.

The War on Terror

Foucault's argument in *Society Must Be Defended*, however, draws our attention to the mobility and contingency of the race war discourse. Most did not need to be convinced that Fukuyama was wrong, but what Foucault allows us to do is to identify the key discourses that can be rearticulated to produce the justification for the state after the cold war. The reconfigured race war discourse allowed the central contradiction of the biopolitical state to be reconciled, but for precisely this reason it means that the race war *cannot* be won. History cannot end because the end of history exposes the fundamental contradiction at the heart of the contemporary normalizing state.

The importance of the contradiction between biopolitics and sovereignty as raised by both Agamben and Butler is difficult to overstate, as it is becoming more and more evident in the politics of contemporary western democracies. In the politics of sovereignty it is a glorious sacrifice to be killed or to send your child to be killed in defense of the state. Biopolitics undermines precisely this willingness to sacrifice, by producing the individual human life as of central value, not only to the individual involved but to the society as a whole. The difficulty this poses to the state has been revealed in stark terms since at least the time of U.S. involvement in Vietnam. As Cristina Masters argues in this volume (chapter 3), the return of American soldiers in body bags was no longer greeted by patriotic outpourings celebrating the noble sacrifice of those inside but rather with protests about the waste of human life. Similar pressures are now faced throughout the industrial west, as governments are increasingly unwilling to lose even a single soldier to combat—particularly if the manner of the loss is anything other than a straightforward, conventional combat casualty.[39] The race war discourse is, therefore, particularly powerful and wide-ranging, as it provides the discursive frame within which this contradiction can be managed, at least as far as it is possible to manage it.

And so we come to the war on terror. With the war on terror there is, once again, a clear articulation of Foucault's race war to the discourse of sovereignty: there is a danger *out there*, and *in here*, a danger that is waging permanent war and that we must fight against constantly. It is, in other words, precisely the permanent war underpinning or undermining the social that Foucault discussed. In the discursive constitution of the war on terror, the state is clearly cast in terms of the defender of the society—and so great is this particular threat that the instrumentality of the state must become extraordinarily extensive and intrusive.

The first thing that is notable about the war on terror is that it is even more complete an expression of the reconfigured race war thesis than was the cold war. As Foucault wrote: "In other words, the enemies who face us still pose a threat to us, and it is not some reconciliation or pacification that will allow us to bring the war to an end. *It will end only to the extent that we really are the victors*."[40] Total victory is the only possibility, but is equally impossible because of the inability otherwise to hide the contradiction at the heart of a normalizing society. Thus when the cold war ended and victory was declared, it was a victory that had to be undermined rather than, as Fukuyama counseled, celebrated. Victory without a new race war exposes the contradiction between sovereignty and biopolitics in a way that is unsustainable. The war on terror fulfills that purpose superbly, for whereas the cold war ultimately allowed for reconciliation—as unexpected as it was—the war on terror simply does not.[41]

Consider first of all, Bush's widely quoted initial mantra of the war: "either you are with us, or you are with the terrorists."[42] That seems precisely prefigured by Foucault. It is a binary stated as starkly as can be imagined that allows no middle ground and no solution other than the eradication of those who stand against us. Remember that in the cold war, there was a third option of "nonalignment." The structure was still fundamentally binary, but there was a relatively significant interstice.[43] No longer.

Second, this enemy cannot give up in the way that the USSR did, nor, in fact, can it be beaten. In part, of course, this is a function of the failure of terrorism to pose as significant a threat as the USSR did. Even by the

U.S. state's own figures, the incidence of terrorism has been in marked decline in the past two decades, since a high point in the early 1980s. The peak was reached in the four years from 1985 to 1988 when the United States counted over 600 incidents a year. By contrast, there were only 199 incidents in 2002 and even in 2001 the total number reached only 355.[44] What is more, even at its peak, terrorism never represented a significant threat to the United States or its allies by any meaningful material measure. As a consequence, terror can never be reduced to an objectively "safe" level—if it is not there now, it will never be until not only are there no more attacks but also no more possibility of attack, and that is, of course, impossible.[45] So, Saddam Hussein or even Osama bin Laden can be captured, but the shadowy threat remains, and if it never actually manages to strike, well then this is simply evidence of how necessary the state and its (ever-more intrusive) security measures are to defending society.

The race war discourse, therefore, allows us to make sense of Butler's incisive recognition of the danger of "indefinite detention":

> "Indefinite detention" is an illegitimate exercise of power, but it is, significantly, part of a broader tactic to neutralize the rule of law in the name of security. "Indefinite detention" does not signify an exceptional circumstance, but, rather, the means by which the exceptional becomes established as a naturalized norm. It becomes the occasion and the means by which the extra-legal exercise of state power justifies itself indefinitely, installing itself as a potentially permanent feature of political life in the US.[46]

Indeed, the potential permanence affects more than just political life in the United States, as Maher Arar's story reminds us. Indeed, Butler provides a clear foundation for understanding the geographic scope of this danger, writing: "[Bush] went on to justify the abrogation of the sovereignty of Iraq . . . by asserting the sanctity of its own extended sovereign boundaries (which the US extends beyond all geographical limits to include the widest gamut of its 'interests')."[47] The indefinite extension of this virulent new iteration of the U.S. sovereign right—indefinite in both space and time— is founded in the war on terror as a near-perfect expression of the race war discourse.

The final point to note about the discourse of the war on terror as an instance of Foucault's race war is the degree to which the enemy is racialized—particularly disturbing in the context of the indefinite extension of the discourse's danger. Foucault argues that only rarely has this discourse been expressed in an overtly racial fashion. It was at times in the colonial period of the nineteenth century. It was in the Nazi period. The discourse of the war on terror, while not explicitly racist in the Nazi sense, is extensively racialized. It has articulated its enemy as people identifiable not just by their religion, as important as that obviously is to their representation, but more particularly by their (racial) appearance.[48] Whether it is the often discussed "racial profiling," or the pervasive, everyday association of Islamist terrorists with the features of Arabs, the war on terror has produced a global discourse more racist than any we have seen since the time of European colonialism. Maher Arar's Syrian origin is central to his extraordinary rendition because the present iteration of race war marks the biological enemy as Middle-Eastern and brown-skinned. Foucault's argument allows us to provide the answer we had expected to Butler's question: "to what extent is there a racial and ethnic frame through which these imprisoned lives are viewed and judged such that they are deemed less than human, or as having departed from the recognizable human community?"[49]

The securing of society is now a securing of "white" society against the Arab other. What makes this move particularly pernicious, of course, is the way in which "white" society has become multihued. While we can racially profile to try to tease out the Arab other, not all terrorists are marked by Semitic looks and long beards; similarly, our more open, plural societies contain innumerable members who look just like the race enemy. As a consequence, these members of the society that the state is supposed to secure are rendered less and less secure in the practices of the state. As Ulrich Beck has argued:

> [Under these conditions] the citizen must *prove* that he or she is not dangerous, for under these conditions each individual finally comes under the suspicion of being a potential terrorist. Each person must thereby put up with submitting to random "security" controls.[50]

What is more, because the line along which the security of society is to be provided is both color-coded and unclear, the measures used to police that line have to be extraordinarily intrusive and severe. Consider this remarkable passage from a U.S. report from 2003 entitled *Nations Hospitable to Organized Crime and Terrorism*, in this case directed at Canada:

> Three broad factors contribute to Canada's position as a favored destination for terrorists and international criminals. First, as a modern liberal democracy Canada possesses a number of features that make it hospitable to terrorists and international criminals. The Canadian Constitution guarantees rights such as the right to life, liberty, freedom of movement, freedom of speech, protection against unreasonable search and seizure, and protection against arbitrary detention or imprisonment that make it easier for terrorists and international

criminals to operate. In addition, a technologically advanced economy and infrastructure facilitate operations and activities as well as providing a myriad of opportunities for abuse.[51]

Notice that what makes Canada a potential danger in the war on terror is that it guarantees "the right to life, liberty, freedom of movement, freedom of speech, protection against unreasonable search and seizure, and protection against arbitrary detention or imprisonment." These are, of course, precisely what makes Canada a free, liberal society that we might want to defend. Society must be defended, even if it means losing what it is that makes that society what it is in the process.[52]

Conclusion: Maher Arar and the Indefinite Future

Maher Arar's story, and the stories of the thousands of nameless others that have been rendered extraordinarily or placed in the sovereign limbo of Guantánamo Bay outrage us. There is an outrage that animates the attempt to understand how this could happen, not just once but repeatedly, systematically. Agamben's answer indicates that we should not be as surprised as we are. This is nothing new; this is the way that sovereign power functions, and we are all subject to its arbitrary expression, all liable to be placed under the sovereign ban. The discovery that the program responsible for Maher Arar's deportation to Syria, the insidious extraordinary rendition, predates the present war on terror seems to support that view. And yet we continue to be outraged. Judith Butler provides voice to the feeling that, as much as sovereign power is expressed in this fashion, something is novel as well.

The turn to Michel Foucault's history of race war seems to provide an answer, the beginnings of a theorization of the present that both captures the continuity Agamben notes and the feeling of novelty Butler expresses. Since the middle of the nineteenth century, race war has enabled the state to maintain its sovereign right expressed in the ability to render bare life, while claiming its legitimacy from the biopolitical capacity to make live. It is this contradiction, when it becomes overt, that outrages us: we are protected from the vicissitudes of power by the rights enshrined at the heart of the state, rights we bear as life far more than bare. When the state violates those rights and renders us as bare life, we feel, and are, violated. Agamben is thus right to note the continuity of the sovereign right, even in contradiction of its biopolitical legitimacy. But Butler is also right to note the novelty of the present condition. The war on terror is a different articulation of race war than those that have preceded it.

I can now begin to answer the questions the extraordinary rendering of Maher Arar demanded. It is clear now what sort of war the war on terror is, and because it is an iteration of race war it enables precisely the story of Maher Arar's rendition. The implications of this argument render the future of global politics profoundly disturbing. Butler recognized in the practice of indefinite detention the indefinite extension of the war on terror's state of emergency. Reading the war on terror as an instance of race war both renders that indefinite extension transparent and exposes the depth of its roots in the constitution of contemporary power. After a series of iterations, race war has found an expression that is in practice, if not in principle, unending; the biological enemy against whom society must be defended cannot be defeated and known to have been defeated. Maher Arar's is the story of an indefinite future, and that is the greatest outrage of all.

Notes

1. Jane Mayer brought the U.S. program of "extraordinary rendition" to public attention in "Outsourcing Torture: The Secret History of America's 'Extraordinary Rendition' Program," *The New Yorker*, February 14, 2005, http://www.newyorker.com/fact/content/?050214fa_fact6 (accessed August 10, 2006).
2. Maher Arar, "Maher Arar: Chronology of Events," 2004, http://www.maherarar.ca/cms/images/uploads/mahersstory.pdf (accessed August 10, 2006).
3. Ibid.
4. Ibid.
5. The government of Canada has announced a public inquiry into the role of Canadian officials and institutions in Mahar Arar's deportation. (Commission of Inquiry into the Actions of Canadian Officials in Relation to Maher Arar, 2004), http://www.ararcommission.ca/eng/index.htm (accessed August 10, 2006).
6. The Center for Constitutional Rights has sued the U.S. government for knowingly sending Maher Arar to a country it believes practices torture. The Center for Constitutional Rights, Canadian Government to Conduct Inquiry into Treatment of CCR Torture Client Maher Arar, http://www.ccr-ny.org/v2/reports/report.asp?ObjID=AJ48mobzZ1&Content=322 (accessed August 10, 2006); One of the lawyers for the CCR has subsequently alleged explicitly that the United States sent Arar to Syria in order to be tortured. See Bruce Demar, "U.S. Wanted Arar to be Tortured, Lawyer Says," *The Toronto Star*, February 29, 2004, http://pqasb.pqarchiver.com/thestar/553756021. html?did=553756021&FMT=ABS&FMTS=FT&date= Feb+28%2C+2004&author=Bruce+DeMara&pub=Toronto+Star&desc= U.S.+wanted+Arar+to+be+tortured%2C+lawyer+says (accessed

August 10, 2006). In addition, the case of Maher Arar led Human Rights Watch to call on the United States to stop the practice of transferring prisoners to countries identified by the United States itself as practicing torture. See Human Rights Watch, "United States: Stop Handing Over Detainees to Torturers," *Human Rights News*, 2003, http://www.hrw.org/press/2003/11/syria110703.htm (accessed August 10, 2006).

7. Mayer (2005).
8. U.K. House of Lords, "Opinions of the Lords of Appeal for Judgment in the Cause: A (FC) and others (FC) (Appellants) v. Secretary of State for the Home Department (Respondent); X (FC) and another (FC) (Appellants) v. Secretary of State for the Home Department (Respondent) ON Thursday 16 December 2004," 2004; http://www.publications.parliament.uk/pa/ld200405/ldjudgmt/jd041216/a&oth-1.htm   (accessed August 10, 2006).
9. Documents released on November 26, 2004 by the Commission of Inquiry into the actions of Canadian officials in relation to Maher Arar suggest that the RCMP, the Canadian federal police service, knew that Maher Arar was not a terrorist when they turned the information over to the United States. See Arar Inquiry Update, December 3, 2004, http://www.maherarar.ca/cms/images/uploads/Arar_Inquiry_Update_Dec_3.pdf (accessed August 10, 2006). For further updates and information on the release of documents, see the Arar Inquiry website, http://www.ararcommission.ca/eng/index.htm.
10. Amnesty International, "Guantánamo Bay—A Human Rights Scandal," http://web.amnesty.org/pages/guantanamobay-index-eng   (accessed August 10, 2006).
11. Amnesty International, "Guantánamo and Beyond: The Continuing Pursuit of Unchecked Executive Power," May 13, 2005, http://web.amnesty.org/library/pdf/AMR510632005ENGLISH/$File/AMR5106305.pdf (accessed August 10, 2006).
12. Amnesty International, "USA: Guantánamo Detentions Enter Fourth Year as Torture Allegations Mount," January 7, 2005, http://news.amnesty.org/index/ENGAMR510032005 (accessed August 10, 2006).
13. Full title: Convention against Torture and Other Cruel, Inhuman or Degrading Treatment or Punishment.
14. In the opinion of the International Committee of the Red Cross, the war on terror is not even a legal armed conflict, as it meets neither the criteria of international or noninternational armed conflict: "the ICRC believes that international humanitarian law is applicable when the 'fight against terrorism' amounts to, or involves, armed conflict. Such was the case in Afghanistan. . . . It is doubtful, absent further factual evidence, whether the totality of the violence taking place between states and transnational networks can be deemed to be armed conflict in the legal sense." See

International Committee of the Red Cross, *International Humanitarian Law and the Challenges of Contemporary Armed Conflicts*, (Geneva: ICRC, 2003), p. 18.

15. Giorgio Agamben, *Homo Sacer: Sovereign Power and Bare Life* (Stanford, CA: Stanford University Press, 1998), pp. 81–112.

16. Ibid., 111.

17. Judith Butler, *Precarious Life: The Powers of Mourning and Violence* (London: Verso, 2004), p. 57.

18. Ibid., p. 63.

19. Mayer (2005).

20. Butler (2004), p. 65.

21. Ibid., p. 53.

22. Ibid., p. 92.

23. Michel Foucault, *Society Must Be Defended*, trans. David Macey (London: Allen Lane and Penguin, 2003), pp. 66–71, 99–107.

24. Ibid., pp. 107–111.

25. "Race war," in other words, argues that politics is a continuation of war by other means. Foucault argues that the famous Clausewitzian dictum, that war is a continuation of politics by other means, is a simple transposition of this much older formulation of race war. See ibid., pp. 47–48.

26. Ibid., pp. 59–60.

27. Ibid., pp. 88–89.

28. Ibid., pp. 58–59, 258–261.

29. Francis Fukuyama's end of history thesis is, of course, a direct descendant of this turn. He returns to Hegel in order to contest not the dynamic of Marxist history, but rather the endpoint, the class content, of the final victor. See Francis Fukuyama, *The End of History and the Last Man*, (New York: Free Press, 1992).

30. Foucault (2003), pp. 61–62.

31. Ibid., pp. 257–261.

32. Regulation is the moment of biopolitics or biopower for Foucault. Biopower operates on people as populations, and is opposed to disciplinary power, which operates on people as individuals. These two forms of power meet in the norm, and so the normalizing society (in which we all live) is structured by discipline and regulation.

33. Thomas Hobbes, *Leviathan*, ed. C. B. McPherson (London: Penguin, 1969), pp. 228–238.

34. Foucault provides a fascinating example, which I will reproduce here in full: The paradoxes become apparent if we look, on the one hand, at atomic power, which is not simply the power to kill, in accordance with the rights that are granted to any sovereign, millions and hundreds of millions of people (after all, that is traditional). The workings of contemporary *politics power* are such that atomic power represents a paradox that is

difficult, if not impossible, to get around. The power to manufacture and use the atom bomb represents the deployment of a sovereign power that kills, but it is also the power to kill life itself. So the power that is being exercised in this atomic power is exercised in such a way that it is capable of suppressing life itself. And, therefore, to suppress itself insofar as it is the power that guarantees life. Either it is sovereign and uses the atom bomb, and therefore cannot be power, biopower, or the power to guarantee life, as it has been ever since the nineteenth century. Or, at the opposite extreme, you no longer have a sovereign right that is in excess of biopower, but a biopower that is in excess of sovereign right. This excess of biopower appears when it becomes technologically and politically possible for man not only to manage life but to make it proliferate, to create living matter, to build the monster, and, ultimately, to build viruses that cannot be controlled and that are universally destructive. This formidable extension of biopower, unlike what I was just saying about atomic power, will put it beyond all human sovereignty." Foucault (2003), pp. 253–254.

35. Ibid., pp. 242–254.

36. Ibid., pp. 87–89.

37. David Campbell, *Writing Security: United States Foreign Policy and the Politics of Identity* (Minneapolis: University of Minnesota Press, 1998), p. 139.

38. The first, and most noted, version of this response was Francis Fukuyama, "The End of History?" *The National Interest* (Summer 1989). Of course, Fukuyama then extended the argument into a book, *The End of History and the Last Man*. It is worthwhile noting that Fukuyama's argument was based in a reading of Hegel, who, in turn, is identified by Foucault as having mutated the "race war" discourse into his conception of the dialectic.

39. One of the effects of the contemporary technological battlefield is that members of Western militaries are rather more likely to be killed by each other than by the "enemy," at least in open combat. Both Canada (in Afghanistan) and the United Kingdom (in Iraq) have recently experienced this sort of loss. In neither case was it accepted as an inevitable part of the risks of waging war. The BBC reported, in relation to the Canadian incident in 2002: "There are signs of growing resentment and even anger in Canada in response to the 'friendly fire' incident in Afghanistan, which killed four Canadian soldiers and injured eight others." BBC World, "Canada Anger at 'Friendly Fire' Deaths," April 20, 2002, http://news.bbc.co.uk/1/hi/world/americas/1940768.stm (accessed August 10, 2006); On the other side, *The Globe and Mail* reported the response to UK friendly fire deaths in Iraq: "There is anger and bitterness among the British soldiers who survived a friendly-fire incident in Iraq in which one of their comrades was killed by a U.S. aircraft, exacerbating broader tensions between the two allies over strategy and the conduct of the war." Alan Freeman, "Survivors Slam Friendly-Fire 'Cowboy,'" *The Globe and Mail*, April 1, 2003, http://www.globeandmail.com/servlet/story/RTGAM.20030401.ubrit0401/BNStory/International (accessed August 10, 2006). The effect, then, is to narrow considerably the legitimate

losses that a state can inflict on its people, even in the name of security or defense.

40. Foucault (2003), p. 51, emphasis added.

41. I am not trying to suggest a reflexivity on the part of the U.S. state managers that allowed them to think in terms of biopolitics and sovereignty, nor a mechanical functionalism. Rather, the need to manage the contradiction finds expression in a series of political pressures: recruitment and (particularly) retention problems within the armed forces, popular support for war, and political support for military budgets are leading such expressions. Clearly, the leading pressure the state faces is the unwillingness of normalizing society to accept the deaths of "their sons" in war.

42. George Bush, "Address to a Joint Session of Congress and the American People," Washington, September 20, 2001, http://www.whitehouse. gov/news/releases/2001/09/20010920-8.html (accessed August 10, 2006).

43. See, inter alia, Andreas Wenger and Doron Zimmerman, *International Relations: From the Cold War to the Globalized World* (Boulder: Lynne Rienner, 2003); A. W. Singham and Shirley Hune, *Non-Alignment in an Age of Alignments* (London: Zed Books, 1986); Steven R. David, *Choosing Sides: Alignment and Realignment in the Third World* (Baltimore: Johns Hopkins University Press, 1991).

44. U.S. Department of State, Patterns of Global Terrorism, 2002 (Washington, DC: Department of State, 2003), www.state.gov/s/ct/rls/ pgtrpt (accessed August 10, 2006).

45. The need for no possibility of attack is clear from since the attacks of 9/11. Those attacks represent the only successful terrorist attack from without on the territory of United States. There have been none since, and yet the level of "security" is unprecedented, and the ratcheting up of color-coded warnings now almost routine. Indeed, if we look at the five years ending in 2002 there were 6 international terrorist attacks in total in North America. Four of those are in the year 2001: the four hijackings on September 11. There is nowhere lower than this to go other than zero, and so there can be no "safe" level other than zero.

46. Butler (2004), p. 67.

47. Ibid., pp. 66–67.

48. George Monbiot, "Race War," *The Guardian*, March 5, 2003, http://www. monbiot.com/archives/2002/03/05/race-war/ (accessed August 10, 2006).

49. Butler (2004), p. 57.

50. Ulrich Beck, "The Silence of Words: On Terror and War," *Security Dialogue*, 34 (2003): 261.

51. Library of Congress, *Nations Hospitable to Organized Crime and Terrorism*, Report Prepared by the Federal Research Division, Library of Congress under an Interagency Agreement with the Director of Central Intelligence Crime and Narcotics Center, October 2003, p. 145.

52. Beck (2003), pp. 260–261.

CHAPTER 9

ABJECT SPACES: FRONTIERS, ZONES, CAMPS

Engin F. Isin and Kim Rygiel

A bject spaces are those in and through which increasingly distressed, displaced, and dispossessed peoples are condemned to the status of strangers, outsiders, and aliens (e.g., refugees, unlawful combatants, insurgents, and the conquered) and stripped of their (existent and potential) citizenship (rights of becoming political) in various emerging frontiers, zones, and camps around the world. There has been a veritable outcry against the fact that these people have been reduced to a status without human rights. Yet their being human has not seemed to matter much to the states and their laws that have condemned them to these states of inexistence (figure 9.1). What is the logic of these abject spaces and how do we investigate the practices that sustain them?

Theorizing Abject Spaces: Arendt, Again

While Guantánamo Bay has become a symbol of U.S. oppression and human rights abuses since 2002, abject spaces—extraterritorial spaces where international and national laws are suspended—have spread throughout the world in the past decade as spaces for holding refugees, asylum seekers, deportees, combatants, insurgents, and others caught in the new global policing and policies net. These spaces include various frontiers controlled by state authorities, zones where special rules and laws apply, and camps where laws are suspended. We refer to these as abject spaces to indicate that those who are constituted through them are rendered as

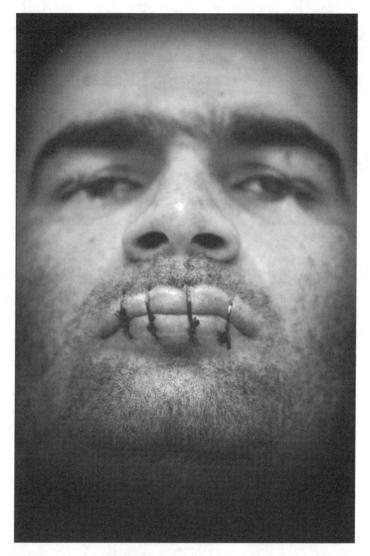

Figure 9.1 Second placed picture in the World Press Photo 2004 contest taken by Reuters photographer Paul Vreeker.

Note: Paul Vreeker, Reuters photographer based in the Netherlands, has won second place in the people In The News Singles catagory at the World Press Photo 2004 contest announced February 11, 2005 with this picture of an Iranian immigrant protesting against proposed Dutch asylum laws. The prestigious competition is the world's largest annual press photography contest.★

neither subjects nor objects but inexistent insofar as they become inaudible and invisible.[1] How do we account for and respond to the production of such spaces? Much has been written about Agamben's consideration of the camp as the *nomos* of the modern. More than a decade ago Agamben suggested that if the camp was the space in which the most inhuman events had happened, the response has been to ask, "how could it happen?" But this question makes it impossible to ask another: "What is a camp? What is its juridico-political structure that such events could take place there?"[2] From this question Agamben proceeds to illustrate that the inhuman could only take place when the camp was constituted as a space of exception, that is to say, a space where the existing juridico-political logic is suspended and replaced by an alternative logic. More significantly, this alternative logic itself becomes the rule. In other words, the camp as a state of exception becomes the rule but, as exception, remains nonetheless outside the normal order. The camp is therefore not simply an external space. Rather, the logic of the camp is its immanence. The state of exception is, by the very fact of its exclusion, included in the juridical order. It is this immanence that enables the camp to conflate its fact and law in and through which anything becomes possible.[3]

For Agamben the state of exception also pertains to bare life. What is significant and dangerous about the modern order, according to Agamben, is that as the state of exception becomes the rule, "the realm of bare life—which is originally situated at the margins of the political order—gradually begins to coincide with the political realm, and exclusion and inclusion, outside and inside, *bios* and *zoe*, right and fact, enter into a zone of indistinction."[4] For Agamben, then, the camp becomes that space where politics becomes biopolitics and "bare life," not the citizen, the subject of politics.[5] Agamben then suggests, "It would be more honest and, above all, more useful to investigate carefully the juridical procedures and deployments of power by which human beings could be so deprived of their rights and prerogatives that no act committed against them could appear any longer as a crime."[6] It becomes impossible to decide between fact and law in the camp because exception and rule become indistinct. If this is true, Agamben says, then we find ourselves in the presence of a camp every time a space is created where it becomes impossible to distinguish between fact and law, exception and rule.[7] Agamben astutely observed almost a decade ago that the logic of the camp as a space of exception had already materialized into most benign spaces in airports and cities.[8] While Agamben is absolutely essential for understanding the frontiers, zones, and camps that have been created since he wrote about the logic of the camp, we suggest that these new spaces cannot be understood with the logic of exception. We want to argue that the logic of the camp as set out by Agamben does not—or cannot—account for the novelty of the kinds of spaces that have been created. The logic of exception that prevailed in the internment camps that Agamben interprets as the *nomos* of the modern, as we shall see, is not quite helpful for understanding frontiers, zones, and camps of our times. This is partly because, as we shall see, Agamben's focus on the logic of the camp is ahistorical; he essentializes the camp, rather than investigating how the camp works in all of its material, experiential, and diverse forms. As abject spaces, frontiers, zones, and camps are often created with the intent of "protecting" the displaced and keeping them simultaneously "away" from both danger *and* state territories. While the camp functioned, as Arendt noted, as a space in which undesirables were eliminated *after* denationalization and denaturalization, frontiers and zones function as spaces where subjects are "processed" as inexistent beings— noncitizens in waiting.[9] If the camp was a *space of abjection* where people were reduced to bare life, the zones, frontiers, and camps of our times are *abject spaces*, spaces in which the intention is to treat people neither as subjects (of discipline) nor objects (of elimination) but as those without presence, without existence, as inexistent beings, not because they don't exist, but because their existence is rendered invisible and inaudible through abject spaces.

It is precisely in this difference that abject spaces are not spaces of abjection but spaces of politics. Thus, it is possible to imagine certain spaces of inexistence where abjection could be resisted. Besides the camp, there are also autonomous and semiautonomous zones where the rule of law is suspended and other logics enacted like the logic of "cities of refuge." Derrida's proposal for a concept of cities of refuge is an example of a space of exception where the rule of law of the state is suspended for hospitality, a hospitality that is not extended by the state but made possible by the city.[10] The revival in recent years of the sanctuary movement in Canada and across Europe are good examples of the sort of practice that "cities of refuge" might include.[11] Agamben, however, is unable to shake himself off from the logic of the camp as the only space of abjection. As a result, he is also unable to imagine spaces of exception that serve against abjection: his conception of the city is nebulous and enigmatic precisely because it is trapped in the camp.[12] Agamben wishes that "European cities would rediscover their ancient vocation of cities of the world by entering into a relation of reciprocal extraterritoriality."[13] Agamben names this space as reciprocal extraterritoriality or even aterritoriality as a new model of international relations in which the guiding concept would no longer be the rights of the citizen but the refuge of the singular. Agamben suggests that "[t]his space would coincide neither with any of the homogenous national territories nor with their *topographical* sum, but would rather act on them by articulating and perforating them *topologically*."[14] The irony is that such spaces are already appearing in Europe and North America as frontiers and zones and in the form of what we call here abject spaces. States are entering into reciprocal relationships to create these spaces in which extraterritorial, or even better aterritorial, relations are being created. European cities too are rediscovering their ancient vocation in sequestering, detaining, and regulating bodies by entering into reciprocal relations with each other.

To understand the logic of what we call "abject spaces" as opposed to "spaces of abjection" such as represented by Agamben's camp requires investigating these spaces as both spaces of abjection as well as spaces of resistance, and the thoughts and practices that sustain them. Our investigations of frontiers, zones, and camps reveal how different kinds of abject spaces employ different strategies to reduce people to abject inexistence, not only creating varying conditions of rightlessness but also making different logics and acts of resistance possible.

We would then be well advised to take Rancière's protest against Agamben (and Arendt) on this issue seriously.[15] Rancière argues that by following Arendt so closely Agamben takes the capacity of being a subject away from those who are caught in the camp, rendering it an altogether apolitical space. The opposition between bare life and political life hinges on an ontological trap. Rancière notes that "[i]n this space, the executioner and the victim, the German body and the Jewish body, appear as two parts of the same 'biopolitical' body."[16] Rancière argues, "Any kind of claim to rights or any struggle enacting rights is thus trapped from the very outset in the mere polarity of bare life and state of exception."[17] He argues that this logical flaw is already present in Arendt.[18] He refers here to Arendt's observation that

[i]f a human being loses his political status, he should, according to the implications of the inborn and inalienable rights of man, come under exactly the situation for which the declarations of such general rights provided. Actually the opposite is the case. It seems that a man who is nothing but a man has lost the very qualities which make it possible for other people to treat him as fellow-man.[19]

Rancière takes issue with Arendt, arguing that for Arendt

either the rights of the citizen are the rights of man—but the rights of man are the rights of the unpoliticized person; they are the rights of those who have no rights, which amounts to nothing—or the rights of man are the rights of the citizen, the rights attached to the fact of being a citizen of such and such a constitutional state. This means that they are the rights of those who have rights, which amounts to a tautology.[20]

As we shall see, Rancière confuses Arendt's observation here regarding the paradox that is human rights with her argument that a politics cannot be founded on human rights. It seems to us that Rancière misses Arendt's essential insight: despite its weightiness as a discourse, human rights are in fact meaningless in and of themselves, becoming significant only within the context of "a right to have rights," that is, with the right to first exist as a political subject. Arendt does not equate the rights of man with the rights of the *unpoliticized* person, as Rancière suggests, but with the person denied the right to become a political subject, an argument that is, as we shall illustrate, very close, ironically, to Rancière's own.

In contrast to his interpretation of Arendt, Rancière argues that "the Rights of Man are the rights of those who have not the rights that they have and have the rights that they have not."[21] Rancière explains that if the rightless "could lose their 'bare life' out of a public judgment based on political reasons, this meant that even their bare life—their life doomed to death was political."[22] He suggests that because Arendt and Agamben begin with the assumption of the clear distinction between *zoe* ("bare life") and *bios* ("political life") they "sort out the problem in advance."[23] Rather, for Rancière, "the point is, precisely, where do you draw the line separating one life from the other? Politics is about that border."[24] The problem lies in assuming that "the rights *belong* to definite or permanent subjects."[25] This approach omits the fact that politics lies precisely in that moment wherein one becomes a political subject by enacting or claiming "the rights one does not have" rather than in some already given status with rights. The consequence of this approach, Rancière suggests, is that "the political space, which was shaped in the very gap between the abstract literalness of the rights and the polemic about their verification, turns out to diminish more and more every day."[26] Rancière's argument here is that the condition of abjection and rightlessness should not be confused with the condition of being political, that is, with the capacity to act as a political subject, for the abject may be without rights but this does not negate their ability to act as political subjects. It is in the very claiming of rights—the rights that one *does not* have—where one enacts one's political existence. Finally, it is precisely in abject spaces like the camp, according to Rancière, where such politics occur "shaped in the very gap between the abstract literalness of the rights and the polemic about their verification."[27] Rancière's argument here is an important corrective to Agamben's interpretation of Arendt and his view of the camp, but we would argue that it is actually much closer to

Arendt's own argument where she insists that what is denied to people reduced to statelessness is the right to have rights, which, she argues, is more fundamental than the specific rights of justice and freedom.

In the insightful chapter "The Decline of the Nation-State and the End of the Rights of Man" in her book *The Origins of Totalitarianism*, Arendt traces the emergence of the question of minorities in Europe and raises questions about the very possibility of human rights, or, rather, the very possibility of founding a politics on human rights. She argues that minority treaties by which "stateless" peoples were to be protected in the early twentieth century were themselves a product of the logic of sovereignty and racialized conceptions of the homogeneity of population and rootedness in the soil that undergirded it.[28] The status of statelessness could only make sense under conditions where freedom was associated with emancipation symbolized by a nation corresponding to a state. For dominant groups in European states the question of minorities dangerously and rapidly converged on assimilation or liquidation.[29] She interpreted this tragic process as the conquest of the state by the nation whereby the state was transformed from an institution of law into one of the nation.[30] She thus arrived at the conclusion that

> [n]o paradox of contemporary politics is filled with a more poignant irony than the discrepancy between the efforts of well-meaning idealists who stubbornly insist on regarding as "inalienable" those human rights, which are enjoyed only by citizens of the most prosperous and civilized countries, and the situation of the rightless themselves.[31]

It was impossible to bring any of these rightless people under state law precisely because the state, now conquered by the nation, produced the condition of statelessness and hence the question of minorities, refugees, and the rightless in the first place. And all efforts to define their rights as inalienable human rights proved ineffective.

Arendt locates the origins of this paradox in the very Declaration of the Rights of Man. While on the one hand the source of the rights of man was "man" himself (as opposed to God or tradition), the guarantor of such rights could only be a people: "man hardly appeared as a completely isolated being who carried his dignity within himself without reference to some large encompassing order, when he disappeared again into a member of a people."[32] Man was man only insofar as he was a member of a sovereign people, and being a sovereign people was increasingly defined as being rooted in soil and with a state. "The whole question of human rights, therefore, quickly and inextricably blended with the question of national emancipation; only the emancipated sovereignty of the people, of one's own people, seemed to be able to insure them."[33]

The significance of her argument, and its poignancy then as now, is that human rights proved ineffective not because of ill will or intention but because of the logic of sovereignty of the nation-state. Her argument was not, Rancière argues, a revival of citizenship rights (civil, political, and social) ensconced in nation-states but to call into question the logic of sovereignty that undergirded citizenship and made the denial of those rights to certain groups possible. Arendt's reference to Burke, which troubles Rancière, was meant to illustrate the prescience of Burke's insight rather than arguing in defense of his conservatism and the return to tradition. On the contrary, as her argument about the definition of citizenship as "a right to have rights" makes clear, Arendt, like Rancière, argued that "something much more fundamental than freedom and justice" is at stake when humans are deprived of the right to have rights; that is to say, the right to speech, opinion, presence, and action, in effect, the rights to being political.[34]

When Arendt speaks about the dark background of mere givenness she means to critique the logic of sovereignty that takes the mere existence of humans and turns it into the foundations of a nation. By contrast, the foundation of a state (not a nation or nation-state) for Arendt would then be to militate against mere existence with what she calls human artifice: the state as a result of our common human labor.[35] When people are forced out of the political, they lose "all those parts of the world and those aspects of human existence" that are the products of human labor.[36] "This mere existence, that is all that which is mysteriously given us by birth and which includes our bodies and the talents of our minds," cannot justify equality because "[w]e are not born equal; [but] we become equal as members of a group on the strength of our decision to guarantee ourselves mutually equal rights."[37] Equality is not given but is a product of human labor—negotiation, struggle, compromise, defeat, victory—all that is human, all too human ways of being.

Approaching frontiers, zones, and camps that have appeared in the past few years reminds us of the emergence of minorities and refugees in the early twentieth century. While the logic of sovereignty that undergirded the camp and the spaces that corresponded to it are similar, the abject spaces that have emerged in the late twentieth and early twenty-first century appear different. As much as we feel horror at the appearance of such spaces, we also argue that investigating the logic that underpins them and the practices that sustain them is absolutely essential for revealing these spaces as *political spaces*. As if responding to Arendt's argument that human rights are meaningless without the ability to first claim political existence, these new abject spaces govern precisely by attempting to prevent individuals from exercising political subjectivity by holding them in spaces of existential, social, political, and legal limbo. *We interpret the rendering of certain people as invisible and inaudible as nothing less than a rendering of these people as inexistent and we understand those spaces in which they are so constituted as abject spaces.*

While this logic of inexistence is common to all forms of abject spaces, frontiers, zones, and camps each intervene in this process of rights making in different ways. In the case of frontiers and zones, the focus is on halting the ability to enact rights. Recalling Rancière here, it is precisely when one enacts "the rights that one does not have" that one becomes a political subject. As Rancière explains, "[t]hese rights are theirs when they can do something with them to construct a dissensus against the denial of rights they suffer."[38] Historically, citizenship has always emerged first as a practice and only after as legal status. Groups excluded from legal definitions of citizenship entitlement (slaves, women, the propertyless, etc.) have always made their claims to citizenship first by acting as political subjects and demanding "the rights that they do not have." Only by acting as citizens in this way has the legal status of citizenship broadened its boundaries to newcomers. Frontiers and zones abject, then, by attempting to halt this very process of citizenship making by incapacitating subjects from claims making. This is done through strategies of silencing such as geographical and social isolation. Abjects, like the Iranian man in the photo with which this chapter opens, know only too well these strategies of silencing. Suturing one's eyelids and lips in protest viscerally marks the pain, which is this denial of subjectivity. But it is also an act of resistance, reclaiming political subjectivity out of this very act of silencing. Denied legal citizenship status, and with it "the onto-political status of a speaking being," abjects "have to interrupt the dominant political (speaking) order not just to be heard, but to be recognized as a speaking being as such."[39] The act of suturing (along with the hunger strike that results) is an act by which the nonspeaking abject transforms his very own body (his own "bare life") into an act of resistance.

If frontiers and zones are designed with the intention of preventing the abject from acting as a political subject, camp spaces work with a different logic of internment. Through internment, political subjects with legal status are turned into those "who have not the rights that they have," a necessary first step in order to be able to strip away this status, thereby turning these political subjects into abjects. As Arendt observed, denationalization and denaturalization were necessary first steps in making the extermination of Jews, gypsies, homosexuals, and other "undesirables" thinkable and possible. Similarly, new forms of the camp, such as Guantánamo Bay, render citizens and nationals in legal limbo as "enemy combatants," denying them the rights that come with citizenship and nationality—even with criminality. After all, as Arendt noted, the status of criminal might be preferable for some since at least a criminal has rights.[40] In other words, the new forms of abject spaces share the same overall governing logic but come at it from different ends: frontiers and zones work to interrupt the *practice* of citizenship while camps aim to strip away citizenship *status*.

In the rest of the chapter we, therefore, propose to investigate these abject spaces and their logics but from outside the logic of human rights. The logic of human rights demands the inalienability of human rights in situations where it has already been determined that certain individuals have lost their rights. But as Rancière notes this "identification of the subject of the Rights of Man with the subject deprived of any right" leads to "an actual process of depoliticization."[41] Perhaps counterintuitively, the power of human rights lies precisely in the fact that there is a gap between the ideal of them as an abstract concept and their realization in practice. For it is this gap that engenders politics, facilitating the process of political subjectivization as abjects claim the rights they do not have and, in so doing, acquire the first condition necessary for having human rights, that of the right to being political. Human rights are problematic, therefore, because in deciding who has, and does not have, rights from the outset they "become humanitarian rights, the rights of those who cannot enact them, the victims of the absolute denial of right."[42] In other words, human rights discourse is used to *give* rights to individuals determined to be without rights, something akin to a charitable donation like medicine or clothes, which are donated to the poor, rather than rights that are already theirs by virtue of being political.[43] Thus, the logic of human rights is such that it makes the case for the inalienable rights of the abject on the grounds that the abject is already other than a political subject, a logic that ultimately works against its own good intentions. Moreover, by investigating abject spaces, we see that often the logic that results in the loss of "the right to have rights" is couched in human rights discourse in arguments, for example, suggesting that abject spaces are designed to offer protection. Thus, while we recognize that human rights may seem like a good tactical tool "on the ground" for negotiating the rights of the abject, we would argue that the logic that they confer is the same problematic logic employed by the abject spaces we wish to analyze. For despite their different intentions, both treat the abject as an exception outside of the realm of politics.

Frontiers

Frontiers are those spaces where the mobility of people is regulated and national and international laws temporarily suspended through the creation of buffer zones through which people can be processed. It should be noted that migration is, for many, simultaneously a strategy of resistance and an attempt to better one's life conditions through mobility.[44] It is in this context, then, that frontiers should be understood as abject spaces; they are, in the first instance, attempts at controlling migrant agency in transit spaces, spaces that migrants have to some extent created.[45]

This section exemplifies emerging frontiers in which various subjects are not only stripped of their citizenship rights (of their origins), but also given ostensibly differentiated citizenship rights (in their destinations). The logic behind such spaces is to prevent the abject from exercising social, political, and economic rights, recognizing that the ability to do so is a first step in becoming political and claiming legal citizenship status. The logic behind such governmental thought in producing such spaces, however, is one of human rights, and more specifically of protection, that is, that indeed new rights are being extended to those who would otherwise remain rightless. This logic condemns those who are caught in its web to a state of being neither objects nor subjects but abjects: those whose inexistence is secured by virtue of their transient and suspended state.

We see this logic, for example, in the U.K. government's new proposal for a global asylum system based on two types of zones:[46] "Regional Protection Areas" and "off-territory Transit Processing Centres."[47] Regional protection areas are areas to be set up near conflict zones producing major flows of people, and under UNHCR responsibility to be located in Turkey, Iran, northern Somalia, and Morocco.[48] In contrast, processing centers are to be located along the external borders of the European Union in countries such as Romania, Croatia, Albania, and Ukraine and are meant to be extraterritorial processing areas where people's asylum claims could be processed, preventing the need to actually travel to the countries in which they wish to request asylum.[49] We can also consider the heavily regulated and controlled border zones such as the U.S./Mexico border as poignant examples.[50] The example we wish to highlight here, however, is Australia's excised offshore places and processing centers. Like the United Kingdom, Australia's plans also depend on creating extraterritorial spaces in which to "house" asylum seekers and other migrants in a space of social isolation away from, and off the territory of, the Australian state where they might more easily exercise certain social, political, and civil citizenship rights.

In 2001, the Australian government passed legislation to deter refugees (especially those smuggled in without valid documentation) from reaching its shores. As part of this legislation, Australia removed certain territories from its "migration zone" as a way of circumventing international refugee law and its own national immigration law and responsibility to process asylum seekers. These territories act as spaces permitting indefinite detention with limited judicial review as a way of bypassing judicial procedures normally applying on the Australian mainland. These territories, called "excised offshore places," include Christmas Island and the Cocos (Keeling) Islands in the Indian Ocean; Ashmore and Cartier Island in the Timor Sea; and "any Australian sea installation or offshore resource (such as an oil rig)."[51]

In addition to "excised offshore places," the Australian government has also made arrangements with several Pacific islands to establish "offshore processing centers," essentially amounting to the "subcontracting of detention to poorer neighbouring states (the so-called 'Pacific Solution')."[52] Here asylum seekers, especially those entering "illegally" or "expelled" by the Australian government (like those arriving by boat) may be turned away to these places and held in facilities similar to detention centers and refugee camps to await the processing of their asylum claims. Persons detained in these camps are denied such civil and political rights as "contact with the outside world," "freedom of movement," and "due process guarantees" like independent legal counsel.[53]

Like zones of protection, these offshore places interrupt the process of citizenship and rights making by rendering asylum seekers into abjects through social isolation in detention centers where they are less likely to be able to exercise citizenship rights such as the right to legal council, speech, and access to social services and community. Whereas zones of protection operate by creating extraterritorial spaces that function as buffers, offshore places work by redefining state territory as either no longer falling under state jurisdiction (e.g., excised offshore places) or as extraterritorial space purchased on a second territory and often under the responsibility of a third party like an international organization. Either way, these technologies create frontiers that keep threats to the state and its sovereignty at a distance.

What is then the logic of all these zones of protection, regional protection areas, excised offshore places, offshore protection areas, and protection borderlands that we call frontiers? It is not that there is an inexorable logic that is enacted through these diverse forms of population control and regulation but that they are assembled together to create frontiers in and through which subjects are denied possibilities of constituting themselves as political subjects without being reduced to objects. These frontiers through which people are constituted as abject have become spaces with their own logic. Rather than focusing on how these spaces violate the human rights of abjects, it makes more sense to us to emphasize the ways in which these spaces attempt to incapacitate these people from constituting themselves as subjects with rights to have rights. These spaces render subjects with an inexistent status that is without voice, without speech, without presence, without reason—in effect, without the capacity of becoming political and thus deserving of even a right to have rights. Yet, it is in these abject spaces that the dominant regimes of democratic states are also made visible—and rendered so by the very same abjects they have tried to constitute. For the abject continue to act as political subjects exercising the rights they do not have whether it is in acts of suturing mouths, setting boats on fire in order to be picked up and brought to the Australian shores, or attempting dangerous border crossings. It is through these acts that they render themselves existent and present while simultaneously exposing the web of strategies and technologies of otherness that attempt to render them inexistent.

Zones

The logic that assembles frontiers can also be found in spaces that we call zones. These zones are spaces where abjects live under suspended rules of freedom as spaces of inexistence. Unlike frontiers, whose logic is to keep out and away those threats to state sovereignty via extraterritorial arrangements, zones are spaces nestled within state and city territories. These include zones within cities to which various subjects are dispersed but then live under some form of conditional freedom and surveillance. These are zones of inexistence insofar as abjects who inhabit them are constituted as inexistent subjects in a state of transient permanence.

While refugees living in many cities of the world have been called "an invisible population" whose needs are often overlooked even under UNHCR programs, the plight of refugees, especially in European cities, concerns us here.[54] In Paris, squatter camps have emerged in downtown centers like Alban-Satragne and near the Channel ports. These "unofficial open-air transit camps" are referred to as "mini-Sangattes" after the infamous, now closed, Sangatte detention center.[55] Young men gather around these sites by day and disperse to nearby building sites to sleep at night.[56] These growing transit camps are, in part, the response of migrants to the crackdown by France and Britain on refugees crossing the Channel to seek asylum in Britain. The asylum seekers find an occasional meal through the Salvation Army but fear staying overnight in hostels because of police harassment.[57]

In Britain, rejected asylum seekers find themselves in similar situations, suddenly turned out onto and left to sleep in the streets, without access to social services. The U.K. government provides housing to some asylum seekers awaiting their claims to be processed. Once a negative decision has been reached, however, they may find themselves suddenly turned out overnight onto the street without a place to sleep, benefits, and even the right to work.[58] In these cases, asylum seekers are literally turned into the homeless without rights to social services and the right to work.[59] What is particular to abject spaces nestled within cities is the way states use these spaces to make the failed asylum claimants "disappear" into the streets by rendering them invisible, inaudible, and ultimately inexistent, thus limiting their access to many of the citizenship rights that become available by virtue of being in and of the city.

Other abject spaces nestled within the city include various detention centers. In the past decade democratic states have introduced increasingly restrictive means of dealing with refugees and migrants including the growing use of detention centers.[60] These detention centers range from "asylum hotels" or "induction centers" to "accommodation centers" to "removal centers."

Removal centers, also known as "closed centers," are often privately run, prison-like holding centers where people are kept behind barbed wire and denied rights of movement, with limited access to legal rights and time outdoors just as in prison, with one well-known example being Scotland's Dungavel Immigration and Asylum Centre.[61] In contrast, "open centers" permit asylum seekers freedom of movement and house both "illegal" immigrants as well as asylum seekers either awaiting deportation or the processing of asylum claims, with one example being Belgium's Le Petit Chateau.[62] There are also "departure" or "expulsion centers" to hold those awaiting deportation such as those being built by the Dutch government which, in 2004, ruled that it would "deport within the next three years 26,000 asylum seekers whose claims have been rejected."[63] Criticized by human rights organizations for violating international refugee law, the law has elicited mass protest and hunger strikes, one Iranian asylum seeker even sewing closed his eyes and mouth in protest.[64] Finally, there are detention camps, like the infamous Woomera camp in Australia, discussed by Anne Orford in chapter 10, or Sangatte in France, which will be further discussed in the section on camps. Of particular interest to us here, however, is the example of "asylum hotels" and "induction or reception centers."

In 2002, the U.K. government announced plans to build new reception or induction centers to house asylum seekers for the first week after their arrival, giving them a physical exam and information on asylum procedures, before moving them to large-scale accommodation centers where they would be housed while waiting for their claims to be processed.[65] The plan was to use various hotels (popularly referred to in the press as "asylum hotels") as induction centers. One such example is the Coniston Hotel in Kent. However, protest from neighborhood residents led to the eventual decision to abandon the project because of a lack of proper public consultation.[66] Yet, the response of public protest also reveals the ways in

which a logic of inexistence—this time enacted through discourses of
hospitality (asylum and accommodation)—is thrown into crisis as local
residents object to asylum seekers as guests in a hotel, "a hospitable space
traditionally reserved for paying guests, such as tourists."[67]

As a result of, and in order to mitigate against, further protests from
inner city neighborhoods around the use of hotels as induction centers, the
U.K. government also proposed building a network of accommodation
centers to house incoming asylum seekers waiting for their claims to be
processed. These centers are to be built in rural communities, the logic
being that since inner cities have shouldered most of the responsibility for
asylum seekers in the past, other parts of the country should now assist.[68]
Moreover, the government notes that such centers would be an improvement to its current practice of housing asylum seekers in leased houses and
flats by enabling faster processing of cases, "lessening the impact on social
services" and "providing closer contact with asylum seekers."[69] The centers
are to provide all the basic services to asylum seekers in one spot so that
they "will not be dependent on local services" such as education, health,
transportation, legal services, and "purposeful activities and voluntary
work."[70] These euphemisms are designed to mask the fact that the authorities want to render asylum seekers inexistent, making it impossible for
them to become subjects by becoming part of the daily life of cities, which
is achieved, in part, by accessing government services. Harkening back to
medieval European cities, these detention centers function as a new form
of the ghetto, a technology of segregation whereby subjects are constituted
as strangers and outsiders rather than subjects with rights to have rights.

Detention centers represent a continuum of holding spaces for asylum
claimants where the logic is initially one of protection and welcoming by
the state. This logic shifts to one of transition, where claimants' lives are put
on hold in accommodation centers that "accommodate" by providing basic
services all in one spot as they await a decision on their status. Finally, at the
other end of the continuum are removal and expulsion centers. Here the
logic is one of incarceration with the state seeking to punish the "bad,"
failed claimants, now no longer deserving of state protection and the
"human rights" that it confers. Detention centers reveal that if the logic of
human rights is to give rights to asylum seekers by granting protection then
the flip side of this is to remove these rights through expulsion centers.

Like frontiers, zones also govern by restricting the ability of people to
enact certain citizenship rights that they may have access to despite not having formal citizenship status and rights. Unlike frontiers, however, which
work through the creation of extraterritorial spaces, zones are nestled within
cities and states. What is particular to these spaces is that cities are spaces

where abjects have been more successfully able to make claims to rights to the city (as compared to the state) by virtue of being able to practice many citizenship rights despite not having formal citizenship status. Thus, the logic of zones is to act as a filter in the citizenship-making process, "weeding out" the "bad" or illegitimate (i.e., "illegal") asylum claimants by segregating them in enclosed spaces where their rights and access to social networks can be severely curtailed. Failing deportation, abjects experience a transition in subjecthood in these spaces from claimants deserving of human rights under the protection of the state to criminals with limited rights to finally being rendered invisible by being made homeless. Because the logic of awarding human rights to some also makes it possible to deny them to others, we would argue that it would be more effective to focus attention on the way these spaces operate as political spaces, that is how they prevent abjects from claims making to the rights that they should, but do not, have.

Camps

We now reconsider Agamben's idea of the camp as a new paradigm of biopolitics.[71] We illustrate different kinds of camps than those Agamben considered as paradigmatic: rather than focusing on camps that reduced subjects to bare life, we consider camps as states of inexistence that function as reserves in which subjects and their rights are suspended temporarily, in transition from one subjecthood to another.

The number of people kept in such reservation zones around the world is staggering. For example, of the 20 million people currently receiving assistance from the UNHCR, approximately 12 million are refugees living in camps or similar conditions.[72] Yet, we are specifically concerned here with refugee camps in democratic states. While we focus in detail on the example of Guantánamo Bay, it is only the most recent example of the type of large-scale detention camp becoming all too common across states. Other examples include the Woomera detention center in the South Australian outback, a desert camp that operated from 1999 to April 2003, designed to hold about 400 people, but holding at times as many as 1,400 asylum seekers, some for as many as three years, in desperately poor conditions.[73] Similarly, France's Sangatte asylum camp (1999–2002) near Calais is yet another example of this type of camp that was designed to house growing numbers of asylum seekers found sleeping on the streets of Calais as they tried to cross to Britain through the Channel to seek asylum.[74] Intended to hold around 800 people before its closure in 2002, it often held between 1,300 and 1,900 in overcrowded conditions, with as many as 67,000 asylum seekers passing through Sangatte.[75]

Following Woomera and Sangatte, Guantánamo Bay is the most recent example of such camps. A U.S. naval base leased from Cuba, Guantánamo Bay has been used since 2002 for military detention camps that imprison suspected al Qaeda and Taliban "terrorists." The U.S. government claims that those being held are beyond U.S. law and the constitutional rights they would be afforded as prisoners on American soil. Guantánamo currently holds some 650 foreign nationals from over 40 different countries, many arrested in Afghanistan in 2002. These men (and some children) are being held without charge or trial, denied the right to legal counsel, and subject to degrading and cruel conditions such as solitary confinement and intensive interrogation without the presence of a lawyer.[76] Not only have most men not been charged but the United States refuses to clarify their legal status, referring to them as "enemy combatants" in order to be able to hold them indefinitely without recourse to the courts.[77] The United States refuses to grant these detainees prisoner of war status or to clarify their legal status in front of a tribune as required under the Third Geneva Convention (Articles 4 and 5).[78] Instead, the United States plans to try detainees by military tribunals, which Amnesty International notes "do not meet international standards for a fair trial" since they are "not independent and impartial courts," "curtail the right of appeal," and "allow a lower standard of evidence than ordinary civilian courts in the USA."[79] These tribunals are capable of handing down the death sentence.

Given the lack of legal rights and due legal process, the United Kingdom, Denmark, and Spain, for example, have negotiated for the rights of their nationals to be repatriated for trial. In other cases, repatriation might expose detainees to the risk of torture or execution in their own states (e.g., China, Yemen, and Russia).[80] On April 20, 2004, the U.S. Supreme Court heard *Rasul v. Bush* and *Habib v. Bush*, two cases brought forth by the Centre for Constitutional Rights (CCR) on behalf of detainees at Guantánamo Bay. The cases are based on the principle of habeas corpus, that is, that no one may be imprisoned without a clear basis in the law.[81] The petitions argued that Guantánamo detainees have the right to know the charges against them and to a fair trial so they may defend themselves against charges.[82] On June 28, 2004, the U.S. Supreme Court ruled that detainees should have the right to access U.S. courts in order to challenge their detention. This challenged the U.S. government position that it has the right to hold indefinitely foreign nationals without due legal process.[83]

Camps function as reservation zones where the rights of subjects can be suspended as a first step in stripping away their status as political subjects in order to render them as abject. In contrast with both frontiers and zones, camps intervene in the process of rights making differently. Rather than focusing on ways to hinder the practice of claims making (although this too is obviously restricted in such spaces), camps intervene by revoking status, that is by transforming the status of those "caught" from subjects to abjects. The logic of refugee camps is one of giving human rights and protection to those who have lost their rights. Yet, this logic condemns these refugees to living in varying degrees of transient permanence in inhospitable conditions, in other words, to living in a state of inexistence. Camps attempt to undermine the politicization of refugees by transforming their status to one of "not-quite-refugees" or "refugees-in-waiting." Similarly, detention camps like Guantánamo are used to remove individuals from their political communities into holding areas where they are kept in legal limbo, without recourse to appeal either as citizens or on the grounds of human rights, except in circumstances where their own countries intervene on their behalf. As Elizabeth Dauphinee argues in chapter 11, the camp as abject space enacts a logic that has as much to do with those of us with legal citizenship status as it has to do with the abject. The camp functions as spectacle—they put the abject on display as a reminder of what can happen when one transgresses outside the boundaries and loses their political community.[84]

Abject Spaces as Spaces of Inexistence

We argued in this chapter that the rights of the rightless ought to be interpreted other than as human rights. The chapter has sought not only to illustrate frontiers, zones, and camps as abject spaces but also to consider the question of how they should be investigated and what kinds of politics they occasion other than human rights politics. Through Arendt and Rancière, we illustrate the kinds of politics and the kinds of new political subjects that emerge in these spaces that render humans neither as subjects nor objects but as abjects—condemned to inexistent states of transient permanence in which they are made inaudible and invisible. Yet abject spaces also expose and render visible and audible various strategies and technologies of otherness that attempt to produce such states of inexistence. The exposure of this logic becomes a significant act of resistance. We see Derrida's "cities of refuge" as acts of resistance, for example, not only through sanctuary movements but also through initiatives such as the "Don't Ask, Don't Tell" campaigns that have been adopted in cities across the United States and underway in Toronto, Canada, and the "Sanctuary City" initiatives adopted by the city of Cambridge, Massachusetts. These initiatives aim to make cities more hospitable to nonstatus peoples by forbidding city workers to ask about a person's status, or reveal it to other government officials, to ensure that all residents of the city, regardless of status, are able to access essential services without fear of arrest and/or deportation.

If such acts of resistance illustrate the way we might begin to think about acts and spaces of becoming political through which to resist abjection, then Arendt's and Agamben's insights about the camp's centrality to the nation-state system also invite us to examine our imaginings of the international system. The camp as state of exception makes the rule of the nation-state system possible by being "home" to all those undesirables left without political community, expelled from their nation-states. This includes more than 10.4 million refugees, 1 million asylum seekers, 9 million stateless peoples, and 20–25 million internally displaced people worldwide.[85] As we demonstrate, the increasing number and the novelty of frontiers, zones, and camps as abject spaces certainly suggest that it may be time to look at the international system from the vantage point of the abject as more appropriately being a much more complex picture. Rather than a system of sovereign, contiguous, discrete, and exclusive nation-states, we are witnessing the reemergence of a patchwork of overlapping spaces of greater and lesser degrees of rights and rightlessness, abject spaces and spaces of citizenship being nestled within each other.

Notes

We would like to thank Agnes Czajka, Peter Nyers, Simon Dalby, William Walters, and an anonymous reader for their helpful comments on an earlier draft of this chapter. We would also like to thank editors Elizabeth Dauphinee and Cristina Masters for their immensely useful critical comments.

* Paul Vreeker, Zaandijk, Netherlands, February 11, 2004 (REUTERS/Paul Vreeker JFL/AA WORLD PRESS ROTTERDAM Photo by Paul Vreeker. 11/02/2005 [X012990020050211e12b00001, x01299]).

1. Julia Kristeva, *Powers of Horror: An Essay on Abjection, European Perspectives* (New York: Columbia University Press, 1982).
2. Giorgio Agamben, *Homo Sacer: Sovereign Power and Bare Life* (Stanford, CA: Stanford University Press, 1998), p. 166.
3. Ibid., p. 170.
4. Ibid., p. 9.
5. Ibid.
6. Ibid., p. 171.
7. Ibid., p. 174.
8. Ibid., p. 175; William Walters, "Deportation, Expulsion and the International Police of Aliens," *Citizenship Studies*, 7 (2002): 285.
9. Hannah Arendt, *The Origins of Totalitarianism* (New York: Harcourt Brace Jovanovich, 1951).
10. Jacques Derrida, "On Cosmopolitanism and Forgiveness," in *Thinking in Action*, trans. M. Dooley and M. Hughes (London: Routledge, 2001).

11. Peter Nyers, "Abject Cosmopolitanism: The Politics of Protection in the Anti-Deportation Movement," *Third World Quarterly*, 24 (2003): 1078; Walters (2002), p. 287.

12. Giorgio Agamben, *Means Without End: Notes on Politics, Theory Out of Bounds*, vol. 20 (Minneapolis: University of Minnesota Press, 2000), pp. 24–25.

13. Ibid., pp. 24–25.

14. Ibid., p. 25.

15. Jacques Rancière, "Who Is the Subject of the Rights of Man?" *The South Atlantic Quarterly*, 103 (2004): 297–310.

16. Ibid., p. 301.

17. Ibid., p. 301.

18. Ibid., p. 298.

19. Arendt (1951), p. 300.

20. Rancière (2004), p. 302.

21. Ibid., p. 302.

22. Ibid., p. 303.

23. Ibid., p. 303.

24. Ibid., p. 303.

25. Ibid., p. 306.

26. Ibid., p. 307.

27. Ibid.

28. Arendt (1951), p. 270.

29. Ibid., 270.

30. Ibid., 270.

31. Ibid., p. 273.

32. Ibid., p. 275.

33. Ibid., p. 279.

34. Ibid., p. 291.

35. Ibid., p. 296.

36. Ibid., p. 300.

37. Ibid., p. 300.

38. Rancière (2004), p. 305.

39. Nyers (2003), p. 1078.

40. Arendt (1951), p. 286.

41. Rancière (2004), p. 306.

42. Ibid., p. 307.

43. Ibid., p. 307.

44. Nandita Sharma, "Travel Agency: A Critique of Anti-Trafficking Campaigns," *Refuge: Canada's Periodical on Refugees*, 21 (2003): 21.

45. Sandro Mezzadra and Brett Neilson, "Né Qui, Né Altove: Migration, Detention, Desertion. A Dialogue," *Borderlands Ejournal*, 2 (2003), para. 8.

46. "Home Secretary's Statement on Zones of Protection: Press Release," London, Home Office, March 29, 2003.

47. Amnesty International, *Australia: Asylum-Seekers—Where to Now?*, AI Index ASA 12/010/2001—News Service Nr. 215, December 5, 2001.

48. UK Home Office (2003), *A New Vision for Refugees*, March 26, p. 26. www.proasyl,info/texte/europe/union/2003/UK_NewVision.pdf. (accessed August 8, 2006).

49. Amnesty International (2001).

50. Roberto L. Martinez, "Immigration, Migration, and Human Rights on the U.S./Mexico Border," *In Motion Magazine*, August 28, 2001; *In Motion Magazine*, "U.S. Border Patrol in South California Developing Deadly but Ineffective Operation Gatekeeper: Interview with Roberto Martinez," December 1999; National Public Radio, "Tunnels Under The U.S.-Mexican Border: Big Increase In Discoveries of Smuggler's Routes," 2004. http://www.npr.org/templates/story/story.php?storyId=1842750. (accessed August 8, 2006). See also Roxanne Doty's contribution to this volume.

51. Amanda Vanstone, "Border Protection: Unauthorized Arrivals and Detention—Information Paper," http://www.minister.immi.gov.au/media_release/ruddock_media01/r01131_bgpaper.htm. (accessed March 10, 2004).

52. Human Rights Watch, *"By Invitation Only": Australian Asylum Policy* (New York: Human Rights Watch, 2002), p. 1.

53. Ibid.

54. Human Rights Watch, "Refugees, Migration and Trafficking" in *Human Rights Watch World Report 2003* (New York: Human Rights Watch, 2003).

55. *The Guardian*, "Would-Be Refugees Make a Mini-Sangatte in Heart of Paris," April 29, 2003.

56. Ibid.

57. Ibid.

58. *The Observer*, "UK: Living in Fear," March 29, 2004.

59. Paul Willis, "UK: Asylum Seekers Face Life on Leeds Streets," *Yorkshire Evening Post*, March 2, 2004.

60. Human Rights Watch, "Refugees, Asylum Seekers, Migrants and Internally Displaced Persons," http://www.hrw.org/campaigns/race/refugeepresskit.html; Jesuit Refugee Service, *Detention in Europe: JRS-Europe Observation and Position Paper* (Europe: Jesuit Refugee Service, 2004); Ruud Lubbers, "Statement to the Third Committee of the General Assembly, 59th Session," November 9, 2002, http://www.unhcr.org/cgi-bin/texis/vtx/admin/opendoc.htm?tbl=ADMIN&id=41922eca4 (accessed August 8, 2006); Llewelyn G. Pritchard, "The INS Issues Detention Standards Governing the Treatment of Detained Immigrants and Asylum Seekers," U.S. Committee for Refugees, 2004, http://www.ilw.com/lawyers/articles/2001,0403-Pritchard.shtm. (accessed August 8, 2006).

61. *The Herald*, "UK: Dungavel Alternative Is Turned Down," March 22, 2004; Dominic Casciani, "Dungavel: Target of Asylum Campaign," *BBC News*, February 19, 2003.

62. Angus Roxburgh, "Belgium's Asylum 'Lottery,' " *BBC News Online*, October 27, 2003, http://news.bbc.co.uk/go/pr/fr/-/1/hi/world/europe/ 3208539.stm. (accessed August 8, 2006).

63. *Worldstream*, "Tough Dutch Measures Bring a New Dimension to Europe's Clampdown on Immigration," March 25, 2004.

64. *The Guardian*, "Dutch Pass Law to Expel Failed Asylum Seekers," February 18, 2004.

65. U.S. Committee for Refugees, *World Refugee Survey 2003 Country Report: United Kingdom* (Washington, DC: U.S. Committee for Refugees, 2003).

66. *BBC News*, "Anger at 'Asylum' Hotel Meeting," February 14, 2003; *BBC News*; "Asylum Hotel Scheme May Be Dropped," January 20, 2003; *BBC News*, "Australia Shuts Asylum Camp," April 17, 2003; *BBC News*, "Politicians Unite Against 'Asylum Hotel,' " February 19, 2003.

67. Sarah Gibson, "Accommodating Strangers: British Hospitality and the Asylum Hotel Debate," *Journal for Cultural Research*, 7 (2003): 372.

68. Bicester Accomodation Centre Gets the Green Light (London: Home Office, April 6, 2004).

69. Accommodation Centres for Asylum Seekers—Your Questions Answered, London: Home Office, April 6, 2004.

70. Home Office (2004).

71. Agamben (1998) and (2000).

72. Hillary Mayell, "World Refugees Number 35 Million," *National Geographic News*, June 16, 2003, http://news.nationalgeographic.com/ news/2003/06/0616_030616_refugee1.html. (accessed August 8, 2006).

73. *BBC News*, "Australia Shuts Asylum Camp," April 17, 2003; Patrick Barkham, "No Waltzing in Woomera," *The Guardian*, May 25, 2002; *CNN*, "UNHCR Attacks Australian Immigration Policy," February 1, 2002. http://archives.cnn.com/2002/WORLD/europe/02/01/unhcr. australia/ index.html. (accessed August 8, 2006).

74. Asylum Rights Campaign, EU Working Group, *Sangatte: Asylum Rights Campaign*, September, 2002.

75. *Agence France Press*, "Now Abandoned French Refugee Centre to Formally Close," December 27, 2002.

76. Amnesty International (2001).

77. Amnesty International, United States of America: Beyond The Law: Update to Amnesty International's April Memorandum to the US Government on the Rights of the Detainees Held in US Custody in Guantanamo Bay and Other Locations, December 13, 2002, p. 1. AI Index: AMR 51/184/2002.

78. Ibid., p. 2.

79. Ibid., p. 5.

80. Amnesty International, "Guantanamo Bay: A Human Rights Scandal," 2004. http://web.amnesty.org/web/web.nsf/print/guantanamobay-index-eng. (accessed August 8, 2006).

81. Center for Constitutional Rights, *Optimistic on Guantanamo after Vigorous Supreme Court Argument*, April 20, 2004, http://www.ccr-ny.org/v2/reports/report.asp?ObjID=rg1zf8P8It&Content=350. (accessed August 8, 2006).
82. Ibid.
83. Ibid.
84. Walters (2002), p. 286.
85. United Nations High Commissioner For Refugees, *Refugees By Numbers*, 2003, http://www.unhcr.org.uk/info/briefings/statistics/documents/numb2003.pdf. (accessed August 8, 2006).

excluded from the community to which the law gives rise.[3] This chapter asks whether human rights offer a mode of resistance for the subject—a way of resisting modernity's "hounding of the subject beyond death, apparently without limit," as Joan Copjec has recently argued[4]—or whether instead the invocation of human rights constrains our capacity to think about and counter the ways in which power circulates in this global politics and economy.

My argument will be that human rights law in its liberal manifestation offers limited means for countering the administration of human life represented by biopolitics, and indeed in some ways supports this mode of governmentality. In other words, some of the foundations of the liberal challenge to the practices of administrative detention may work to strengthen the efficacy of these practices. However, this is not to say we should (or indeed could) simply forget human rights. Human rights law also incorporates an earlier natural law tradition, one that can be traced to the Greek tragedies of Sophocles.[5] This tradition offers rich possibilities for thinking about the politics of our time and suggests a range of critical practices and relations that may provide more useful means for understanding and resisting the excesses of biopolitics.

The Administration of Suffering

COMMISSIONER OZDOWSKI: But it was a culture of self harming, which was impacting on children?

MS. BENDER: There was very visible self harm, constant talk of it. The children for example when I arrived would have seen people in graves—when I first arrived there were people in dug graves with children seeing this. Some of the children—it was their parents or people they knew. They knew why the parents were doing this. They knew that the parents were talking about possibly dying. They were on a hunger strike. There was visible self-harming on the razor wire. People were taken to the medical centre at regular intervals having slashed. People taken to hospital. There were attempted hangings that children would have seen.

COMMISSIONER OZDOWSKI: What were the other three case circumstances?

MS. BENDER: Two little boys who were very close friends. One was brought to the medical centre. When I arrived he had attempted to hang himself and I spent quite a lot of time with him and his family and as I was doing that another little boy who was his best friend had been brought in who had also attempted to hang himself.

COMMISSIONER OZDOWSKI: And the last case?

MS. BENDER: Another child of 13 who attempted to hang himself and his family at that point was quite disintegrated. His mother was in an almost

CHAPTER 10

BIOPOLITICS AND THE TRAGIC SUBJECT OF HUMAN RIGHTS

Anne Orford

I nternational law is a regime that recognizes certain entities as s
In doing so, it helps to produce a world of legitimate violer
territorially bounded. International law, through the institutiona
human rights, also produces the techniques by which the law a
mediate that violence. The appeal to human rights is a means
many lawyers and activists attempt to constrain the power e
states over the individuals within their territory or jurisdiction.
standing of power which informs this legal tradition is largely
Michel Foucault has described as juridical power—power und
commodity held by a sovereign and dependent upon control o
and its products.[1] Yet human rights law is increasingly resorted
a struggle against the globalization of disciplinary power an
mechanisms of power exercised through bodies, and wh
International human rights law is one field in which internat
and others try to make sense of the ways that modern states
life as a project and a problem. This is clearly visible in the e
the human rights community with the American treatment
part of the war on terror, and with the related detention of
in Australia as part of an Australian immigration control po
deter "economic refugees." In other words, lawyers invok
when confronted with the fate of human beings who are ab
law of the sovereign state—included as subjects of law

immobile depression. She had been hospitalised. His sister who I saw in my room that day just sat there tearing up paper from—hand towel paper and saying, "I am dead don't touch me"[6]

This extract is taken from the transcript of one of the public hearings conducted as part of the National Inquiry into Children in Immigration Detention, undertaken by the Australian Human Rights and Equal Opportunity Commission from 2001 to 2003. Human rights activists and human rights inquiries such as this one played a major role in publicizing the suffering caused by the Australian government's practice of detaining asylum seekers in remote detention centers.[7] This regime of mandatory detention was designed to dissuade asylum seekers from making the dangerous trip by boat to Australia, and to deter the activities of "people smugglers." From mid-1999, increased numbers of unauthorized asylum seekers began to arrive in Australia, often landing in the mainly island territory across the north. Most of these people came from Afghanistan, Iran, and Iraq and were later found to be refugees. During this period, increasing numbers of people were taken into immigration detention. For example, 2,716 people were detained in 1997–1998, 8,205 in 1999–2000, and 7,808 in 2001–2002.[8]

Most of these detainees were taken to one of the "remote location detention centres," including the infamous Woomera Immigration Reception and Processing Centre located in the Simpson Desert, 487 km from the nearest city.[9] In summer, the temperature often passed 50 degrees centigrade.[10] Although the center was set up to house 400 people, by April 2000 it had almost 1,500 detainees.[11] The witness interviewed in the dialogue above, Ms. Bender, had been employed as a psychologist by Australian Correctional Management [ACM], the private corporation responsible for running the Woomera center. Bender testified before the Inquiry that at Woomera she witnessed daily acts of self-harm, daily acts of distress, detainees being forcibly physically restrained, chronic complaints from a majority of detainees of symptoms consistent with posttraumatic stress, severe symptoms of stress-related bodily pain such as chronic headaches, and verbal expressions of intense despair and hopelessness. Many detainees spent more than a year in detention, with some detained for periods longer than five years. The *average* length of detention for children as at December 2003 was one year, eight months, and eleven days.[12] The physical structure of centers such as Woomera, with high security fences, razor wire, and restricted access, promoted a culture of incarceration amongst detainees and staff. Detainees spoke of a longing for greenery, trees, and flowers. On rare excursions to Woomera township, they referred to joy in being able to touch grass and "because there are no fences." Bender testified that she had done a lot of work with suicide and worked in prisons and she had never experienced an environment like that in Woomera. She commented:

> The intensity and the prevalence is outside all my experience. . . . it was like an environment where, really, everyone I spoke to spoke about death. I don't actually recall someone not mentioning death.[13]

While the treatment of detainees in some ways seems to be modeled on prison conditions, the human rights of prisoners are far more clearly protected than those of detained asylum seekers. As Richard Harding, the Inspector of Custodial Services for Western Australia, commented in response to the detainee deaths, confrontations, and riots that had occurred in the centers run by ACM:

> Prisoners in Australia are actually very much aware of their entitlements, their rights, and they know that now, as opposed to perhaps 50 years or 100 years ago, they are not the civil dead, they are actually people who can expect to be treated properly, and the history of prison riots in this country is the history of managements forgetting that. When they do so, you get riots. When there is inequitable treatment, you get riots. The conditions at the detention centres are redolent of lack of respect, inequitable treatment, and injustice, and if you put a bunch of Aussie prisoners in Port Hedland or Curtin, or in some of the other detention centres, the place would go up in quite a short time.[14]

This distinction between the rights of prisoners and of detainees resonates with the work of Giorgio Agamben, who has compared the prison to the concentration camp. Agamben argues that while prison law is a space in which a version of penal law operates, the space inside the concentration camp is "the absolute space of exception." The law's relation with those who are inside such camps is one of abandonment—they are included as subjects of law only by being excluded from the community to which the law gives rise. A similar argument can be made about detention centers. The razor wire walls not only detain asylum seekers but also encircle this space of abandonment of the civil dead.

Agamben suggests that this law grounded on the management and transformation of human life founds the democratic human rights state more generally. Agamben here builds on Foucault's notion of biopolitics. Foucault argues that power operates in liberal states in ways that differ from what he terms the juridical model of power that is accepted in much political and legal theory.[15] For Foucault, coercive juridical or sovereign power is no longer the dominant form of power operating within liberal states. It has been replaced as the central mode of exercise of power by what he has termed "disciplinary power," a new mechanism of power that emerged in the seventeenth and eighteenth centuries in Europe.[16] Biopower designates that which

> brought life and its mechanisms into the realm of explicit calculations and made knowledge-power an agent of transformation of human life. It is not that life has been totally integrated into techniques that govern and administer it; it constantly escapes them. . . . But what might be called a society's "threshold of modernity" has been reached when the life of the species is wagered on its own political strategies. For millennia, man remained what he was for Aristotle: a living animal with the additional capacity for a political existence; modern man is an animal whose politics places his existence as a living being in question.[17]

The sovereignty of the nation-state is grounded on the inclusion of the bodies of its subjects through the management and transformation of human life.[18] The transformation of human life into a task or project for governance thus marks "the biopolitical turn of modernity."[19] It is through assuming the bare life of *homo sacer* "as a task" that this life becomes "explicitly and immediately political."[20] Agamben makes of this a warning of the price that we all must pay to be included in democratic societies. The concentration camps of Nazi Germany are for Agamben (merely) a localization of this broader relation of subject to sovereign in the modern state. For Agamben, the story of the holocaust and of the genocidal states of our age is *not* a story about sacrifice. Rather, he insists that the relation between subject and sovereign in such regimes is one already premised on the body of *homo sacer*, the person who can be killed lawfully but not sacrificed. The true horror of the camps and of genocide is not that their administrators were willing to sacrifice their victims, but rather that the acts of administrative killing that they undertook so efficiently were *not* acts of sacrifice, which would at least vest them with religious significance.

The statements of the Australian government and the Department of Immigration and Multiculturalism and Indigenous Affairs (DIMIA) bureaucrats point to just such a mode of administration. According to a DIMIA "fact sheet" on border control, "Australia is a sovereign country and has the right to decide who can enter and stay on its territory. . . . The Australian Government is firmly committed to ensuring the integrity of Australia's borders and to the effective control and management of the movement of people to and from Australia."[21] The immigration detention

policy was a central part of this practice of "effective control and management."
It was premised upon calculations about what kinds of environments would
serve as a deterrent to those seeking asylum or entry into Australia. In a discussion about the Woomera detention center, the Minister for
Immigration, Philip Ruddock, explained:

> We will be briefing people when they come in here on the nature of the
> facility, the environment in which it's been placed. It's not a holiday camp,
> nor should it be seen as one.[22]

One doctor from Woomera who told a meeting of DIMIA officials that
conditions at the center were having catastrophic effects on detainees and
that there was a mass psychiatric disaster inside the center was advised at the
end of two hours: "That sounds all well and good to us, Simon, but we
don't want to make it so nice for them in detention that they won't want
to leave."[23] The National Inquiry found that conditions in detention centers
failed to ensure that children were treated with humanity and respect for
their inherent dignity. These conditions included harsh physical environments with an absence of trees and grass in some centers, periods during
which children were addressed by number rather than name, absence of
clear procedures to ensure special protection of children when tear gas,
water cannons, and other security measures were used, instances of obtru-
sive head count procedures, periods of great overcrowding, instances of
unsanitary toilet facilities, failure to promptly send children to school and
ensure education appropriate to the needs of the children, failure to make
routine assessments regarding the mental health of children on arrival in
order to ensure that services were provided to recover from past trauma or
torture, and failure to act upon repeated recommendations from health
professionals that certain children be removed from detention to protect
their mental health. The Minister for Immigration, in a joint press release
with the Attorney General, responded to these findings by explaining the
relationship of such practices to the overall policy goals of the government:
"The government's strong but fair border protection policies have had an
impact. The number of unauthorized arrivals has dramatically reduced."[24]
With its commitment to "effective control and management of the movement of people," its calculation of human suffering as a form of deterrence,
and its grounding of politics on the transformation of human life, the practice of immigration detention is a model biopolitical project.[25]

    The dominant legal response to this situation, in Australia as elsewhere,
has been to attempt to make use of liberal notions of human rights as a
counter to the excesses of executive action. The practice of mandatory and

indefinite detention of unauthorized arrivals, suspected terrorists, or "unlawful combatants" has been challenged as an unwarranted infringement of the freedom of the individual in a democratic society. In the Australian context, a series of legal cases brought on behalf of detained asylum seekers have unsuccessfully sought to challenge the practice of indefinite detention on the basis, inter alia, that it infringes Australia's international human rights obligations.[26] Numerous investigations by the Human Rights and Equal Opportunity Commission, parliamentary committees, and the United Nations High Commissioner for Refugees have found that the conditions under which detainees have been held violate international human rights obligations.[27] The detention by the United States of foreign nationals suspected of involvement in terrorist activities has also been widely challenged as seriously violating international human rights and humanitarian law.

This human rights discourse has been extremely effective at maintaining public awareness of the treatment of detainees. Human rights texts make use of a series of techniques in their address to the reader. One is the reference to an international legal system, premised upon universal values and objectively verifiable standards, which exists outside the positive law of any given state. It is this aspect that receives most attention in the work of lawyers. Yet these texts also deploy moving and intimate first person accounts of the experience of detention or of administering detention (such as that extracted above), images of desolation or humiliation (such as the infamous scenes of hooded and chained detainees at Guantánamo Bay), and detailed records of the administrative and legal language used by state officials in explaining the practices under challenge. The texts often end with suggestions directed to state decision makers and the practice of statecraft—they offer recommendations as to how management of detained or other populations must be made more humane. This discourse about the human rights of people in detention has preserved a space institutionally from which to speak and write about the people who refuse to sort themselves smoothly into their allotted places in the international division of labor, or who are hostile to the U.S. military.

Yet despite (or, as I think in my more pessimistic moments, because of) this public awareness of the situation facing those detained in these remote camps, despite the activism of many Australians who showed their solidarity with asylum seekers by lining up for hours outside the camps to bring food or letters or telephone cards or company to those detained, despite the media and activist campaigns to make the horrors of these conditions politically unacceptable, the Australian people reelected the government responsible for this situation. On October 9, 2004, the conservative coalition of the Liberal Party led by Prime Minister John Howard and the National Party of Australia won a fourth term in office, with a gain of 3.7 percent of the vote over the previous election. At a press conference on August 29, held to announce the election, John Howard told journalists that the election would be about trust. "Who do you trust to keep the economy strong and protect family living standards? Who do you trust to keep interest rates low? Who do you trust to lead the fight on Australia's behalf against international terrorism?"[28] It is in the context of this politics that I want to think about how human rights work in the liberal democratic state.

Human Rights and the Memorialization of Sovereignty

I don't actually recall someone not mentioning death.[29]

Human rights and democracy are regularly invoked in the texts of liberal legalism as a response to administrative excesses of the modern state. Human rights are understood as being granted to all human beings "on the basis of the inherent dignity of all persons."[30] Where bureaucrats or governments might treat individuals as "objects rather than as holders of rights," able to be sacrificed to achieve some larger purpose, human rights treats individuals "as political actors in the full sense."[31] Thus the human rights tradition, at least as translated into the declarations and covenants of modern law, would seem to challenge the legal regimes of administrative detention and other excesses of the war on terror by refusing to accept that individuals are mere objects to be acted upon and subject to the calculations of state decision makers. According to the liberal view of the war on terror, we are witnessing a reversal in the progress of humanity. The past 200 years has seen the emergence of a commitment to notions of respect for human dignity and constraints on the power of the sovereign state to intervene in the sphere of individual freedom. Indefinite detention and other illiberal measures invoked in the name of defending against terrorism pose a challenge to the human rights of the liberal individual.

In these liberal formulations of history, we can see an echo of the "tragic humanism" which emerged from the German romantic tradition.[32] Michelle Gellrich argues that this vision has had a major (if little studied) influence on the sense of tragedy which became popular in the twentieth century. For German romantics such as Friedrich Schiller, the essence of tragedy involves the individual's "confrontation with oppressive or hostile forces" inimical to his "moral freedom."[33] This theory of tragedy involves several key ideas that are assimilated from the philosophy of Kant: "the dignity of the person, nobility through conflict, conformity to inner purpose or personal law, and freedom from external constraint."[34] In his essays on tragedy, Schiller stresses "the individual hero and his isolation in the face of potentially annihilating powers."[35] This experience of what Kant termed the sublime "may arise either in the face of an extreme magnitude that suggests infinity or in the face of a powerful natural force."[36] Much of the writing on the remote detention centers—both texts produced by the government and those produced by human rights lawyers—is infused with this sensibility. The individual is "assaulted and threatened by a violent external force, which appears to have no . . . boundaries."[37] That force is imagined both as the unrestrained power of the sovereign state or its military, and in a more Kantian spirit, as the natural forces of the environment (the desert, the awesome power of the tropical rains).

In order to understand the political effects of this, we might turn to Foucault's discussion of tragedy in his lectures published as *Society Must be Defended*. Foucault suggests that tragedy reemerged in the Europe of Shakespeare and Racine as a genre that reproduced the juridical concept of power and the related vision of sovereignty, society, and the subject. Tragedy is "one of the great ritual forms in which public right was displayed and its problems discussed."[38] Like the earlier royal annalists, the writers of tragedy show "that what sovereigns and kings do is never pointless, futile, or petty, and never unworthy of being narrated."[39] Human rights texts also memorialize the acts of sovereigns from whom power is supposedly emanating and who abuse this power to bloodthirsty or unjust effect. What emerges is a narrative about the sovereign state and its overwhelming power.

Liberal legal thought thus takes as givens the model of power as repressive and the principle of the sovereignty of the nation-state. This sovereign state, its rights, its power, and the possible limits on that power, are the key elements of this mode of thought.[40] These assumptions make it difficult to understand other mechanisms of power that operate within the institution of the detention center and through the practices of administrative detention. The mechanisms of power involved in administrative detention can better be understood in terms of the characteristics of political rationality which, Foucault argues, emerged at the end of the eighteenth century in the liberal states of Europe. From this time, the nation ceases to be organized and united through the figure of the monarch, but instead around the figure of the state.[41] The "defining characteristic of a nation" will become "its ability to administer itself, to manage, govern, and guarantee the constitution and workings of the figure of the State and of state power."[42] Control rather than domination becomes the sine qua non of power.

Central to this control is the new technology of biopower:

> [T]he state has essentially to take of men as a population. It wields its power
> over living beings as living beings, and its politics, therefore, has to be a
> biopolitics. Since the population is nothing more than what the state takes
> care of for its own sake, of course, the state is entitled to slaughter it, if neces-
> sary. So the reverse of biopolitics is thanatopolitics.[43]

Biopolitics introduces into statecraft regulatory and security mechanisms
designed to control "the random element inherent in a population of living beings so as to optimize a state of life."[44] While sovereign power "took
life and let live," these mechanisms of regulation involve "making live and
letting die."[45] In the detention centers of Australia and Guantánamo Bay,
as in the concentration camps of Nazi Germany, these mechanisms manage
death in life. We sense this in the report of the speech of the sister in
Woomera: "I am dead don't touch me," and in Bender's description of
Woomera as a space saturated by death.

   Yet in other ways the detention centers seem to depart from the logic of
biopower. This mechanism or technology of power requires "maintaining
intimacy and continuity with its governed population."[46] The state must
act to "control the series of random events that can occur in a living mass"
and attempt to predict (and where possible modify) these events.[47] As a
technology for "managing" the movement of people across Australia's borders, the centers were championed as highly successful by the Australian
government. Yet as became clear during the course of the serial inquiries
into the conditions in the centers, the strategy of the government was to
withdraw from the populations concentrated within the razor wire fences.
These people suffered in part as a result of their confinement within a space
offering no administrative care or intimacy. Indeed, the privatization of the
running of such centers, a phenomenon that has proved to offer major
businesses opportunities for the global detention industry, has meant that
governments take little responsibility for the provision of services to those
within immigration detention centers or private prisons. This withdrawal
was only acceptable as a result of the mobilization of a certain discourse of
the (white) nation. While the people within the detention centers were
within the control or under the management of the Australian state, they
were also and at the same time characterized as posing a threat to the
"nation." In this way, the centers represent what Lauren Berlant has in
other circumstances called "a particularly brutal mode of . . . *hygienic
governmentality*"—that is, the deployment by the ruling elites of the notion

that "an abject population threatens the common good" and is "exemplary of all obstacles to national life."[48] Unlike the concentration camps of Nazi Germany, where an "abject population" was governed and monitored rigorously so as to protect the rest of the nation from the threat that they were taken to pose, here the Australian state withdrew from this population. The centers represent a point where the logic and extension of biopower "will put it beyond all human sovereignty."[49]

Human rights lawyers respond to this situation by attempting to link this mechanism of power back to human sovereignty. The dominant strategy is to describe the effects of biopower as emanating from an all-powerful sovereign and to try to find ways within existing legal regimes to hold that sovereign responsible for human rights violations. Behind the ill-coordinated and inept actions of the private corporation or the immigration officer is the brooding intelligence of the state. To the extent that human rights lawyers have both taken as given and tried to found a sovereign model of power,[50] they have not been able to address the operation of the mechanisms of biopower. The effect of focusing only on the juridical or sovereign form of power is to mask the operation of power in its biopolitical form and thus to make that form of power all the more effective. By abandoning sovereign power as a central premise of analysis, it may become easier to analyze the ways in which local effects of power and local tactics combine to make what we call politics possible.

Death and the Politics of Mourning

> Another child of 13 who attempted to hang himself and his family at that point was quite disintegrated. His mother was in an almost immobile depression. She had been hospitalised. His sister who I saw in my room that day just sat there tearing up paper—hand towel paper and saying, "I am dead don't touch me."[51]

In order to reclaim something of the human rights tradition that precedes its relationship with the modern state and declarations of the rights of man, we might turn to *Antigone*. This tragedy is one of the conventional places with which to begin an exploration of the natural law tradition. The play concerns an order passed by Creon, the King of Thebes, prohibiting the burial of Polynices, who perished in an attack on the city. While his brother, who died defending Thebes, was given full funeral honors, Creon decreed that Polynices should be left "unburied and unwept." Antigone, the sister of Polynices and a daughter (and sister) of Oedipus, determines to

disobey the King's order. When she is brought before Creon and charged
with her disobedience, she responds:

> I did not think your edicts strong enough
> To overrule the unwritten unalterable laws
> Of God and heaven, you being only a man.
> They are not of yesterday or to-day, but everlasting,
> Though where they came from, none of us can tell.
> Guilty of their transgression before God
> I cannot be, for any man on earth.
> I knew that I should have to die, of course,
> With or without your order. If it be soon,
> So much the better. Living in daily torment
> As I do, who would not be glad to die?
> This punishment will not be any pain.
> Only if I had let my mother's son
> Lie there unburied, then I could not have borne it.[52]

These "unwritten unalterable laws" govern Antigone's conduct. At least
since the time of Hegel, the audience of the play has been "asked to
shadow the action of the tragedy and sit in judgment."[53] In *The
Phenomenology of Spirit*, Hegel reads Antigone as embodying the inevitably
tragic nature of the pull between two laws.[54] Hegel's influential interpretation sees "the conflict in the play in pervasively binary terms: Antigone
versus Creon, family versus state, female versus male, unwritten divine law
versus written civic edicts."[55] The notion of this conflict between the individual and the state links Antigone to the modern conception of human
rights law. For Hegel, the tragic result of Antigone belongs to a moment in
Greek history when these oppositions could not be overcome. Each pro-
tagonist "sees right only on one side and wrong on the other, that consciousness which belongs to the divine law sees in the other side only the
violence of human caprice, while that which holds to human law sees in
the other only the self-will and disobedience of the individual who insists
on being his own authority."[56]

Human rights law follows this tradition. It invites us to listen to the
speech of the state and that of the victim, and to sit in judgment. In order
to avoid a tragic outcome, the aim of modern international human rights
covenants is to find a way to reconcile the two perspectives—the positive
law of the state and the autonomy of the individual. Human rights become
caught up in the practice of statecraft. Rights are never absolute but can be
limited to the extent necessary in a democratic society to protect other values
or interests such as public morals or security. Human rights inquiries record

the state endlessly talking about itself and make recommendations as to how the state can better engage in tasks of management and control in a humane fashion.

Yet there is another reading of Antigone that is called forth by the words "I am dead don't touch me." This reading focuses upon Antigone's love for her brother and "the unspeakable wrong against the love object that the institution commits."[57]

> In her own excessive love for her brother and death, Antigone may be the eternal reminder of an abyss that enfolds and enforces all law.[58]

The passage in which Antigone declares this excessive and singular love for her brother has been much debated—the authenticity of this passage has been questioned by many, including perhaps most famously by Goethe when he wrote "I would give a great deal . . . if some talented scholar could prove that these lines were interpolated, not genuine."[59]

> ANTIGONE: Never I tell you.
> if I had been the mother of children
> or if my husband had died, exposed and rotting—
> I'd never have taken this ordeal upon myself,
> never defied our people's will. What law,
> you ask, [is my warrant for] what I say?
> A husband dead, there might have been another.
> A child by another too, if I had lost the first.
> But mother and father both lost in the halls of
> Death, no brother could ever [bloom for me].
> For this law alone I held you first in honor.[60]

This love leads Antigone to defy Creon. Her action is ethical—not in the sense of linking ethics with universal form in the Kantian tradition but in a sense much closer to the Jewish tradition in which the demand by the Other is associated with singularity, otherness, and unmediated duty.[61] Antigone responds to the demand to bury her irreplaceable brother, a demand produced through the uniqueness of her relationship with him. In contrast to the state law represented by Creon, Antigone might stand for a different vision of the social:

> Someone dies and leaves behind his place, which outlives him and is unfill-able by anyone else. This idea constructs a specific notion of the social, wherein it is conceived to consist not only *of* particular individuals and their relations to each other, but also *as* a relation to these unoccupiable places.

The social is composed, then, not just of those things that will pass, but also of relations to empty places that will not.[62]

We might think then of "mourning" as related to human rights in the insistence on defying the state's injunction to leave its victims "unwept" and on remembering that which has been lost. Mourning is both a politics and an ethics. There is something ethical in the quality of the relation set up by mourning, relations with the potential presence always figured by absence.[63]

> [I]f loss is known only by what remains of it, then the politics and ethics of mourning lie in the interpretation of what remains—how remains are produced and animated, how they are read and sustained.[64]

In trying to understand the stakes of this politics of death and mourning, it is necessary to think about that which separates us from the world of the fifth-century Greek city-state. Both Antigone and the sister in the detention center appear at the point where state power reaches its limits.[65] Yet the nature of that power and those limits has shifted since the time of Antigone. Death is ritualized in cultures where it represents a transition—from this world to the next, one law to another. When Antigone scatters dust over the body of her brother in the manner of a holy burial, she performs her fidelity to her family, the domain of the dead, and the laws that govern there.[66] With the emergence of biopower, death moves "outside the power relationship."[67] Death in the era of biopolitics has become privatized, "the moment when the individual escapes all power, falls back on himself and retreats, so to speak, to his own privacy."[68] The theme is taken up by Agamben:

> Every attempt to rethink the political space of the West must begin with the clear awareness that we no longer know anything of the classical distinction between *zoē* and *bios*, between private life and political existence, between man as a simple living being at home in the house and man's political existence in the city.[69]

When Antigone "covers the exposed body of her brother," she refuses the "conditions of naked existence to which Creon remains bound."[70] Perhaps we might understand "I am dead don't touch me" as a similar refusal to be subjected, this time to the disciplining forces of modern medicine and psychology in their engagement with biopolitics—a profound rejection of the invitation to join a community of the living on such terms. Despite the move to grasp life as something to be evaluated and weighed as part of a mechanism of power, "life has [not] been totally integrated into techniques that govern and administer it; it constantly escapes them."[71]

Tragedy and Its Audience

ISMENE: I fear for you, Antigone; I fear—
ANTIGONE: You need not fear for me. Fear for yourself.[72]

The tragic tradition that infuses human rights might offer us one more lesson. As Page duBois argues, to read Greek tragedy with a focus on the individual, interpreting it as the forerunner of "humanitarian individualism," is to "ignore the dialectic between part and whole, between individual and collective, and erase, polemically, context and history."[73] She urges us rather to see in Greek tragedy "a moment before the closure of the individual subject that might speak to its dissolution now."[74] Tragedy was a form that mattered as a political site of engagement in the new democracy of Athens. Tragedy was a "social institution," and in the staging of tragedy Athens "turned itself into a theatre."[75] Michelle Gellrich argues that this sense of the political and disruptive aspect of Greek tragedy has been lost. Philosophical readings "so digest tragedy into a form both intelligible and safe that its threatening, enigmatic aspects are transformed."[76] For Jean-Pierre Vernant, Greek tragedy should be understood as emerging from a very specific "historical moment," contemporary with the Athenian city and the problems of law and radical changes to the social order encountered there.[77] It developed at a particular moment in Greek history, in which the human world and the religious world were understood as distinct yet inseparable. In tragedy, "every action, as if double, unfolds on two levels, on the one hand that of men's ordinary lives, on the other that of the religious forces that are obscurely at work the world over."[78] Tragedy is an inquiry into what it meant to be responsible under such conditions. It takes place "in that border zone where human actions are intermeshed with divine power."[79]

> [T]ragedy at the outset positions the individual at the crossroads of action, facing a decision in which he becomes totally committed. But his ineluctable choice takes place in a world full of obscure and ambiguous forces, a divided world in which "one justice is in conflict with another," one god with another god, in which right is never fixed but shifts even within the course of the dramatic action, is "twisted" and transformed into its contrary. Man believes he is choosing for the best; he commits himself heart and soul; and it

turns out to be a choice for evil that, through the defilement attached to the crime committed, reveals him to be a criminal.[80]

The meaning of each expression, action, and subject is radically uncertain under such conditions. Tragedy is thus marked by ambiguity. Developing this theme, Page duBois urges modern readers to attend to the disruptive voices of the Chorus and the shifting play of language in Antigone and in Greek tragedy more generally:

> The foreign, the collective, the ecstatic, the enslaved are always there, from tragedy's beginnings, disrupting efforts to isolate the solitary, masterly self attempting heroically to grapple with fate.[81]

The tragedy that results from the administration of suffering in detention centers and other places of incarceration is also a politics. How we understand that politics remains as complicated a question for us as it was for the Athenians of the fifth century.

To illustrate this, I want to conclude by returning to the story of the children in Australian detention. In a strange twist, the turning point for this practice of detaining "unlawful arrivals" was the report of an inquiry into the management failures of DIMIA and the immigration detention centers, initiated in the aftermath of the discovery that a schizophrenic Australian woman had been in immigration detention for a year in the mistaken belief that she was an unauthorized arrival.[82] The report's author Mick Palmer did not seek to challenge the government's detention policy or raise any human rights questions. He did not paint a picture of the state as all-powerful or overwhelming. Instead, the *Palmer Report* adopts a management consultant perspective. In its main findings, it criticizes the lack of a "corporate policy" for reviewing the continued validity of the "reasonable suspicion that Ms Rau was an unlawful non-citizen,"[83] the effect of understaffing on the high individual workloads and stress of DIMIA staff,[84] the absence of "operation systems and processes designed to ensure integrity of application and demonstrable accountability" in the operation of the immigration detention policy,[85] the "overly self-protective and defensive" culture within DIMIA's immigration compliance and detention areas,[86] the "process rich" and "outcomes poor" approach of DIMIA management,[87] the lack of formal training of DIMIA's operation and field staff and their "poor understanding of the legislation they are responsible for enforcing, the powers they are authorised to exercise, and the implications of the exercise of those powers,"[88] the lack of "even basic investigative and management skills" amongst those officers directly responsible "for detaining people suspected of being unlawful non-citizens and for conducting identity and immigration status inquiries,"[89] the inadequacy of the mental health care delivered to Ms. Rau while in detention,[90] and the "lack of any focused mechanism for external accountability and professional review of standards and arrangements for the delivery of health care services."[91] Forget bloodthirsty sovereigns and tragic tales of individuals subject to boundless power, these people just weren't good managers. In the words of the report:

> With a performance management regime that does not manage performance or service quality or risks in any meaningful way, it is not surprising DIMIA was caught unaware. The system did not "fail": it was ill-conceived and could never deliver to the Commonwealth the information on performance, service quality and risk management that DIMIA was confident it would.[92]
>
> DIMIA officers are authorised to exercise exceptional, even extraordinary, powers. That they should be permitted and expected to do so without adequate training, without proper management and oversight, with poor information systems, and with no genuine quality assurance and constraints on the exercise of those powers is of concern. The fact that this situation has been allowed to continue unchecked and unreviewed for several years is difficult to understand.[93]

This had extraordinary political effects. Where Australians had grown used to imagining the state as all-powerful, we were suddenly presented with a picture of the state as weak and bumbling. Ryszard Kapuscinski tells a similar story about a moment in Iranian politics which marked the beginning of the revolution and the overthrow of the shah.[94] The event occurred at an intersection in Teheran, when a man on the edge of a crowd refused to obey the order of a policeman to go home. News of this refusal immediately spread. While the prior experience of these two ordinary men and of the crowd surrounding them suggested that when the policeman raised his voice, the man would run, this time things turned out differently:

> The policeman shouts, but the man doesn't run. He just stands there, looking at the policeman. It's a cautious look, still tinged with fear, but at the same time tough and insolent. So that's the way it is! The man on the edge of the crowd is looking insolently at uniformed authority. He doesn't budge. He glances around and sees the same look on other faces. Like his, their faces are watchful, still a bit fearful, but already firm and unrelenting. Nobody runs though the policeman has gone on shouting; at last he stops. There is a moment of silence. We don't know whether the policeman and the man on the edge of the crowd already realize what has happened. The man has stopped being afraid—and this is precisely the beginning of the revolution. Here it starts. Until now, whenever these two men approached each other,

a third figure instantly intervened between them. That third figure was fear. Fear was the policeman's ally and the man in the crowd's foe. Fear interposed its rules and decided everything. Now two men find themselves alone, facing each other, and fear has disappeared into thin air. . . . The two men have now grown mutually indifferent, useless to each other; they can go their own ways. Accordingly, the policeman turns around and begins to walk heavily back toward his post, while the man on the edge of the crowd stands there looking at this vanishing enemy.[95]

According to Slavoj Žižek, the fear that is described in this passage is in fact fear of the "big Other"—the policeman is feared as a representative of the social order and his acts are feared as acts of power in that sense.[96] In a similar way, both human rights lawyers and conservative voters imagine that the careless, violent, or abusive acts of the minor functionaries who staffed the detention system are acts of power, proof that the government is indeed the powerful and terrifying sovereign manager of the nation. This management was "not necessarily about excluding/destroying otherness but about regulating the modality of its inclusion."[97] The surprising challenge to the capacity of the conservative government to run the detention system seemed to have destroyed this fantasy of the white Australian as legitimate manager of the nation, or as the sovereign which decides who can enter its territory and on what terms. Within weeks of the *Palmer Report* being released, the government had begun the process of emptying the detention centers and granting protection visas to the majority of the former detainees.

The *Palmer Report* also drew attention to a paradox at the heart of the biopolitical state. How can such a state, drawing its legitimacy from its capacity to protect, guarantee, and cultivate the life of the individual and the population, justify its exercise of the old sovereign power to kill or expose some people to the risk of death? Since the nineteenth century, this tension inherent in the coexistence of sovereign, disciplinary, and biopower has been resolved through the notion of a threat to the nation.[98] If such a state seeks to exercise the power to kill or to expose life to the risk of death, it does so through speaking about threats to the purity and survival of the nation, the population, and the economy under its care. Within this logic, killing is acceptable if it can be justified in terms of the elimination of such a threat.[99] The only way the state can appear at the same time as the mighty sovereign and as the manager, protector, and cultivator of life is if the population is fragmented, so that some people within its jurisdiction or territory are understood to be properly subject to the power to kill (or detain or torture), and some are subject to its powers of normalization, regularization, and cultivation of life.[100] In the context of the detention centers, it became necessary in this way to justify the application of conflicting techniques of power. In order to regularize and manage the movement of peoples and in order to decide who enters Australian territory, the state counted on the deterrent effect of the human suffering within the centers. In order to produce this suffering, it withdrew from the detained populations and suspended the disciplinary mechanisms by which the life of the broader Australian community was normalized and regularized, such as education, medical care, psychological treatment, counseling, and control over hygiene. This could only be justified on the basis that the people within the centers posed a threat to the nation. Because the *Palmer Report* was concerned with exploring the treatment of a detained Australian citizen, this conflict between the forms of power exercised by the state was revealed. The decision of the Australian government to withdraw from its role as cultivator of life within the space of the detention centers appeared as a failure of the art of managing life, rather than a triumph of the sovereign power to kill.

I do not mean to conclude with an ode to management consultants. Rather, I mention the strange effects of the *Palmer Report* to suggest that reaching automatically for the juridical tools that liberalism offers may leave us without the necessary conceptual or strategic means to understand and counter the techniques of power involved in these new detention regimes. By adopting the liberal programmatic vision of human rights, the shape of the politics of our time seems predetermined—all over the world, the individual confronts the all-powerful apparatus of the state. We know already the nature of the problem, the nature of the recommendations that will be necessary to solve the problem. We lose our sense that there may be alternative ways of thinking about politics that may have been lost in the rush to celebrate or bemoan the omnipotent sovereign of liberal imagination. By acting as if the problem is one that can be understood only in terms of repressive power, we risk constituting the world in those very terms— acting as if we are confronting an omnipotent sovereign authority helps to make it so.[101] As scholars, we may become part of the problem if we make politics seem programmed and predictable. As Žižek comments, "the circle is closed when the new social pact establishes itself in its necessity and renders invisible its 'possibility,' the open, undecided process that engendered it."[102] In the face of new social pacts that seek to close the circle of community in the name of waging wars on terror, critique needs to work at keeping visible this openness of politics, this possibility. And fear may yet disappear into thin air.

Notes

Thanks to Andrew Robertson for his helpful comments on earlier drafts of this chapter.

1. On juridical power and its relation to a theory of sovereignty which takes as given the subject, unitary power and law, see Michel Foucault, *Society Must Be Defended: Lectures at the Collège de France*, trans. David Macey (London: Penguin, 2003), pp. 12–40.

2. Ibid., pp. 239–262.

3. On abandonment as involving inclusion through exclusion, see Giorgio Agamben, *Homo Sacer: Sovereign Power and Bare Life*, trans. Daniel Heller-Roazen (Stanford: Stanford University Press, 1998).

4. Joan Copjec, *Imagine There's No Woman: Ethics and Sublimation* (Cambridge: MIT Press, 2002), p. 47.

5. See generally Costas Douzinas, *The End of Human Rights* (Oxford: Hart, 2000).

6. National Inquiry into Children in Immigration Detention, "Transcript of Hearing," Melbourne, Friday May 31, 2002, http://www.hreoc.gov.au/human_rights/children_detention/transcript/melbourne_31may.html (accessed November 30, 2005).

7. The practice of detention of asylum seekers is authorized by Australia's *Migration Act 1958* (Cth), which provides that if an immigration compliance officer or a police officer knows or reasonably suspects a person to be an unlawful non-citizen, the officer must detain that person. An unlawful non-citizen is a person who does not hold a current visa: *Migration Act 1958* (Cth), section 189(1).

8. Department of Immigration and Multicultural and Indigenous Affairs (DIMIA), "Fact Sheet 82: Immigration Detention," July 12, 2006, http://www.immi.gov.au/media/fact-sheets/82detention.htm (accessed August 1, 2006).

9. National Inquiry into Children in Immigration Detention, *A Last Resort?* (Sydney: Human Rights and Equal Opportunity Commission, April 2004), pp. 26, 59.

10. The remote location of these centers functioned both to cut detainees off from urban services and to expose them to climatic extremes, such as the wet season of far north-west Australia which faced those sent to the Curtin detention center located 2,643 km north-west of Perth, or the desert conditions of Woomera. On the extreme conditions in the Curtin center, see the comments by Richard Harding in "Experts Respond to the Video," Australian Broadcasting Corporation (ABC) Lateline, April 22, 2002, http://www.abc.net.au/lateline/stories/s537864.htm (accessed November 30, 2005).

11. "About Woomera," ABC Four Corners, May 19, 2003, http://www.abc.net.au/4corners/content/2003/transcripts/s858341.htm (accessed November 30, 2005).

12. National Inquiry into Children in Immigration Detention (2004), p. 68.

13. National Inquiry into Children in Immigration Detention (2002).

14. "Worse than Prisons? Managing Detention Centres," ABC Background Briefing, http://www.abc.net.au/rn/talks/bbing/stories/s697195.htm (accessed November 30, 2005).

15. Michel Foucault, *The History of Sexuality: An Introduction*, trans. Robert Hurley (London: Allen Lane, 1980).

16. Michel Foucault, "Two Lectures," in *Power/Knowledge: Selected Interviews and Other Writings 1972–1977*, ed. Colin Gordon, trans. Colin Gordon et al. (New York: Harvester Wheatsheaf, 1980), p. 105.

17. Foucault, *History of Sexuality* (1980), p. 143.

18. Agamben (1998), pp. 126–143.

19. Ibid., p. 153.

20. Ibid., p. 153.

21. DIMIA, "Fact Sheet 70: Border Control," July 12, 2006, http://www.immi.gov.au/media/fact-sheets/70border.htm (accessed August 1, 2006).

22. "About Woomera" (2003).

23. "Woomera Detention Centre Doctor Speaks Out," ABC Lateline transcript, October 27, 2004, http://www.abc.net.au/lateline/content/2004/s1229335.htm (accessed November 30, 2005).

24. Joint media release by the Minister for Immigration and Multicultural and Indigenous Affairs, Senator the Honorable Amanda Vanstone, and the Attorney General, the Honorable Philip Ruddock, MP, May 13, 2004, http://www.minister.immi.gov.au/media_releases/media04/v04068.htm (accessed November 30, 2005).

25. For further discussion of the calculation of human suffering and death as a form of deterrence, see Roxanne Doty's contribution to this volume.

26. In the 2004 decision of Al-Kateb v Godwin (2004) 219 CLR 562, the High Court found that there was no limitation to be found in the Commonwealth constitution or under international law on the power of the executive government to detain unlawful arrivals, potentially for life.

27. For a list of such investigations, see National Inquiry into Children in Immigration Detention (2004), p. 26.

28. "PM Calls October 9 Poll," August 29, 2004, http://www.abc. net.au/news/newsitems/200408/s1187484.htm (accessed November 30, 2005).

29. National Inquiry into Children in Immigration Detention (2002).

30. Philip Alston, "Resisting the Merger and Acquisition of Human Rights by Trade Law: A Reply to Petersmann," *European Journal of International Law*, 13 (2002): 815–844, 846.

31. Ibid., p. 846.

32. See generally Michelle Gellrich, *Tragedy and Theory: The Problem of Conflict since Aristotle* (Princeton: Princeton University Press, 1988), p. 246.

33. Ibid., p. 246.

34. Ibid., p. 251.

35. Philip Alston, p. 246.

36. Ibid., p. 248.

37. Ibid., p. 247.

38. Foucault (2003), p. 174.

39. Ibid., p. 67.

40. Ibid., p. 26.

41. Ibid., p. 223.

42. Ibid., p. 223.

43. Michel Foucault, *Technologies of the Self*, ed. Luther H. Martin, Huck Gutman, and Patrick H. Hutton (Amherst: University of Massachusetts Press, 1988), p. 160.

44. Foucault (2003), p. 246.

45. Ibid., p. 247.

46. Lauren Berlant, *The Queen of America Goes to Washington City: Essays on Sex and Citizenship* (Duke: Duke University Press, 1997), p. 278.

47. Foucault (2003), p. 249.

48. Berlant (1997), p. 175.

49. Foucault (2003), p. 254.

50. Ibid., p. 44.

51. National Inquiry into Children in Immigration Detention (2002).

52. Sophocles, "Antigone," in *The Theban Plays*, trans. E. F. Watling (London: Penguin, 1947), pp. 493–506.

53. Costas Douzinas and Ronnie Warrington, *Justice Miscarried: Ethics, Aesthetics and the Law* (New York: Harvester Wheatsheaf, 1994), p. 60.

54. G. W. F. Hegel, *The Phenomenology of Spirit*, trans. A. V. Millter (Oxford: Clarendon, 1977).

55. Gellrich (1988), p. 46.

56. Hegel (1977), para 466.

57. Douzinas and Warrington (1994), p. 79.

58. Ibid., p. 80.

59. Costas Douzinas, "Law's Birth and Antigone's Death: On Ontological and Psychoanalytical Ethics," *Cardozo Law Review*, 16 (1994–1995): 1325–1362, esp. p. 1353.

60. Sophocles, *The Three Theban Plays*, trans. Robert Fagles (London: Penguin, 1984), II. 995–1004, as cited in Douzinas (1994–1995), p. 1353.

61. Douzinas (1994–1995), pp. 1360–1361.

62. Copjec (2002), p. 23.

63. David L. Eng and David Kazanjian, "Introduction: Mourning Remains," in *Loss*, ed. David L. Eng and David Kazanjian (Berkeley: University of California Press, 2003), p. ix.

64. Ibid., p. ix.

65. For a discussion of "the paradoxes that appear at the points where the exercise of this biopower reaches its limits," see Foucault (2003), p. 253.

66. See Jean-Pierre Vernant, "Oedipus without the Complex," in *Myth and Tragedy in Ancient Greece*, ed. Jean-Pierre Vernant and Pierre Vidal-Naquet (New York: Zone Books, 1988), pp. 101–102.

67. Foucault (2003), p. 248.
68. Ibid., p. 248.
69. Agamben (1998), p. 187.
70. Copjec (2002), p. 47.
71. Foucault, *History of Sexuality* (1980), p. 143.
72. Sophocles (1947), pp. 126–127.
73. Page duBois, "Toppling the Hero: Polyphony in the Tragic City," *New Literary History*, 35 (2004): 63–81, p. 65.
74. Ibid., p. 65.
75. Jean-Pierre Vernant, "Tensions and Ambiguities in Greek Tragedy," in *Myth and Tragedy in Ancient Greece*, ed. Jean-Pierre Vernant and Pierre Vidal-Naquet (New York: Zone Books, 1988), pp. 29, 33.
76. Gellrich (1988), p. 111.
77. Vernant, "Tensions and Ambiguities in Greek Tragedy" (1988), p. 29.
78. Vernant, "Oedipus without the Complex" (1988), p. 93.
79. Ibid.
80. Ibid., p. 91.
81. duBois (2004), p. 76.
82. Commonwealth of Australia, *Inquiry into the Circumstances of the Immigration Detention of Cornelia Rau*, July 2005 (Palmer Report). According to the Minister for Immigration, 200 other cases of mistaken detention of citizens in immigration detention centers have been referred to the Commonwealth Ombudsman: see further the press release available at http://www.minister.immi.gov.au/media_releases/media05/v05087.htm (accessed November 30, 2005).
83. *Inquiry into the Circumstances of the Immigration Detention of Cornelia Rau* (2005), p. viii.
84. Ibid.
85. Ibid., p. ix.
86. Ibid.
87. Ibid., p. x.
88. Ibid.
89. Ibid.
90. Ibid., p. xii.
91. Ibid.
92. Ibid., p. 70.
93. Ibid., p. ix.
94. Ryszard Kapuscinski, *The Shah of Shahs* (London: Picador, 1986), pp. 109–110.
95. Ibid., pp. 109–110.
96. Slavoj Žižek, *Tarrying with the Negative: Kant, Hegel, and the Critique of Ideology* (Durham: Duke University Press, 1993), p. 234.
97. Ghassan Hage, *White Nation: Fantasies of White Supremacy in a Multicultural Society* (Sydney: Pluto Australia Press, 1998), p. 174.
98. Foucault (2003), p. 256.
99. Ibid., p. 256.

100. Ibid., pp. 254–255.
101. See further Ian Duncanson, "Law as Conversation," in *International Law and Its Others*, ed. Anne Orford (Cambridge: Cambridge University Press, 2006), pp. 57–84.
102. Žižek (1993), p. 228.

CHAPTER 11

LIVING, DYING, SURVIVING II

Elizabeth Dauphinee

Perhaps every word, every writing is born, in this sense, as testimony.[1]
One must do justice, which is the source of theory.[2]
Peace, peace to him who is far off, and to him who is near, says the Eternal.
—(Isaiah 57:19)

Manuel Bravo committed suicide yesterday. I learned about it just after I left the Job Centre Plus in Rusholme, where I had attended a compulsory interview for a National Insurance Number—the last step in a stunningly facile work permit process that whisked me from Canada to the United Kingdom in exactly 12 weeks. It was a daunting process, to be sure, and fraught with an insomniac's anxiety. I had to pack up my apartment, say goodbye to friends and family, and worry about which of my new colleagues at the University of Manchester might collect me from the airport with my 140 pounds of overweight baggage. The National Insurance Number interview was one of the strangest experiences I have ever had—I was asked to bring essentially all of the documentation I have ever been issued. I arrived there with my two blue passports (one Canada, one U.S.), my U.K. visa, my work permit, my birth certificate, the lease agreement for my flat in Manchester, a connection agreement with British Telecom and another with UK Online to prove my address (the signed lease agreement was apparently not sufficient), my employment contract with the university along with a letter from Human Resources that essentially recapped the important details of the contract, namely, that I would be paid and would, in turn, pay taxes. They copied my U.S. social security number and my Canadian social insurance number; they copied every page in both of my passports and asked me to sign each of these pages in order to confirm that I had traveled to the countries corresponding to the entry and exit stamps. They called in a pleasant but serious man who introduced himself as a trained expert in the detection of fraudulent passports. He spent a particularly long time scrutinizing my U.S. passport—it was issued in April 2005 and there were some subtle differences between the new issue and the old one, with which he was evidently not yet familiar. He took the passport off for a consultation with another colleague.

I was there for an hour and a half. I sipped my tea and gazed out the window into the soft autumn rain while they methodically filled out an application form that was so long it needed an industrial staple to keep it all together. This is the process through which one becomes politically human in the United Kingdom. This is the process through which one becomes intelligible as a capital-earning, tax-paying, rights-bearing thread in the weave of the sociopolitical fabric. When I stepped out onto the street again, the documentation that testifies to my existence safely bundled away in my briefcase, I saw Manuel Bravo's face staring out from the front page of the *Independent*. The grainy color photograph portrayed a young, unsmiling man who, it seemed to me, had a look of mistrust in his eyes. But sometimes it's possible to look at something for too long—a photograph, a sentence, a man's eyes—and to read something which is not there.

Witnessing

Manuel Bravo arrived in the United Kingdom with his son, Antonio, just as I was getting ready to write my PhD qualifying examinations in International Relations at York University in Toronto in 2001. He appeared before an asylum tribunal in Leeds in October 2002 with the support of his parish priest when the lawyer he had retained failed to show up. He waited for news of the outcome of his application, but the priest says that none came. Manuel and Antonio Bravo waited. Then, in the thin light before morning on Wednesday, September 14, 2005, while I was still sleeping off my jetlag in my new flat in Manchester's city center, Manuel and 13-year-old Antonio were arrested and taken to a place called Yarl's Wood—a detention center for asylum seekers in Bedfordshire—where they learned that their deportation to Angola was imminent. When he was informed that they would be deported, Manuel hanged himself in a stairwell. The *Independent* explained his suicide with a perverse, painful twist: "hemmed in by British asylum laws, [Manuel's suicide] was a final, astonishing act of parental love. If he had remained alive, his son would have been returned to Angola with him. Now that Mr. Bravo is dead,

Antonio will have a chance to achieve their dream of building a life in Britain."[3] According to a statement from the Home Office, Antonio, now an orphan, cannot be deported before his eighteenth birthday.

Perhaps, when the time comes, Antonio's asylum application will be successful. Perhaps not. It is likely that, by the time those five years have passed, this story will have been forgotten and Antonio's application—should he make one at all—will be just another slip of paper in a machinery fed by exile. I want to hope that this is not the case; I want to hope that Manuel and Antonio Bravo will not be forgotten. But I can see that they were designed to be forgotten in an asylum system that removes them both physically and conceptually from the sphere of public life. They were designed to be forgotten in the structure of a juridical system that relies fundamentally on the identification of those who are unwelcome; they are the obverse—the unbelonging—that makes possible the celebration of sovereign subjectivity as *the* historical achievement of human political community. They are the alibi that vests the quest for security with its legitimacy—with its raison d'être: the protection of those whom it claims are its own, whose claims, in turn, can only be made in the terminology of sovereign subjectivity—which is to say, in the case of Manuel Bravo, not at all. While I was being fast-tracked through the U.K. visa process in order to provide what the Human Resources Department at the University of Manchester referred to as my "expert services," Manuel Bravo was getting ready to die.

There are so many ways to express Manuel Bravo's living, dying, and surviving in Leeds that to reduce my narrative to only one or two aspects risks a second, equally unforgivable erasure. A man is never what can be said about him. A man is never wholly contained by the confines of political space, or even within the narrative contours of his own life—his friends, his children, the depth of his love, his hopes and aspirations, his fears, and his grief—in short, his living and his dying and his surviving. And so I proceed knowing that I can never capture these things despite my best intentions and attempts to do so. There is always this opacity, and it is opacity to ourselves, the opacity of our intentions.[4] Plagued by the awareness that there is no pure witnessing, nor complete portrayal, I begin this ending.[5] One cannot witness from the inside of death; one narrates, or attempts to narrate, only from the outside—from the obverse of death, which is to say, from my life made possible by another's death. I begin, sensing that there is something fundamentally inadequate here—sensing that I can never really approach this man or this death. This is therefore my exposure to him; I want justice, fully cognizant of the disembodied nature of this desire—fully cognizant of the risk that Manuel Bravo becomes in this narrative not himself, but a representation of himself. I proceed, knowing that my justice is also a violence, trying to make sense of questions even as I refuse them. I proceed on supposition and rumor, but I am doing the best I can.

James Hatley writes that "[i]n the end, one does not choose *whether* one will witness but *how* one will witness. . . . In this witness, even the attempt to cover over one's witness witnesses. . . . In ethical witness . . . one finds a witness of self-accusation, a witness unsure of its own sincerity, insecure in its own memory, but brought into insomnia, into a consideration of the other's plight that cannot be undone."[6] This is not the structure of command given to oneself, which is no command or obligation at all, but the accountability that lies in the address of the other—a command to witness what cannot be witnessed; that is, the command to the living to witness the surviving, the command to the surviving to witness the dying, from which there is no return or recompense. Here, I am a reluctant witness. I want no part of this witnessing. I want to go home. But that is no escape. In a moment of despair or courage (I don't know which), Jacques Rolland writes that "[t]he necessity of fleeing, of hiding oneself, is put in check by the impossibility of fleeing oneself."[7] And so I begin.

There are at least two ways in which the living, dying, and surviving of Manuel Bravo can be explored. On the one hand, we can identify the ways in which asylum seekers in Britain and elsewhere are reduced to what Agamben and many of the contributors to this volume have identified as "bare life." Stripped of their capacity to be political, claims-making subjects, asylum seekers face a juridical system that denies them the politically meaningful use of their own voices. Like the concentration camps of Australia, the detention centers of the United Kingdom produce and profit from the influx and transit of human beings whose arrival is cast as inherently suspect.[8] Their logic is one of boundary making and marking. But we also know that even the most violently enclosed systems of sovereignty are unavoidably leaky. They cannot securitize against every challenge that might be launched—both because it is never possible to anticipate every site from which resistance might come (for resistance is already everywhere), but also because the very logic of this closure always already implies a breach. Through the instrumental use of his own bare-life-in-death, Manuel Bravo exercised political subjectivity in a place where he was presumed to have none and thus reclaimed, for a time at least, the subjectivity of his son. In the lexicon of bare life, Manuel Bravo's assertion of political agency is probably the reason why his death was worthy of the front page of the *Independent*. I don't think it was the trauma of his death that earned his suicide national attention. I think it was the scarcely believable fact that he managed to disrupt the edifice of the law whose job it was to silence him. In this sense, the trauma that was logged was that done to sovereign power, and not to Manuel Bravo. His suicide, at least for a moment, exposed the logic of biopower for what it is: the permissible violent inscription of sovereignty on the bodies of those who have been reduced to bare life—on those who have been identified as occupying a zone beyond the human— those whose abjection is so complete that their deaths no longer have any political meaning. They die and do not die. They are present, but their presence is absence.[9]

Even in the face of this elemental exposure, I don't want to narrate Manuel Bravo's life as one of abjection. Manuel Bravo built a life in Leeds. His son went to school. He had friends, he found a parish and attended services there. He was living, even if his living can also be narrated as a mere surviving, and even if his surviving reached its culmination in his dying. The point is that his dying was a profoundly political undertaking. Manuel Bravo knew the law. He knew that if his son was orphaned, he would become a charge of the state. Antonio would be taken into foster care, he would escape Yarl's Wood, he would avoid deportation to Angola, and he would have another chance to remain in the United Kingdom. And so, whether Manuel Bravo's decision to commit suicide was borne out of calculation or desperation or both, or something else, one fact starkly remains: he knew what the legal implications would be for his son. He had worked out the terrible imbalance between the costs and the benefits, and he paid with the currency of his own life. He had bought his son five more years, and another chance. He had refused the judgment of the law, refused its sentence, refused the very logic of its incarceration and excision by escaping from it through his death—and he had snatched his son back from the silence imposed upon him by the exigencies of sovereign power, even if only for an instant. Indeed, following the rupture that Manuel Bravo's suicide enacted, the logic of detention and asylum reasserted itself, and Yarl's Wood remains. Trapped in the logic of a biopower that erases and renders invisible as it sucks both peoples and individuals into its narrative claim of their absence, Manuel Bravo, through his death, managed to rearticulate himself as visible, as present, as un-erased.

The point here is not to celebrate Manuel Bravo's suicide as a heroic act of resistance. It was, to my mind, not a heroic act of resistance, but rather a last-ditch, desperate effort to save his son in the moment when it became apparent that this was the last choice that could be made. In this sense, I think the *Independent* narrated at least one accuracy, that this was "a final, astonishing act of parental love." And while the act of suicide in such circumstances appears to be exceptional, the fact is that Manuel Bravo's suicide, singular in the life that was lost, is *not* exceptional. Thirty-five asylum seekers either in detention or under deportation orders in the UK have taken their own lives over the last five years. The day before Manuel's suicide, a 26-year-old Zimbabwean man, Edmore Ngwenya, jumped to his death in a Manchester canal while the police and staff in a nearby office building looked on.

Forgetting

What made the story of Manuel Bravo particularly photogenic for the *Independent* was an incomplete awareness of a complex phenomenon: *Manuel Bravo exercised his political subjectivity despite the fact that he had none.* In an asylum logic that requires an ethos of forgetting and erasure to operate successfully, how could this be? The law operates on the excision of those who are carefully *not remembered.* Our collective sense of liberal space as inherently welcoming is made so by the forgetting of the fact that the logic of liberal space as welcoming space is built on the concealed identification of those who are rendered unwelcome. And there are always the unbelonging—those who disrupt the coherence of national narratives and who must be subsequently managed through a logic of forgetting in order to successfully maintain those narratives: the Mexican and other Latino migrants who die of thirst in the Sonoran Desert, the "transfer tubes" full of dead American soldiers who undermine the myth of American militarized masculinity, the detention centers of Australia and France and Britain, the offshore excised places in the Pacific, the interrogation rooms at JFK through which Maher Arar (and countless others) experienced his own obliteration. In the grammar of the biopolitical, "one not only forgets the face of the other, but one must also forget that one has forgotten."[10] This is the double imperative that makes possible the narration of excision as "necessary excision." Embedded in this forgetting is a delusion "concerning one's own responsibility for the other even as the face of the other continues to haunt one's every gesture."[11]

But the space between discourses of belonging and unbelonging blurs, one bleeds into the other, and the logic that informs dichotomous hierarchies of being is exposed for what it is: an alibi for the legitimacy of the project of sovereignty. After all, we are produced as intelligible subjects through this forgetting in which we are all implicated. The law that enshrines must also exclude. The law that protects must also destroy. The law that makes live must also let die. The law that makes me eligible for political personhood in the United Kingdom (and in Canada and in the United States) is built on the doomed applications of thousands—of hundreds of thousands—who are not eligible. This much seems clear: in its desire to make live, the law is a producer of death—it is a veritable assembly line of excision, exception, erasure, absence, abjection, and unbelonging. In the gravity of its orbit, one lives or dies or survives, each precarious space informing the other, but none being permanent sites of existence. And the logic that makes all this living, dying, and surviving possible is immediately forgotten—it is *de-remembered*. This de-remembering, this turning away from the liquidity of the other man's eyes, is the required elision that makes all this living, dying, and surviving possible.

Any failure to interrogate the political and philosophical practices that make possible these livings, dyings, and survivings validates the destruction of human lives and bodies through a profound historical omission; that is, the omission of life lost itself, the tacit understanding that it did not, in fact, exist at all. This was the logic of the camps: the annihilation of generations, of space and time, the *rendering invisible* of those who found themselves in the orbit of its logic.[12] This is an attack on the future itself. This is an attack on the very possibility of constructing future memory. It denies memory as a paradigm through which the past can be made present and through which the present can be resisted in the future. It aspires to produce a total loss. The production of death requires first the political intelligibility of the bodies on which death is inscribed as worthy of being given death—because this is a biologic that appends worthiness and value as the identifying tag—the biometric, if you will—on the bodies it produces, encounters, and seeks to manage. The work of mourning never need be assumed because in the structure of bare life, the dead did not die. Yet, at the same time, mourning is all there is left to do—the mourning of and for Manuel Bravo, the grief of his son, the grief of his priest, the grief of those whose names I do not know and will never know, the grief that I felt when I saw the paper as I was leaving the Job Centre in Rusholme. This stark juxtaposition— not complex, not difficult, not even particularly academic—is lodged in my throat like a needle: *the accident of birth in a world absurdly rent.*

This pure accident of birth is fashioned into the rational adjudicative technology through which sovereign power asserts itself as a necessary historical mode of political existence and belonging. The apparent rational seamlessness of its justification is, at the core of its logic, purely accidental and contingent. Giorgio Agamben points out that "[i]f refugees (whose number has continued to grow in our century, to the point of including a significant part of humanity today) represent such a disquieting element in the order of the modern nation-state, this is above all because by breaking the continuity between man and citizen, nativity and nationality, they put the originary fiction of modern sovereignty in crisis. Bringing to light the difference between birth and nation, the refugee causes the secret presupposition of the political domain—bare life—to appear for an instant within that domain."[13] The figure of the asylum seeker illuminates the disjuncture between sovereign power and the fictive basis of its legitimacy; it exposes the absurd fact that it is simply *accident of birth* that affords the technology to underwrite the legitimacy of boundary making: political, topographical, linguistic, racial. We know it. But if we are to go on bearing it, we must simultaneously forget.

In the logic of the sovereign ban, death does not happen. The dead did not die if they were constituted as subjectless in the first place. It is not that they are "inhuman," which connotes something else—something equally excising—but de-subject-ed, undone, the ephemeral occupants of a constructed core of nothingness that relies on a political logic which employs them as alibis for the myth of our shared human political community. The abject do not die in the grammar of this political lexicon. They are *erased*. No amount of address will evoke an answer. The adjudication of asylum claims is just that: it is the relationship of a technology to its applications; it is the bits of paper that undergo judgment, and those who stand behind those bits of paper are denied their own faces, their own voices, their own skins. They appear before tribunals and are erased. This is a suffering and an abjection compounded by a profound betrayal.[14] One approaches sovereign power in the only way one can, as a supplicant, seeking refuge under the law, and is betrayed in the discovery that the very language of one's being is unintelligible outside the matrix of the right to lay claim.[15]

The Biopolitics of Dying

In the structure of the suicide of Manuel Bravo, the British state is exempted from murder, and in this sense avoids this death as murder entirely, not because it is suicide but because the life that was extinguished was already stripped of all political subjectivity *and so could not be killed*. It is this logic that protects all the British and American and Canadian judges who knowingly return those who appear before them to countries where they will be incarcerated, tortured, or executed. In this way, the giving of death is rendered apolitical; the returning of refugees to zones of death is without political or moral consequence. This sentencing to death is, in the algorithm of biopolitics, an outcome without outcome. Manuel Bravo was supposed to have accepted his sentence of death and was presumed incapable of enacting resistance. Whatever personal, emotional, private grief might accompany his consignment to abjection was supposed to remain just that. He was not supposed to have been capable of claiming that death for himself, and even less so to have managed to repoliticize his life through this claiming. His death was simultaneously an indictment and an escape, but it was an escape from a power which renders suicide the last possible option in a biopolitical logic that denies the possibility of life. And so, while the death of Manuel Bravo stands as an intensely personal experience—an experience that is impossible to bear witness to from inside—it is also a political wail leveled against an edifice of law that produces and strips life down to the bone—that simultaneously hides and reveals the mechanisms of its interventions through the desire to contain that which is by definition uncontainable: life, which, however bare, *is still life*. This is the interplay between the imperative and the impossibility to witness. One cannot bear witness, but one yet witnesses. We witness all throughout the pages of this volume. We witness death, and we witness the witnesses of death.

It is the intensely private nature of death in the biopolitical regime that marks the subversion when death is thrown back in the face of sovereign power. Through his suicide, Manuel Bravo both confirmed and denied what the state had already decreed: that his was a life that could not be lived; yet the subversion lies precisely in this fact: in order for the biopolitical ban to function, death must remain *concealed* as the originary activity of sovereignty. In the instant of his death, Manuel Bravo held up the mirror in which the logic of sovereign power was captured and exposed. He reasserted death, even if only for an instant, as the fundamental task of sovereignty. Regardless of intention, Manuel Bravo's suicide exposed the crisis at the heart of sovereign biopower, forcing the recognition that the biopolitical project of "making live and letting die" is, fundamentally, an active, willful giving of death to those identified as ineligible for life.[16]

Manuel Bravo is not a tragic hero, since he acted in a space where he was nevertheless denied both subjectivity and the capacity to decide his own fate (beyond the narrowest of confines, which is, to be sure, almost no decision at all). The paradox here is significant: Manuel Bravo could kill himself, but this was also *all* he could do, which is to say, that this was essentially his only option; and his decision was also decided *for* him in a biopolitical logic that produces bare lives for whom the only remaining option of exercising political power is through death. There is still a limit space between being offered death and assuming it oneself. To formulate the paradox another way, sovereign power can regulate death, but it cannot regulate suicide, even though it consistently produces a limit condition in which suicide becomes the only possible political option for those caught in the sovereign ban. In a perverse and terrifying way, then, suicide becomes the limit condition of resistance, paradoxically expressing the capacity to refuse the logic of death that lies at the core of biopower.[17]

Exposure

Drawing on the work of Adriana Cavarero, Judith Butler argues that "we are beings who are, of necessity, *exposed* to one another in our vulnerability and singularity, and that our political situation consists in part in learning how best to handle—and to honor—this constant and necessary exposure."[18] This exposure remains despite our best attempts to secure ourselves from it, and all our attempts to secure are aimed at achieving this originary desire: to deny our vulnerability, to minimize our exposure, to contain, control, and excise what is other in the same. The constancy—the infinity—of this exposure is such that no politics can ever fully regulate or deny it. Indeed, the imperative to forget the life that was lost is the awareness of the forgetting that has taken place—and precisely because of this forms the possibility of the beginning of remembering. James Hatley points out that "the very activity of forgetting the other . . . becomes itself an insistent witness to the contrary that the other could not be forgotten."[19] In this sense, this rupture cannot be sealed over because the rupture is constantly reenacted, and because the contours of the rupture are not static. In this sense, also, the question Who are you? can ever only be answered in a partial and fragmented manner, and this answering is an ongoing, and necessarily incomplete, project.

We can never give a full accounting, no matter how stuffed with documentation our briefcases might be. We try to account, as Judith Butler points out, and come to find that

> [t]here are clearly times when I cannot tell the story in a straight line, and I lose my thread, and I start again, and I forgot something crucial, and it is too hard to think about how to weave it in. I start thinking, thinking, there must be some conceptual thread that will provide a narrative here, some lost link, some possibility for chronology, and the "I" becomes increasingly conceptual, increasingly awake, focused, determined. At this point, when I near the prospect of intellectual self-sufficiency in the presence of the other, nearly excluding him or her from my horizon, the thread of my story unravels. If I achieve that self-sufficiency, my relation to the other is lost.[20]

This desire to account in full measure, forgetting nothing, sealing over the cracks in the plaster, is the desire through which we lose the one who faces us. In this case, the losing of the other man is a total loss, because there is no way back from death. Here, the imperatives of the political imaginary of the British state to secure and to adjudicate are concluded in a narrative that holds the line, so to speak, that holds the one who seeks refuge over the horizon, literally and figuratively. It desires a narrative in which there is no rupture, an identity in which there is no ambiguity (or in which ambiguity can be managed and marginalized). Here, Levinas finds the "vanity of vanities: the echo of our own voices, taken for a response to the few prayers that still remain to us; everywhere we have fallen back upon our own feet, as after the ecstasies of a drug. Except the other whom . . . we cannot let go."[21]

The exposure to which we are given over is an elemental condition of human relationality, and it is in this exposure that the political takes shape. This exposure cannot be completely contained because its impact can never be calculated beforehand. Manuel Bravo and I came before the adjudicative apparatus of the British state, but we had vastly different things at stake, and in our exposure to sovereign power, we came also to be exposed to one another in ways and with impacts that could not be fully anticipated. He, exposed to me because the British state requires the imaginary of the good immigrant to provide the basis on which his application could be rejected wholesale (or ignored, as the priest attests). I, exposed to him because I know that I took his place, I made his death possible, and because he haunts me in a semipermanent insomnia over which I cannot get control. This is that exposure: the structure of grief, because we are hemmed in on all sides by a biopolitical power that denies this exposure, that denies that we are at each other's mercy and as such are obligated, despite our best attempts at autonomy, to trust one another. There is no trust or faith in the sovereign ban—only a technology of knowledge and its application. In the condition of the biopolitical, then,—in the space of the sovereign ban— our exposure remains, but the dangers are more extreme because the categories of intelligibility are narrower and narrower. It is precisely because biopolitical exposure is exposure to specified modes of living, dying, and surviving that we need to dwell on the possible meanings of this exposure more carefully. The arrival of the stranger, who is unknown and unknowable, the arrival of the seeker of refuge, who gives no name and no place, stretches the limits of self and subjectivity. Refugees are refugees before the law, but are also refugees *from* the law, which enacts the most devastating betrayals against those who have no choice but to trust in it. It is only outside of the law—indeed, despite the law and in contravention of it—that the gesture of hospitality in the face of our exposure to one another can be made.

Welcoming

Derrida argues that the host as host is only made possible through the arrival of the guest; what can be given is made givable only by the one who receives: "sovereignty can only be exercised by filtering, choosing, and thus by excluding and doing violence. Injustice, a certain injustice, and even a certain perjury, begins right away, from the very threshold of the right to hospitality."[22] It is only outside of the bounds of sovereignty—in those liminal, imaginative spaces—that the possibility for hospitality begins to emerge. In the sphere of sovereign power, one inquires after names, dates and places of birth and residence, of confession and faith and language. One is born here or there, uses this or that language, is young or old, speaks to and longs for one God or many. One emerged in the red or black or yellow clay of a bounded place—an ancestral land—a hill, a plain, a valley, a riverside. The state attempts to embrace, repel, mediate, and otherwise control hospitality through its ability to exercise and perform sovereign space—through its ability to confer and deny political subjectivity—through its claim to be able to confer an unopposable meaning to the color of the clay, to the color of the skin, to the caliber of the qualification.

The law legislates the contours and limits of hospitality, working to limit the limitless exposure to one another that hospitality entails. This is no hospitality. Decision is made, as Kierkegaard laments, through the application of a certain rule or premise which is no decision at all, but only a server-side application concerned with breaches and firewalls and quotas. Hospitality, adjudicated and administered as part of the "right" of sovereign power is already always suspect. (Witness here that asylum is a gift, and not a right.) We claim the right to be hospitable, which is our meager gift to those we have identified through the deployment of our (bio)technologies of knowledge as worthy of entrance. The hospitality that claims to welcome is driven by the command to intelligibility.[23] This country offers hospitality neither to Manuel Bravo nor to me, and this is the paradox through which we are connected. There was no mercy here, and no welcoming. We underwent the technical application of a preexisting adjudicative procedure that was designed in such a way that it would make (me) live and let (him) die. Derrida argues that

> absolute hospitality requires that I open up my home and that I give not only to the foreigner, but to the absolute, unknown, anonymous other, and that I *give place* to them, that I let them come, that I let them arrive, and take place in the place I offer them, without asking of them either reciprocity (entering into a pact) or even their names. The law of absolute hospitality commands a break with hospitality by right, with law of justice as rights.[24]

It is in the utter vulnerability of one before another that the imperative to hospitality emerges and does not ask Who are you? before making offer. It is an ethos of offering lodged in the recognition that this offering is made possible only through our own vulnerability, and through the impossibility of ever knowing one another or ourselves.

In the context of this logic, what might it mean to be responsible? Might it mean that we learn to see differently? To write differently? To explode the line, already so tenuously maintained, between narrative and scholarship? Between mimesis and aesthetics? Between fiction and philosophy? Agamben posits that we are all bare life; that we are all exposed through the logic of biopolitics to the possibility of elimination without punishment.[25] Might this be the call to break the law? To break this perverse contract in which we are all caught, and in which we have everything at stake? Might this be the Foucauldian call to refuse what we are?

Manuel Bravo is not solely representative of the plights of others, even though his living, dying, and surviving is also a representation. Reducing his singularity to a representation denies his specific place—his specific decision. The generality is the asylum law, which is generic in its gift of death—but this same generality appended to the plight of asylum seekers risks the impossible figure—the impossible singularity of the exposure of thousands of men, women, and children, of all of us—it is the generality appended to them that denies them the contours of their subjectivities and of their relationalities. It denies them their names. At the same time, there is a need to speak of the scale of the human destruction—the inexorable logic of the production of unlivability en masse—there is a need to accept the paradox that Manuel Bravo is unique and yet not unique. Singular, and yet not singular. Solitary, and yet not solitary. Erased, and yet still visible. Forgotten, but remembered. Contained herein is the imperative "to be addressed by and to remember those who were being crushed, so that their annihilation might be witnessed, so that the truth of their plight might address the succeeding generations of humanity."[26]

Here is the list of proper names of the asylum-seekers who have taken their own lives in the United Kingdom (the ones we know about, and can name) over the last five years. Their deaths continue, and necessarily so, to haunt our ethical and political imaginings about who we are. We are in large measure what the bodies of these dead have identified us as—a political imaginary lodged in the exercise of a sovereign biopolitical power whose continued intelligibility hinges on their disappearance. *What might it mean to recover them?*

They are:

Manuel Bravo
Edmore Ngwenya
Babak Ahadi

Ramazan Kumluca
Kenny Peter
John Kanau Manana
Majid Rafieei
Ceife Yimene
Ako Mahmood Ahmed
Tran Quang Tung
Sergey Barnuyck
Hussein Nasseri
Zekria Ghulam Mohammed
Liang He
Mohammed bin Duhri
Tema Kombe
Israfil Shiri
Vasiliy Todchuk
Liu Jin Wu
Mikhail Bognarchuk
Sirous Khajeh
Beverly Fowler
Forsina Makoni
Shiraz Pir
Mohsen Amri
Nariman Tahamasbi
Souleyman Diallo
Nasser Ahmed
Shokrolah 'Ramin' Khaleghi
Saeed Alaei
Glynnis Cowley
Robertas Grabys . . .

Notes

1. Giorgio Agamben, *Remnants of Auschwitz: The Witness and the Archive*, trans. Daniel Heller-Roazen (New York: Zone Books, 2002), p. 38.
2. Emmanuel Levinas, *Of God Who Comes to Mind* (Stanford: Stanford University Press, 1998), p. 82.
3. Ian Herbert, "Asylum-Seeker Made Ultimate Sacrifice for Son," *The Independent*, September 17, 2005, p. 2.
4. See Judith Butler, *Giving an Account of Oneself* (New York: Fordham University Press, 2005).
5. James Hatley shows that there are multiple ways of witnessing, some of which are entirely unintentional and all of which are inherently fragmented.

For Hatley, witnessing is ambivalent, often unintentional, an incessant corrective to narrative history; persecution, self-accusation, and silence are also modes of witnessing. See James Hatley, *Suffering Witness: The Quandary of Responsibility after the Irreparable* (Albany, NY: Suny Press, 2000).

6. Ibid., p. 99.

7. Jacques Rolland, quoted in Emmanuel Levinas, *On Escape*, trans. Bettina Bergo (Stanford, CA: Stanford University Press, 2003), p. 36.

8. See Engin Isin and Kim Rygiel, and Anne Orford in this volume.

9. See Jenny Edkins in this volume for another exploration of the ways in which absence is managed and inscribed.

10. Hatley (2000), p. 92.

11. Ibid., p. 92.

12. James Hatley argues that the Shoah was an aenocide—a destruction of the generations and of the connectivities between generations such that it also involved an assault on time and the future itself.

13. Giorgio Agamben, *Homo Sacer: Sovereign Power and Bare Life* (Stanford, CA: Stanford University Press, 1998), p. 130.

14. Hatley (2000), p. 158.

15. For an analysis of the "right to claim rights" see Engin Isin and Kim Rygiel in this volume.

16. Michel Foucault, *Society Must Be Defended: Lectures at the Collège de France 1975–1976*, trans. David Macey (New York: Picador, 2003), particularly lecture 11.

17. One might assert that suicide as political resistance is not dissimilar to a range of activities that are understood as self-injuring: the sewing of lips, hunger strikes, refugees' acts of setting their own boats alight in order to force the assistance of national coast guards, and so on.

18. Butler (2005), pp. 31–32.

19. Hatley (2000), p. 92.

20. Butler (2005), p. 68.

21. Levinas (1998), p. 12.

22. Jacques Derrida, *Of Hospitality: Anne Dufourmantelle Invites Jacques Derrida to Respond*, trans. Rachel Bowlby (Stanford, CA: Stanford University Press, 2000), p. 55.

23. Ibid., p. 41.

24. Ibid., p. 25.

25. Agamben (1998), p. 140.

26. Hatley (2000), p. 68.

CONTRIBUTOR BIOGRAPHICAL INFORMATION

Editors

Elizabeth Dauphinee is Lecturer in International Politics at the University of Manchester. Her research interests include critical security studies, nonstructural approaches to international politics, Levinasian ethics, biopolitics, and trauma. She completed her PhD at York University (Toronto) with fellowship support from the Social Sciences and Humanities Research Council of Canada and the Canadian Consortium on Human Security.

Cristina Masters is Lecturer in International Politics at the University of Manchester. She is the author of "Bodies of Technology: Cyborg Soldiers and Militarised Masculinity" (*International Feminist Journal of Politics*, March 2005) and "Gendered Defences, Gendered Offences: What is at Stake in the Politics of Missile Defence?" (*Journal of Canadian Foreign Policy*, Spring 2005).

Contributors

David Campbell is Professor of Cultural and Political Geography at the University of Durham, where he convenes the Politics-State-Space research group and serves as Associate Director of the Durham Centre for Advanced Photography Studies and Associate Director of the International Boundaries Research Unit. Professor Campbell's research deals with the visual culture of international politics, political theory and global geopolitics, and U.S. security policy. He is currently researching a book (tentatively entitled *Humanitarian Visions*) that is concerned with the pictorial representation of atrocity, famine, and war, as well as curating a photographic exhibition on "Imaging Famine" to be held in London in August–September 2005.

Roxanne Lynn Doty is Associate Professor of Political Science at Arizona State University. She is the author of *Imperial Encounters: The Politics of Representation in North/South Relations* (University of Minnesota Press, 1996) and *Anti-Immigrantism in Western Democracies-Statecraft, Desire, and the Politics of Exclusion* (Routledge, 2003). She has contributed articles to *International Studies Quarterly, Review of International Studies, European Journal of International Relations, Security Studies, Millennium, and Alternatives.* Her research interests include IR theory, immigration and border issues, race, and the politics of writing.

Jenny Edkins is Professor of International Politics at the University of Wales Aberystwyth. Her most recent books are *Sovereign Lives: Power in Global Politics*, with Véronique Pin-Fat and Michael J. Shapiro (Routledge); *Trauma and the Memory of Politics* (Cambridge University Press) and *Whose Hunger? Concepts of Famine, Practices of Aid* (University of Minnesota Press).

Kyle Grayson is Lecturer in the Department of Geography, Politics, and Sociology at the University of Newcastle-Upon-Tyne. Previously, he has served as the Associate Director of YCISS and as a Postdoctoral Fellow of the Canadian Consortium on Human Security. His current research is undertaking a genealogy of assassination with a focus on how the practice has been understood and interpreted in the dominant discourses of global politics.

Engin F. Isin is Professor and Canada Research Chair in the Division of Social Science at York University. His research has focused on the origins and transformations of "occidental citizenship" as a political and legal institution that enables various ways of being political. He is the author of *Cities Without Citizens: Modernity of the City as a Corporation* (Black Rose Books, 1992), *Citizenship and Identity* with Patricia K. Wood (Sage, 1999); *Democracy, Citizenship and the Global City*, ed. Engin F. Isin (Routledge, 2000) and *Being Political: Genealogies of Citizenship* (University of Minnesota Press, 2002). He has also written numerous journal articles, book chapters, technical reports, and public lectures and editorials. His most recent books are coedited with Bryan S. Turner, *Handbook of Citizenship Studies* (Sage, 2002) and with Gerard Delanty, *Handbook of Historical Sociology* (Sage, 2003). His more recent research is on "oriental citizenship and justice" with a focus on Islamic and Ottoman institution, *waqf.*

Mark J. Lacy teaches International Relations at Lancaster University. He is author of *Security and Climate Change: International Relations and the Limits of Realism* (Routledge, 2005) and editor, with Peter Wilkin, of *Global Politics in the Information Age* (Manchester University Press, 2005). He has published articles on cultural politics and International Relations theory in *Alternatives: Local, Global, Politics* and *Millennium: Journal of International Studies.*

David Mutimer is Principal Research Fellow in the Centre for International Cooperation and Security of the Department of Peace Studies, University of Bradford (United Kingdom), and Associate Professor of Political Science, York University (Canada). His work aims to bring critical international theory to bear on issues of traditional concern to security studies. Much of his work has concerned weapons proliferation, and more recently issues of small arms and also the American war on terrorism. He has recently published, with a colleague, a piece on popular culture and the contemporary American self, and is completing a book on the production of a post-cold war international security agenda.

Anne Orford is Professor of Law at the University of Melbourne. She researches, teaches, and supervises doctoral students in the areas of international economic law, international human rights law, international law and security, postcolonial theory, legal theory, psychoanalysis and law, and feminist theory. She is Director of Studies for the Master of Law and Development and the Graduate Diploma of Human Rights Law in the Law School's Graduate Program. Anne is the author of *Reading Humanitarian Intervention: Human Rights and the Use of Force in International Law* (Cambridge University Press, 2003), and has published many articles and reviews on critical theory and international law, including in the *American Journal of International Law*, the *European Journal of International Law*, the *German Law Journal*, the *Leiden Journal of International Law* and the *Harvard International Law Journal.*

Kim Rygiel is a doctoral candidate in the Department of Political Science at York University. Her doctoral research investigates post-9/11 citizenship policies and practices as part of a global governing regime regulating mobility. She is coeditor of *(En)gendering the War on Terror: War Stories and Camouflaged Politics* (Ashgate, 2006) and has also published on diasporic citizenship and gender and Turkish and Kurdish nationalism.

Cynthia Weber is Professor of International Relations at Lancaster University. Her work is located at the intersections of international politics, American studies, gender and sexuality studies, and cultural studies.

INDEX

Abbey, Edward, 10
abject spaces, 181, 184–186, 188–189, 193–194, 198–199
Abu Ghraib, xvi, 49–50, 52–55
Afghanistan, 26, 69, 71, 93, 96, 101, 125, 137, 197, 207
Agamben, Giorgio, xii, 13, 14, 37, 46, 53, 55, 135, 163–165, 168, 174, 184–185, 196, 199, 208, 218, 232, 235
  on bare life, 37, 51, 163–164, 183, 241
  on *homo sacer*, 13, 18, 163
  on the camp, 13, 183, 184, 208
  on the mobility of power, 15
  on the sacred man, 19
  on sovereign power, 165
agency, political, 44, 46, 49, 52, 63, 85, 191, 232
Agnew, John, 110
Al Qaeda, 92, 94, 96, 98, 115, 125, 161, 197
Amnesty International, 52, 162, 197
Antigone, 215
Arendt, Hannah, 184–188, 198–199
  on the logic of sovereignty, 187
Armitage, Richard, 68
Ashcroft, John, 68
Australia, 192
automobility, 131–132, 138, 147–149

Baker, Lori, 20
Bare life, xv, 14, 18, 20, 34, 36–39, 48, 52, 85, 103, 162, 164, 169, 174, 185–186, 196, 209, 232, 233, 235–236, see also *homo sacer*
  as an act of resistance, 189
Barthes, Roland, 29, 67
Baudrillard, Jean, 64
Beck, Ulrich, 173
Berlant, Lauren, 214

Berlin Wall, 6
Bin Laden, Osama, 63, 172
biopolitical state, 166, 170, 222
biopoliticians, U.S., 47, 49, 52
biopolitics, xii, xv, 13, 37, 46, 77, 79–80, 85, 134–136, 138, 147–149, 165, 168–169, 174, 183, 196, 205, 209, 218, 236
  micropolitics of the body, 17
  Woomera as a model biopolitical project, 210
biopower, xiii, 5, 15, 77–80, 134–135, 205, 214, 218, 222, 233, 237, 239–241
body politics, among others, 103
Breton, Andre, 99
Burke, 188
Bush doctrine, 84, 102
  of pre-emption, 109, 116
  hegemonic narrative of, 126
Bush, George. W, 19, 35, 47, 54, 66, 67, 71, 83, 87, 109, 115, 121, 124, 165, 171
  administration of, 68, 85, 95, 98, 100, 110, 115, 124–126, 137, 140
Bush, Laura, 71
Butler, Judith, 61–66, 70, 76, 79, 98, 164, 165, 168, 172, 173, 174, 238
  on governmentality, 165
  on hegemonic consensus, 65
  on indefinite detention, 172, 175
  on imagined wholeness, 62, 64
  on sovereignty, 165–166
  on sublimity of destruction, 66

Campbell, David, 84, 91–92
camp, the, 14, 17, 18, 52, 183–184, 185, 186, 188, 189, 192, 196, 209, 235
Canada, 160–163, 173–174, 184, 198, 229, 239

capitalism, 27, 65, 77, 99, 170
Carter Doctrine, 137
Castillo, Otto Rene, 4
Cavarero, Adriana, 238
Cheney, Dick, 68, 137
citizen, 14, 185
    Citizen/human dichotomy, 20
    Citizenship rights, 191
communism, 169, 170
concentration camp, 51, 208–209, 214–215,
    232
contradiction, of sovereignty and
        biopolitics, 168, 170
Copjec, Joan, 206
Coulter, Ann, 70

Dada, 99
Dali, Salvador, 86–87, 100, 102, 103
    Paranoia-critical method, 100, 101, 103
    on the psychic anamorph, 101, 103
death, xi, xii, xiii, xvi, xviii, 3–20, 26–28,
        32, 35–39, 43–52, 54–55, 61–63, 72,
        74, 76–78, 89–90, 93, 107, 111, 117,
        119–120, 135, 140, 168–169, 178,
        186, 197, 206, 212, 214–218, 222,
        231–239, 241
De Cauter, Lieven, 136, 145
dehumanization, 160
Deleuze, Gilles, 77
    on society of control, 135
democracy, 212
Derrida, Jacques, 13, 62, 65, 239–240
    on cities of refuge, 184, 198
deterrence, border control theory, 16–17, 19
deterritorialization, 131
Desubjectification, xiii
Dillon, Michael, 18
drugs, 7–9, 111, 120, 131, 134, 162
    war on, 129
duBois, Page, 219, 220

Extraordinary rendition, 161, 163, 165,
        173, 174

Fascism, 93
Fahrenheit 9/11, 68, 70, 71
feminine, the, 120–121, 125
    disruptive potential of, 123
Freud, Sigmund, 99
foreign policy, U.S., 86, 110, 129, 132, 137

economistic assumptions of, 136
    as boundary producing, 133–134
    writing of danger, 134
Foucalt, Michel, xii, 77, 134, 165, 166, 171,
        174, 205, 208, 213, 241
    on biopolitics, 13, 46, 135, 208, 214
    on biopower, 13, 46, 209, 214
    on disciplinary society, 135
    on governmentality, 15
    on race war discourse, 166–173
    on sovereign power, 51
    on the camp, 15
    on tragedy, 213
Fox, Vincente, 19
Franco, Jean, 49
Franks, Tommy, 44
Freedom of Information Act, 7
frontiers, 134, 181–190, 192, 197–199
Fukuyama, Francis, 170, 171

Guantanamo Bay, xvi, 50–52, 54–55, 85,
        115, 161, 164, 174, 181, 189,
        196–198, 211, 213
Gellrich, Michelle, 212, 219
geopolitics, 66, 85, 95, 99–101, 103,
        110, 131, 133, 137–138, 144,
        147–148
    of energy security, 138
    of identity, 132
    of oil, 137
Gitlin, Todd, 134
globalization, 131, 205
global panopticon, 100
Greenberg, Judith, 36
grief, 36, 42, 239, see also *mourning*
    as doing, xv
Goddard, Jean Luc, 76
Guattari, Felix, 65, 71, 76–79

Hadley, Stephen, 68
habeas corpus, 51–52, 115, 197
Habermas, Jürgen, 64
Hardt, Michael and Antonio Negri,
        134, 147
    distinction of disciplinary society and
        society of control, 135
Hatley, James, 232, 238
Hegel, 167, 216
hegemony, 46, 48, 62, 65, 83, 86, 99
Hitler, Adolph, 63

homo sacer (sacred man), 18–20, 163, 209,
  see also *bare life*
Howard, John, 212
Hughes, Karen, 68
Humane Borders, 6, 7
human spirit, 16, 17
Human Rights law, 205
humanitarianism, 19
Hurricane Katrina, 79
Hussein, Saddam, 94, 116, 119, 120, 125,
  137, 172

identity/difference, 133
illegal immigrants, 18–19
imagined whole, 66, 76
immanence, 183
indigenous communities, 131
instrumentalization, 39
International Law, 205
Iran, 182, 189, 191, 199, 207, 221
Iraq, 26, 44, 48, 69, 76, 92, 94, 101, 130,
  132, 136, 137, 145, 207

Kant, 212–213
  ethics in the Kantian tradition, 217
Kapuscinski, Ryszard, 221
Kerry, John, 69
Kierkegaard, 240
Krauthammer, Charles, 70
Kyoto protocol, 140

Lévinas, Emmanuel, 76, 239
Lincoln, Abraham, 112, 114–116, 121, 124
live burial, 50
Lorca, Garcia, 4

Mackell, Tommy, 30
materialism, 136
memory/facts dichotomy, 90, 91
Middle East, 130, 137
militarism, 99, 103
Moore, Michael, 69, 71
mourning, 50, 51, 218, see also *grief*
Mussolini, 63

narrative, 36, 46, 67, 71, 74, 83–84, 87–89,
  119, 122, 126, 137, 231–234, 239, 241
  of war, 45
  of identity, 133
nation (state), 187, 209

Nazi Germany, 209, 214, 215
Nazism, 51, 93
Nazi state, 169
Neoliberalism, 99
networks, 77, 95–97, 131, 134–136, 138,
  145, 148–150, 196
  in biopolitical context, 140, 150
Nietzsche, Friederich, 74, 79
Nolan, Christopher, 86
nomos, 183

obscene underside, 54
oil, 130, 131, 136–138, 148
  paradoxical dependence on, 146
ontological security, 88, 91

Patriot Act, 26
Perez, Fidel Velasquez, 9
Piestewa, Lori Ann, 48
Pinter, Harold, 43, 49
polemic, 186
political life, 35, 185
postmodernization, 134
Powell, Colin, 36, 68, 125–126
precarious life, 61–65, 76–78, 80, 162
preemptive justice, 115, 121
prism 9/11, 98
production, 138
  biopolitical, 135
  change in relations of, 134
  of death, 235
  of desire, 132
  of the home, 123
proposition 200, 10

race war discourse, 171, 172, 175
Rancière, 185–186
  on the rights of man, 190
Rapaille, Claude, 143, 145
reborder, the state, 132
refugees, 79, 181, 187–189, 193–196, 198,
  205, 207, 211, 235, 239
resistance, 20, 185, 189, 191, 198–199, 232,
  237, 233
Rice, Condoleeza, 68
Ridge, Tom, 68
rights, 14, 186–187, 189, 195
  Canadian Charter of Rights and
    Freedoms, 161, 163, 174
  Declaration of the Rights of Man, 187, 215

rights—*continued*
    French Declaration of the Rights of Man
        and the Citizen, 14
    human, 186–188, 207–208, 212, 215
    liberal notion of human rights, 210, 223
Rolland, Jacques, 232
Rove, Karl, 68
Rumsfeld, Donald, 68, 125

sacred life, 14 see also *homo sacer*
Sangatte, 193–194, 196–197
Saudi Arabia, 137
Schiller, Friedrich, 212–213
Schmitt, Carl, 163
security/identity nexus, 86, 99, 132
September 11, 2001, vii, 5, 19–20, 25–26,
    33, 38, 45, 61, 65, 67, 83, 93–97, 129,
    144, 165
Shapiro, Michael, 110
Sheehan, Casey, 48
Sheehan, Cindy, 49
Shtetl, Yaffa Eliach, 33
social body, 17
Sontag, Susan, 29, 70
Sonoran desert, 3, 5, 10, 12, 234
sovereign, 163, 164, 199, 205
    authority, 18
    ban, 162–165, 174, 236–237, 239
    biopower, vii
    citizens, 17
    politics, 35, 37
    power, 14, 37, 45–47, 51, 53, 85, 135,
        163–164, 222, 232–233, 236–237,
        239–240
    state, 213
sovereignty, 99, 134, 135, 168–170, 187,
    188, 192, 232
    Hobbesian theory of, 168
    human, 215
    imperial, 134
    of Iraq, 172
space(s)
    of abjection, 184–185
    biopolitical, 13
    of exception, 183
    nonmoral, 14
    outside juridico-political order, 18
    of politics, 184, 196
    of transit, 191
statecraft, 5, 8, 10, 15, 211, 214, 216
Strauss, David Levi, 47

surrealism, 86–87, 99, 103
Syria, 160

Taliban, 93, 95, 96, 197
trauma, 39, 45, 65, 84, 86, 88, 91, 95, 102,
    210, 232, 233
    posttraumatic, 210
    and time, 28
Tarantino, Quentin, 76
Taussig, Michael, 3
technology, 95
territorial politics, 20
territorialization, 132
terror, 19, 55, 66, 72, 124, 131, 134
    war on, 45, 55, 101, 121, 125, 129, 162,
        165, 166, 171, 173, 205, 212, 223
terrorism, 12, 94–97, 130, 144, 171–173, 212
terrorists, 12, 30, 70, 93–97, 101–102, 115,
        121, 129, 160, 162, 171, 173, 197, 211
topography, 13

Urry, John, 131
United Kingdom, 161

Vanity Fair, 66–67, 69, 71
Vernant, Jean Pierre, 219
Vestal virgin, 50–51
Virilio, Paul, 72, 77
virtuous war, 62

Washington, D.C., 16
war
    Afghanistan, 115, 162
    Cold War, 102, 162, 169, 171
    Gulf War I, 45, 144
    Gulf War II, 109, 125
    Iraq, 116, 162
    Korean War, 48
    World War I, 27, 67
    World War II, 63, 122, 141
    Vietnam, 27, 45, 48, 69, 120, 142, 170
Weapons of Mass Destruction (WMD), 97,
    119, 120, 125, 130
Weber, Max, 27
West Wing, The, 68
Wolfowitz, Paul, 68, 115, 125
Woomera, 196–197, 207–208, 210

Zehfuss, Maja, 86, 98
Žižek, Slavoj, 55, 222–223
    on obscene underside, xii
zones, 184, 185, 188–189, 193, 233